The Scientist Within You:™

Women Scientists
from Seven Continents

Biographies and Activities

Instructor's Guide

for use with students ages 10 - 15

By

Rebecca Lowe Warren
and
Mary H. Thompson

ACI Publishing
P.O. Box 40398
Eugene, OR 97404-0064

The Scientist Within You:™
Women Scientists from Seven Continents — Biographies and Activities
By Rebecca Lowe Warren and Mary H. Thompson

 The activities in this book have been tested and are safe when carried out as suggested. The authors and publishers can accept no responsibility for any damage caused or sustained by use or misuse of ideas or materials mentioned in the activities.

Publisher's Cataloging in Publication Data
Warren, Rebecca Lowe.
The Scientist Within You: Women Scientists from Seven Continents — Biographies and Activities/by Rebecca Lowe Warren and Mary H. Thompson.
p. cm.   (The Scientist Within You; 2)
Includes bibliographies and index.
An instructor's guide for use with ages 10 through 15 features 29 women scientists, 7 continental summaries, hands-on activities and experiments, *Scientific Gazette* newsletters, photos and drawings and bibliographies.
1. Women in science - Juvenile literature. 2. Science - Experiments - Juvenile literature. 3. Women scientists - Biographies - Juvenile literature. [1. Women in science. 2. Science - Experiments. 3. Women scientists - Biographies]
I. Thompson, Mary H. II. Title. III. Series.
Q130.W255 1995   920.72 W [B]   95-78055
ISBN 1-884414-12-5; $24.95 Softcover

The Scientist Within You™ series is available at special discounts for bulk purchases for sales promotions, premiums, fund raising, or educational use. For details, contact the publisher.

Published by
ACI Publishing
P.O. Box 40398
Eugene, OR 97404-0064 U.S.A.
(503)689-2154 Fax: (503)689-1369 — through December 31, 1995
(541)689-2154 Fax: (541)689-1369 — beginning January 1, 1996
Printed in the United States of America.

In honor of our daughters

Kimberly Thompson Leeper
Holly Myers Warren

Acknowledgments

The phrase, "It takes a village to raise a child" is akin to writing a book. Two people's names appear on the cover as authors but a "village" of persons have made the gathering of information and its publication possible.

Dr. Dominique Homberger, International Committee Chair of the Association for Women in Science and Professor of Zoology at Louisiana State University, enthusiastically provided names of women scientists in Asia, Africa, and South America.

Dr. Sondra Schlesinger from the Department of Molecular Microbiology, Washington University School of Medicine, contacted Dr. Pham Thi Tran Chau of Vietnam and forwarded photographs and information to us.

Nessy Allen, School of Science and Technology Studies, University of New South Wales, served as a go-between for us and marine biologist Dr. Isobel Bennett.

Marie Barth suggested Dr. Eva Cudlínová and Irena Hanousková and hand-delivered our letter to the Czech Republic. Alisa Coffin, who was determined to have Bolivia represented, placed us in contact with Sonia Alconini.

Frances Caldwell, Equity Resource Center Coordinator, continued to lend encouragement and much-needed resources.

Many thanks to Vivian Wiser, Historian with the U.S. Department of Agriculture, and Thomas Berkemeier who helped locate women scientists.

William Harms with the University of Chicago News Office, Robert and Dawn Dressler, Doug Wise, Christopher Thompson, and Diane Ogdahl provided valuable information.

Friends Anne Larkin Cook, Dorothy Schmidt, Esther Matthews, and Mary Sailada offered helpful suggestions and a sympathetic ear.

Penny Paine, Judith Cobbs, Allana Elovson, and Mindy Bingham shared information and resources.

Alia Gustafson agreed to be our model for the cover illustration.

Jana Triskova Thompson provided research and translating and Jarvis Thompson handled research, editing, artwork and everything else he was asked to do.

Roger Warren and Holly, as always, lent encouragement and incredible patience.

We offer our thanks to the members of Oregon American Association of University Women (AAUW) who have supported us every step of the way.

And to the women scientists who shared their stories through personal letters and telephone conversations, we express our gratitude. Their narratives made this book possible!

Table of Contents

Preface

Agriculturist Grace Ngemukong Tima from Cameroon, Africa, believes that "God never created anybody without a purpose. All we need to do is to find out what each person has the aptitude for, and develop it." These words express the authors' sentiments: **Women Scientists from Seven Continents** reflects our pride in women's accomplishments and our hope for every student.

The lives of these women scientists span a time-line from 1868 to the present. Their fields of work range from microbiology to astrophysics. On each continent these women have collected valuable data, conducted groundbreaking experiments, and shared their discoveries with fellow scientists and appreciative communities.

Their lives and work provide both information and inspiration:

- Dr. Helen Hogg was not only a brilliant educator, notable author, and an accomplished astronomer but a warm, genuine person who believed "anyone can follow the beautiful and interesting events in the sky . . .";
- Entomologist Dr. Ana Aber from Uruguay specializes in termites but in her advisory work with the National Ministry of Environment she encourages each person to recycle — to become "un consumidor responsable";
- While Zdenka Samish abandoned her original dream of becoming a horticulturalist, her work as a researcher in Food Technology helped develop the food industry in Israel; and
- From Dr. Rose Nesbitt, whose childhood in Tanzania was one of her greatest challenges, we hear "Usikate tamaa" (oo-si-ka-tay) (ta-mah-aa), Swahili for "Never give up."

Women Scientists from Seven Continents features full biographies on 29 women scientists, mathematicians, and engineers.

24 Discovery Units offer extensive class activities, experiments, or projects. Each scientist is presented through:

- a biography that may be read to students or summarized by the teacher,
- a photograph,
- a hands-on experiment/activity that duplicates the scientist's work or demonstrates an idea relevant to her work, and
- a bibliography.

Discovery Units also include:

- an introduction page listing key points, supplies needed, and order of events,
- an instructor's guide with background information and comprehensive instructions,
- "My Notes" sheets for students to record observations, information, hypotheses, and experiments, and
- a newsletter that can be duplicated and shared with students and parents.

6 Bridging the Continents pages highlight women whose work in science has intercontinental significance.

7 Continental Summaries emphasize an aspect of that continent's scientific history. Each summary features:

- continental facts unique to that land mass,
- continental curiosities to pique student interests,
- exploration questions for classroom or individual research, and
- suggested enrichment activities.

Unit maps pinpoint key locations in that scientist's work. We also encourage the use of a world map as a focal point for recording each scientist's name and a memento of her work. Such mementos not only give pizzaz to the map but jog the memory.

We encourage you to begin with "Welcome to a World of Possibilities" (Unit 1) and close with "Entering the World of Possibilities in Science and Mathematics" (Unit 24). Since the Continental Summaries are excellent backdrops, consider presenting this information before studying the scientists from that continent. Otherwise, this is a flexible curriculum. Feature as many of these women as your time, energy, and lesson plans allow. Information and activities are appropriate to ages 10 through 15.

Women Scientists from Seven Continents is intended to celebrate the global successes of women in a variety of scientific fields. These women provide life stories and career images that positively impact girls' expectations of themselves and their performance in math and science. Each woman's enthusiasm may inspire both girls and boys to develop an interest in science that will be sustained throughout their educational experience. And to teachers, parents, and leaders who have chosen to "find out what each person has the aptitude for, and develop it," we repeat our heartfelt "thank you!"

◆ ◆ ◆

When girls are steered away from science and mathematics, courses essential to their future employability and economic well-being, we are losing more than one-half of our human potential. **The AAUW Report: How Schools Shortchange Girls** is a synthesis of the available research on the subject of girls in school. To order this 128 page report contact the **American Association of University Women** Sales Office, P.O. Box 251, Annapolis Junction, MD 20701-0251. For phone order call: 800/225-9998, ext. 91.

The Authors

Rebecca Lowe Warren is an author and college instructor living in Portland, Oregon. Her

science class at Marylhurst College spotlights the contributions of women in science and mathematics. She is co-author of **The Scientist Within You, vol. 1** and of **Celebrate The Wonder: A Family Christmas Treasury** published by Ballantine/Epiphany in 1988. Her interests include running, hiking, mountain biking, and volunteer work with Habitat for Humanity. Husband Roger is a salesman and daughter Holly, a freshman at Occidental College, Los Angeles.

Mary H. Thompson is a publisher, teacher, and journalist. An advocate for excellence in

education, she conducts workshops and writes reports on educational equity issues. She is co-author of **The Scientist Within You, vol. 1.** She lives with her husband Jarvis in Eugene, Oregon. They have three sons and a daughter. She has lived in Greece and enjoys foreign travel. Her favorite pastimes are reading mysteries and playing an occasional game of Mah-Jongg.

Rebecca and Mary became acquainted through the American Association of University Women (AAUW) when both were serving on the Oregon State Board of Directors. Inspiration for **The Scientist Within You** series originated following AAUW's release of the report **Shortchanging Girls, Shortchanging America**. Sharing a commitment to gender equity, Rebecca and Mary have pooled their talents to create a curriculum series that highlights the contributions of women in science and inspires girls and boys to discover the scientist within themselves.

Discovery Unit No. 1

Welcome to a World of Possibilities
An Introduction
CONTINENTAL FACTS and SCIENTIFIC THOUGHT

Time-line:

• 1868 - Today — Scientists featured in **Women Scientists from Seven Continents**.

Key points:

☞ Women have traveled to and lived in various parts of the world in order to gain the education and experience necessary to make contributions in the fields of mathematics, science, medicine and engineering. Their influence has encompassed the seven continents.

☞ In the CONTINENTAL FACTS Game, students will get a sense of the global community represented by these women in science.

☞ Scientists tend to follow certain steps to find answers to their questions.

☞ In the SCIENTIFIC THOUGHTS Activity, students will be introduced to some of the women scientists featured in this book and will become familiar with steps of scientific inquiry. Students will use some or all of these steps in Discovery Units 2 through 23.

Supplies:

✓ A world map

✓ CONTINENTAL FACTS Game instruction sheet for the instructor (page 3)

✓ SCIENTIFIC THOUGHT Activity Answer Sheet for the instructor (page 4)

✓ SCIENTIFIC THOUGHT Activity sheet for each student (page 5)

✓ Quote sheet for SCIENTIFIC THOUGHT Activity for each student (page 6)

✓ Scissors

Steps:

1. Locate the "seven" continents.
2. Play the CONTINENTAL FACTS Game.
3. Distribute the SCIENTIFIC THOUGHT Activity and quote sheets.
4. Complete and discuss activity sheets.
5. Assist students in clean-up.

For next time:

• Announce the first scientist.

Exploration idea:

The "globe" at the top of this unit is called **A Map in a Circle.** Until a person looks closely at it, one might think it is a sphere. This is just one projection of a world map. The more common projections are "Robinson" and "Mercator." Other interesting projects are variations of "Mollweide" and "Sinusoidal."

The global projections shown at the top of Discovery Units 2 through 23 show the world from different perspectives depending on the continent that is being featured.

Use map projections as an exploration topic. Have students share their discoveries.

Instructor's Guide:

CONTINENTAL FACTS and SCIENTIFIC THOUGHT

Background:

As an introduction to the activities in **Women Scientists from Seven Continents** there are two subjects with which the students should have some familiarity: the geography of continents and thinking in a scientific manner.

In the first instance, the authors have chosen the geographic distribution of continents to be Africa, Antarctica, Asia, Australia, Europe, North America, and South America — seven continents. Another way of classifying the continents is to consider North and South America as one continent and Antarctica, Australia, New Zealand, and the surrounding islands as the continent Oceania — making five continents in all. The Continental Summaries in **Women Scientists from Seven Continents** provide geographic descriptions, a history of science, facts and curiosities, exploration questions, and enrichment activities. The CONTINENTAL FACTS game will spark their curiosity about places in the world.

This book is filled with activities, projects, and experiments written to open a world of possibilities to the students. The SCIENTIFIC THOUGHT activity will introduce the steps that will assist them in thinking scientifically.

Instructions:

> **Explain ...**
> *You will be exploring science from a global perspective based on the work of women scientists from seven continents. To get a sense of this global community, we will play the CONTINENTAL FACTS Game.*

1. Present a map of the world. Find each continent. Mention that as a new scientist is studied, her name and a memento will be placed on the map on the continent she represents.

2. Form four teams and play the CONTINENTAL FACTS Game (page 3).

3. After the game is over, distribute copies of page 6 (quotes about/by scientists) to students. Ask them to cut on dotted lines.

4. Distribute blank SCIENTIFIC THOUGHT Activity sheets to students. (Page 5)

> **Explain ...**
> Throughout these Discovery Units you will be asking questions and looking at possibilities. Here is a list of steps that will aid you in thinking like a scientist. Each step correlates to an experience or observation made by one of the scientists you will be studying. Match the statement from a scientist to the "Step" it most closely represents.

5. Allow time for students to complete the SCIENTIFIC THOUGHT Activity.

6. As you give the students the correct answers, find the Discovery Unit for that scientist, show her picture and mention her field of science.

Continental Facts Game:

Divide the students into four teams. Starting with team one, give the first fact on this list. If they can name the correct continent, then they get a point and another turn.

If the team answers incorrectly, the question passes to the next team. The winning team will have the most number of points at the end of the game.

These facts are taken from the Continental summaries.

- The native wildlife on this continent includes 520 species of birds including the emu and cassowary both of which cannot fly.
  Australia
  • • • • • • • • •
- This continent's name is a shortening of "anti-Arctic" since this continent rests opposite the Arctic region.
  Antarctica
  • • • • • • • • •
- The Bug River empties into the Black Sea.
  Europe
  • • • • • • • • •
- The shore of the Dead Sea (-1,310 feet below sea level) between Israel and Jordan is the lowest place on dry land in the world.
  Asia
  • • • • • • • • •
- The okapi, a relative of the giraffe, uses its 14-inch tongue to wash out its ears.
  Africa
  • • • • • • • • •
- This is the only continent without national borders.
  Antarctica
  • • • • • • • • •
- Recent findings place the longest river in the world on this continent. (Amazon River)
  South America
  • • • • • • • • •
- Indonesia has 167 active volcanoes.
  Asia
  • • • • • • • • •
- The largest city in the world is located on this continent. Its population numbers more than 17 million people. (Mexico City)
  North America
  • • • • • • • • •

- Of the 230 mammal species on this continent, almost 50% are marsupials whose young are born in very early stages of development and are "matured" in the mother's pouch.
  Australia
  • • • • • • • • •
- In its dry valleys snow evaporates before it hits the ground.
  Antarctica
  • • • • • • • • •
- There are mountains on this continent that have veins of salt 600 feet thick.
  Europe
  • • • • • • • • •
- Its largest land animal is a wingless mosquito.
  Antarctica
  • • • • • • • • •
- Mt. Everest (29,023 feet above sea level) in the Himalayas is the highest peak in the world.
  Asia
  • • • • • • • • •
- The world's longest freshwater lake is Lake Tanganyika.
  Africa
  • • • • • • • • •
- Over 13,000 plant species are native to this continent.
  Australia
  • • • • • • • • •
- Two species of monotremes (egg-laying mammals) live on this continent. They are the duckbilled platypus and the spiny ant-eater.
  Australia
  • • • • • • • • •
- The name of one of the countries on this continent possibly came from the Huron-Iroquois word, Kanata, which means "village" or "community."
  North America
  • • • • • • • • •
- The country of England was separated from this continent 8,000 years ago.
  Europe
  • • • • • • • • •
- One-sixth of the globe's runoff into the ocean comes from a river on this continent.
  South America
  • • • • • • • • •
- Over 600,000 domestic camels roam the Gobi in Mongolia.
  Asia
  • • • • • • • • •

Scientific Thought Activity
Answer Sheet

Make an observation
Crayfish grow and molt in experiments conducted in summer but fail to grow and molt in experiments conducted in winter.
Dr. Mary Alice McWhinnie
(Antarctica - Unit 5)

Ask questions
"Why does bovine meat when cooked with pineapple, gradually become ground down?"
Dr. Pham Thi Tran Chau
(Asia - Unit 10)

Gather information
-Talk with others
- Read books
- Make observations
"It is the possibility to work in a team of scientists from different disciplines instead of solving the whole problem only by myself. . ... I enjoy this style of work."
Dr. Eva Cudlínová
(Europe - Unit 15)

Build a theory
Archaeologist Dr. Aslihan Yener theorizes that ancient Anatolians mined and smelted tin.
Dr. Aslihan Yener
(Asia - Unit 8)

Create a hypothesis to test theory
If olives are rinsed too often, then sugars necessary for fermentation are removed.
Zdenka Samish
(Asia - Unit 9)

Design experiment(s) to test hypothesis
Dr. Ocampo-Friedmann designed experiments to "feed" the "endolithic" samples she collected in Antarctica.
Dr. Roseli Ocampo-Friedmann
(Antarctica - Unit 7)

Conduct experiment(s)
At the Tanga Tsetse Research Institute, Dr. Nesbitt reared and released sterile tsetse flies.
Dr. Symphorose Tarimo Nesbitt
(Africa - Unit 3)

Interpret experiment results
When Dr. Hahn, a scientist from Germany, confessed that the results of an experiment puzzled him, Dr. Meitner studied the results and concluded that her former co-worker had split the uranium atom!
Dr. Lise Meitner
(Europe - Unit 14)

Evaluate theory
Observing that math games have generated enthusiasm for and competence in mathematics among elementary students, Mildred Bennett continues to include math games in her tutoring programs.
Mildred Bennett
(North America - Unit 17)

Repeat process
Since sediment samples from the floors of seas, lakes, and other bodies of water provided valuable data, Dr. Klenova participated in geologic expeditions every year for 50 years.
Dr. Marie Klenova
(Europe - Unit 16)

Publicize findings
Dr. Ana Aber has written more than 30 articles about termites, conducted seminars, and organized a Conference of Termite Specialists/Scientists.
Dr. Ana Aber
(South America - Unit 21)

Enjoy the scientific process
"So far, the scientific world has been a happy-ending story for me."
Maria Elena Diaz
(North America - Unit 19)

Scientific Thought Activity

Make an observation

Ask questions

Gather information
    -Talk with others
    - Read books
    - Make observations

Build a theory

Create a hypothesis to test theory

Design experiment(s) to test hypothesis

Conduct experiment(s)

Interpret experiment results

Evaluate theory

Repeat process

Publicize findings

Enjoy the scientific process

Cut apart and use with SCIENTIFIC THOUGHT Activity

Crayfish grow and molt in experiments conducted in summer but fail to grow and molt in experiments conducted in winter.
Dr. Mary Alice McWhinnie
(Antarctica - Unit 5)

Archaeologist Dr. Aslihan Yener theorizes that ancient Anatolians mined and smelted tin.
Dr. Aslihan Yener
(Asia - Unit 8)

"So far, the scientific world has been a happy-ending story for me."
Maria Elena Diaz
(North America - Unit 19)

"Why does bovine meat when cooked with pineapple, gradually become ground down?"
Dr. Pham Thi Tran Chau
(Asia - Unit 10)

"It is the possibility to work in a team of scientists from different disciplines instead of solving the whole problem only by myself....I enjoy this style of work."
Dr. Eva Cudlínová
(Europe - Unit 15)

Dr. Ana Aber has written more than 30 articles about termites, conducted seminars, and organized a Conference of Termite Specialists/Scientists.
Dr. Ana Aber
(South America - Unit 21)

Since sediment samples from the floors of seas, lakes, and other bodies of water provided valuable data, Dr. Klenova participated in geologic expeditions every year for 50 years.
Dr. Marie Klenova
(Europe - Unit 16)

Observing that math games have generated enthusiasm for and competence in mathematics among elementary students, Mildred Bennett continues to include math games in her tutoring programs.
Mildred Bennett
(North America - Unit 17)

Dr. Ocampo-Friedmann designed experiments to "feed" the "endolithic" samples she collected in Antarctica.
Dr. Roseli Ocampo-Friedmann
(Antarctica - Unit 7)

When Dr. Hahn, a scientist from Germany, confessed that the results of an experiment puzzled him, Dr. Meitner studied the results and concluded that her former co-worker had split the uranium atom!
Dr. Lise Meitner
(Europe - Unit 14)

At the Tanga Tsetse Research Institute, Dr. Nesbitt reared and released sterile tsetse flies.
Dr. Symphorose Tarimo Nesbitt
(Africa - Unit 3)

If olives are rinsed too often, then sugars necessary for fermentation are removed.
Zdenka Samish
(Asia - Unit 9)

Africa covers 20% of the earth's land surface. Geologically some areas are more than 3.2 billion years old. Volcanic activity created most of its mountains, including snow-capped Mount Kilimanjaro (19,340 ft.) located near the equator. The Great Rift Valley, a deep divide in the earth's surface, extends almost 4,300 miles.

Forty percent of Africa is desert. Its Sahara Desert stretches the breadth of the continent and is the world's largest. In some places rain does not fall for six or seven years in a row. Savannas, or grasslands, also make up 40% of the continent's land mass and, unlike deserts, support a variety of wildlife ranging from the largest four-legged animal in the world, the elephant, to the 5-inch-long insect-eating golden mole. In the continent's tropical rain forests, trees grow so closely together that each leaf competes for sunlight and the forest floor is dark and quiet.

Africa and Science:

Like its geography, science in Africa enjoys an ancient, varied, and impressive history. Eighteen thousand years ago Africans grew barley, wheat, lentils, and dates along the Nile River; 15,000 years ago they domesticated cattle; and 7,000 years ago at agricultural sites along the Niger River in the Sudan, Africans harvested millet, sorghum, yams, okra, watermelon, sesame, and African rice.

Ancient Egyptians:

- made glass,
- wove flax fibers into textiles, and
- navigated the Nile in reed boats.

Their city of Alexandria was a center of learning in the ancient world.

Achievements in **architecture** and **engineering** include the familiar pyramids of Egypt and the lesser known Great Zimbabwe (Zim - BOB- way), an ancient "stone city." More than 800 years old, Great Zimbabwe was the seat of a civilization that flourished for 300 years and included more than 200 stone villages throughout present-day Zimbabwe and Mozambique. Great Zimbabwe has:

- secret passageways and large rooms,
- an enclosing wall 750' in length and 6' thick, and
- approximately 15,000 tons of granite blocks.

In **navigation**, Africans constructed a variety of boats including dugouts as large as Viking ships. They used compasses and constellations to guide them through waterways and across the Sahara Desert. In **metallurgy**, between 1,500 to 2,000 years ago, they produced carbon steel in furnaces whose temperatures exceeded 1,700 degrees C. In **astronomy**, Africans in Kenya around 300 BC constructed an observatory. Egyptians could determine the time during the night by looking at the stars.

These achievements were impossible without mathematics. The first written numerals come from ancient Egypt. Their calendar had 365 days with each day being 24 hours long. Annual flooding of the Nile River required remeasurement of the land when the waters receded. This remeasurement was the origin of geometry (*geo* = "land" and *metry* = measurement). Our mathematical concepts of distance, area, volume, and weight originate with the Egyptians.

Africans were knowledgeable and competent healers. They:

- performed autopsies and Caesareansections,
- developed a smallpox vaccine centuries before the Europeans,
- used traction to set fractured limbs,
- removed cataracts,
- practiced antiseptic surgery, and
- administered anesthesia.

Both men and women practiced medicine. In ancient Egypt women were physicians and surgeons. As early as 2700 B.C. a woman practitioner named Merit Ptah served as the "Chief Physician." In central and south Africa, Bantu-speaking tribes had their own aspirin. The Mali used kaolin (the active ingredient in Kaopectate) to cure diarrhea, and the Zulus knew the medicinal uses of 700 plants.

In contemporary Africa the role of women in science is expanding. This unit will spotlight three women scientists from Africa. They are **Dr. Letitia Obeng** (Ghana), **Dr. Symphorose A. Nesbitt** (Tanzania), and **Grace N. Tima** (Cameroon).

Continental Facts:

- The world's longest freshwater lake is Lake Tanganyika.
- Wadi Halfa, Sudan, receives an average 0.1 inch of precipitation each year; Debundscha, Cameroon, has an annual average of 404.6 inches.
- The okapi, a relative of the giraffe, uses its 14-inch tongue to wash out its ears.

Continental Curiosities:

- A clariid catfish can live out of water for several days while it wriggles across dry land to reach another body of water. Its ability to locate this other water source remains a mystery.
- In the Middle Ages the Dogon, a people living in the mountains of West Africa, knew about Saturn's rings, Jupiter's moons, and the spiral structure of the Milky Way Galaxy. They studied the Canis Major (Big Dog) constellation and noted the elliptical 50-year orbit of the small star Sirius B around Sirius A. Present-day scientists remain puzzled by the Dogon's ability to make these accurate astronomical observations.

Exploration Questions:

- What forces changed the Sahara from a rich grassland with fish-filled streams to a desert?
- What national parks and game reserves exist in Africa?

Enrichment Activities:

- Collect postage stamps from Africa. Explore the continent's history and culture, and research the plants and animals featured in the colorful illustrations.
- Create an *Animals in Africa* alphabet book. Letter "X" can be an animal that the student creates.

Add information and ideas here:

Bibliography:

America Online, **Compton's Encyclopedia, Online Edition** (downloaded January 3, 1995).

Bass, Thomas A. **Camping with the Prince and Other Tales of Science in Africa.**

Carr, Archie, and The Editors of LIFE. **The Land and Wildlife of Africa**.

Van Sertima, Ivan, Editor. **Blacks in Science: Ancient and Modern.**

Dr. Letitia Eva Obeng, internationally known hydrobiologist, founded the Institute of Aquatic Biology in Ghana.

Discovery Unit No. 2

Dr. Letitia Obeng
Hydrobiology

BECAUSE OF WATER Institute

Time-line:

- 1925 - Dr. Letitia Eva Obeng is born in Anum, Ghana.
- 1941 - Marine biologist Rachel Carson writes **Under the Sea-Wind**.
- 1957 - The Independent Republic of Ghana is established on March 6, 1957.
- 1963 - African Universities Press of Lagos, Nigeria, publishes J. H. Kwabena Nketia's **Folk Songs of Ghana**.
- 1970 - Aswan Dam in Egypt is completed.

Key points:

☛ Dr. Obeng lives in Accra, Ghana. She is an internationally known hydrobiologist, a scientist that studies plants and animals that live in water.

☛ As far back as she can remember, Dr. Letitia Obeng has been curious about living things.

☛ In 1965 Dr. Obeng founded the Institute of Aquatic Biology in Ghana.

☛ For over 30 years, Dr. Obeng has promoted environmental management. She has worked to make clean water available to communities and to educate people about water-related parasitic infections.

☛ In the BECAUSE OF WATER Institute, students will independently explore water topics, and share and celebrate their discoveries.

Supplies — today:

✓ A large sheet of butcher paper
✓ "My Notes" for each student (page 16)

✓ Library and/or science resource center

Supplies — 4 to 6 days later:

✓ Dr. Obeng's poem, "Because of Water"
✓ Writing pens
✓ A sheet of paper (approximately 5" x 8") for each student
✓ Background music [Optional]
✓ A roll of masking tape or push pins

Steps — today:

1. Point out Accra, Ghana, on a map.
2. Share highlights of Dr. Letitia Obeng's life.
3. Create the BECAUSE OF WATER Institute. (See instructor's guide, page 14)
4. Visit the library. Assist/join students in research.

Steps — 4 to 6 days later:

1. Reconvene the institute for students to share their discoveries.
2. Distribute the sheets of paper.
3. Each student writes a poem.
4. Unfold newsprint with Obeng's poem.
5. Add students' poems.
6. Add Dr. Letitia Eva Obeng's name and a memento to the world map.
7. Distribute *The Scientific Gazette* .

For next time:

- Introduce the next scientist.

Bibliography:

Obeng, Letitia Eva. **Curriculum Vitae**, 1989.

Obeng, Letitia Eva. **Letter**, November 21, 1994.

Obeng, Letitia E. "The Right to Health in Tropical Agriculture," **Outlook on Agriculture**, Vol. 21, No. 4, 1992.

Biography of
DR. LETITIA EVA OBENG
b. 1925

Dr. Letitia Obeng from Accra, Ghana, is an internationally known hydrobiologist, a scientist who studies plants and animals that live in water. As far back as Dr. Obeng can remember, she was curious about living things.

In school her favorite subjects were general science, literature, and poetry. She liked biology and zoology. From Achimota College in Ghana, Letitia Obeng traveled to England to attend the University of Birmingham where she graduated with a B.Sc. in Zoology (1952). She was "particularly fascinated by the invertebrates" — animals without backbones. But it was the "strange and intriguing" parasites that captured Obeng's attention and lifelong interest.

"Strange and intriguing" parasites

Parasites live in or on other organisms. They generally cause harm to their host. Although Obeng describes them as unpleasant creatures who are "nobody's friend," she finds them an academic joy. Parasites have "amazing characteristics, devious intrigues and clever machinations." Why parasites "would want to live hidden in others" when it is "so much more interesting and beautiful outside" intrigues this nature-loving scientist. While studying for her M.Sc. in Parasitology (University of Birmingham, 1962), Obeng pursued her special interest in parasitic worms in rodents.

"A whole new world in water!"

Schistosomes (SCHISS-toe-soams) are flukes (or worms) that live as parasites in the blood of mammals and birds, and cause diseases that affect internal organs. Schistosomiasis (SCHISS-to-so-my-a-sis) is prevalent in Africa killing approximately 200,000 people each year. The aquatic snail plays a role in the transmission of this disease so Letitia Obeng had to "understand the physical and chemical nature of the water which formed the habitats of the snails." This was her introduction to freshwater ecosystems with their "fantastic array of living things." She discovered "a whole new world in water!"

Institute of Aquatic Biology

For her Ph.D. she studied the aquatic stages of the black fly and its role in causing river blindness. In 1964 Obeng received her Ph.D. in Freshwater Sciences from the University of Univerpool, United Kingdom. In 1965 she founded the Institute of Aquatic Biology in Ghana and served as its director until 1974 when she began work with the United Nations Environment Program (UNEP). From 1980 - 1985 Dr. Obeng was the Director of the UNEP Regional Office for Africa. Two years later she participated in the World Bank's Sanitation Project Evaluation, a project including Malawi, Botswana, Kenya, Lesotho, Nigeria and Zimbabwe.

Environmental management

The common thread running through these responsibilities is Obeng's commitment to environmental management. Industrial and agricultural progress in tropical areas often bring disease in their wake: reservoirs created by the construction of dams provide breeding grounds for insects that transmit disease; irrigation canals expose rural communities to water-borne parasites that penetrate the skin; and chemicals contaminate drinking water, soil, fish, and even crops.

Dr. Obeng believes that environmental management offers a solution that balances progress with the health needs of agricultural workers and rural communities. Self-help programs and education also improve waste treatment programs and discourage widespread unsanitary practices.

Influence beyond her country

Her work extends beyond the borders of Ghana. Through her efforts a network of African National Environmental Officers discussed regional problems and drew up a realistic program of action for environmental management on the continent. Obeng was a senior adviser to the secretary general of the 1992 Earth Summit in Rio de Janeiro as well as a member of the International Irrigation Management Institute and the Stockholm Environmental Institute.

Healthy water for people

"I am not an environmentalist," Obeng writes. "I am a scientist with experience in freshwater ecological changes which affect both the quality and availability of water and I do care about water for meeting human needs - and protecting human health." For over 30 years Dr. Obeng has worked to make clean water available to communities and to educate people about water-related parasitic infections.

Dr. Obeng has three grown children all of whom hold doctoral degrees: her daughter Letitia (Washington, D.C.) has a Ph.D. in Public Health Engineering; son, Ernest (Monaco and France), a Ph.D. in Agricultural Chemistry; and son, Edward (United Kingdom), a Ph.D. in Chemical Engineering.

"As far back as I can remember, I have always been curious about living things — ants which scurry along small ant-made paths carrying pieces of matter several times their size; millipedes whose many tiny legs move in synchronized rhythm and never get confused; caterpillars which seem to eat quantities of leaves much bigger than themselves; dull looking grasshoppers which turn beautiful when in flight because they spread out their many colored wings; sedentary larvae and darting beetles in streams; birds with long iridescent tails; mosquitoes and their annoying humming noise; seedlings pushing through the soil; delicate designs on flowers of "weeds" — I have always been conscious of such things. I did not choose science as a subject to study — I suppose I naturally glided into the field"

Add information and ideas here:

Instructor's Guide:

BECAUSE OF WATER Institute

Background Information:

"A whole new world in water!" greeted Letitia Obeng as she worked on her doctoral degree. This enthusiasm for water and its biodiversity underlies her science as well as her poetry. Poetry and art in nature are her hobbies.

This unit encourages students to become hydrobiologists (in the BECAUSE OF WATER Institute) and discover that "new world in water." They will independently explore water topics of their choice, share these discoveries in creative formats (science experiment, slide show, video, etc.), and write poems about the liquid that covers nearly 75% of the earth's surface and constitutes almost 60% of every human body!

Instructions:

Establishing the Institute

1. Generate a list of ideas (topics) by completing the sentence — "Because of Water there are . . ."

> *Because of Water*
> *there are . . .*
> *· puddles of rain*
> *· canoe trips*
> *· storm drains*
> *· steam irons*
> *·*
> *·*
> *·*
> *·*

- Post sheet of newsprint with "Because of Water there are . . ." written at the top.

- Give students time to look around the classroom, school, home, or outdoors for ideas.

- Brainstorm a list of ideas (topics) on this sheet of paper.

> **Explain . . .**
> *We are now forming an institute to explore ideas about water. The name will be the BECAUSE OF WATER Institute. An institute holds a series of meetings to explore and share ideas about a cause. The cause of this institute is "Water."*

2. Ask each student to choose an idea (topic) from the idea list.

   Note: Students can work individually or in teams of 2 or more.

   Write students names beside the topic they will be exploring.

3. Hold a discussion on creative ways the topics can be shared. Suggest artwork, charts, experiments or demonstrations, videos, skits, etc.

4. Pass out "My Notes." Give students time to complete.

5. Determine a schedule.

   - Schedule research and preparation time.

   - Set the dates and times for reconvening the BECAUSE OF WATER Institute. Assign student presentations to a specific meeting. (Allow several days for sharing of discoveries.)

Preparation

1. Visit library or resource room. Assist/join students in research.

2. Encourage and help students use a variety of resources.

3. Explore a water topic yourself. Schedule your presentation along with the students'.

Reconvening the Institute

1. Prepare an agenda for each meeting. Write agenda on chalkboard.

2. Choose a person to preside.

3. Students present their information.

4. After presentations are completed, allow for discussion of ideas generated during that session of the institute.

The Final Day

1. Prior to the meeting:
   - Copy Dr. Obeng's poem onto a large piece of newsprint.

2. For the final day of the BECAUSE OF WATER Institute:
   - Distribute a sheet of paper (appx. 5" x 8") to each student.
   - [Optional] Play soft background music.
   - Ask each student to write a poem about water.
   - Write a poem yourself.
   - Reveal Dr. Obeng's poem (after all have completed writing) and read aloud.
   - Attach students' poems to newsprint.
   - Display on wall or bulletin board.

3. Ask students about subjects they would like to use for future institutes.

4. Distribute *The Scientific Gazette*.

Add notes here:

Poem — Because of Water:

This poem by Dr. Letitia Eva Obeng is her response to the question, "What advice would you like to share with children?"

Remember as you grow up,
and forever, that --

Because of water, flowers bloom,
lilies, pure and white,
hyacinths, richly violet,
orchids, strange but exquisite,
roses, velvety and red,

Because of water,
orange blossom aromas,
clinging scents of jasmine
and blends of musky perfumes
fill the evening air

Because of water,
ponds have daphnia and bosmina
and streams have mayfly, stonefly,
delightfully clumsy crabs, and graceful fish;

Because of water we hear
the gentle gurgle of streams,
tinkling drops of springs,
roaring tumbling rivers,
booming waterfalls and
exhilarating blustering rains

Because of water there are
serene lakes,
cool breezes,
brilliant rainbows and
multi-coloured sunsets,

Don't ever forget --
these wonderful, beautiful things
uniquely, are all, water!

— *Dr. Letitia Eva Obeng*

Topic Development Sheet — BECAUSE OF WATER Institute

Topic: _____

Team Members: _____

Where we will find information on this topic? _____

_____

_____

How much time is allocated for research? _____

_____

How are we going to present our research? _____

_____

_____

Assignments:

Who *is going to do*	**What**	*by* **When**
_____	_____	_____
_____	_____	_____
_____	_____	_____

What supplies are needed?   Who will furnish them?

_____   _____

_____   _____

_____   _____

Date of our presentation at the Institution: _____

The Scientific Gazette

Poetry and literature inspire hydrobiologist from Ghana

Dr. Letitia Eva Obeng is an internationally known hydrobiologist, a scientist that studies the plants and animals that live in water. Born in Ghana in 1925, Obeng's father was a teacher and minister who served as the Head (or Moderator) of the Presbyterian Church of Ghana. Her mother was an "excellent mother, home and family manager." Letitia had three brothers and four sisters.

Her favorite subjects in school were general science, literature, and poetry. She attended college in the United Kingdom earning her Ph.D. in Freshwater Sciences from the University of Univerpool.

For over 30 years Dr. Obeng has worked to make clean water available to people and to educate populations about water-related parasitic infections. Her work in environmental management stems from her concern for people and her love of nature.

Writing poetry and seeing art in nature are Dr. Obeng's hobbies.

> *"I did not choose science as a subject to study - I suppose I naturally glided into the field."*
> — **Dr. Letitia Eva Obeng**

Dr. Obeng was the first . . .

- woman appointed lecturer at the University of Science and Technology in Kumasi, Ghana.
- Ghanaian woman to obtain a M.Sc. degree in Parasitology.
- Ghanaian woman to obtain a Ph.D. degree.
- woman to build a new Research Institute for the Academy of Sciences, Ghana.
- Ghanaian Woman Fellow and Silver Medalist of the Royal Society of Arts, United Kingdom.
- African woman to address the Royal Swedish Academy of Sciences.
- woman appointed Director of the Regional Office (Africa) of the United Nations Environment Program.

Dr. Obeng studies parasites. She learned that hookworms live up to 7 years and lay 10,000 to 20,000 eggs a day. If a hookworm lived 5 years and laid 15,000 eggs a day, how many eggs would it lay in its lifetime? (Plan for one leap year in your answer.) Answer: 27,390,000 eggs

Like Dr. Obeng, I studied water. My topic was

_____

I learned _____

_____

I felt _____

_____

_____

Multicultural Mathematics by Claudia Zaslavsky (J. Weston Walch, Publisher) is a book of 58 activities using mathematical concepts from ancient civilizations and other cultures. From the Egyptian method of multiplication to magic squares and number codes, these cooperative-learning activities will arouse curiosity and encourage critical thinking.

Dr. Symphorose A. Tarimo Nesbitt, entomologist, was born in Kilimanjaro, Tanzania.

Discovery Unit No. 3

Dr. Symphorose A. Tarimo Nesbitt
Entomology

SHOO, FLY, DON'T BOTHER ME Experiment

Time-line:

- 1952 - Dr. Symphorose (Rose) A. Tarimo Nesbitt is born in Kilimanjaro, Tanzania.
- 1960 - Jane Goodall travels to Tanzania to begin her study of the chimpanzee.
- 1970 - The International Center of Insect Physiology and Ecology (ICIPE) opens in Kenya.
- 1984 - Archaeologist Mary Leakey retires from "field work" and writes, among other things, a book on the rock paintings of Tanzania.

Pronunciation guide:

- Usikate tamaa (oo-si-ka-tay) (ta-mah-aa), Swahili for "Never give up."
- tsetse (TET-see) fly

Key points:

- ☛ Born in Kilimanjaro, Tanzania, Dr. Nesbitt believes that her childhood was "one of the greatest challenges I have had."
- ☛ Her determination to study insect-caused diseases began when she had malaria at age nine.
- ☛ Dr. Rose Tarimo Nesbitt is a lecturer at Howard University, Washington, D.C.
- ☛ Many insects, including the common housefly, transmit disease.
- ☛ In the SHOO, FLY, DON'T BOTHER ME Experiment, students will use Anna Botsford Comstock's suggestion to design an experiment that will increase their knowledge of the common housefly.

Supplies — today:

- ✓ "My Notes" Part A for each student (page 23)
- ✓ A sheet of newsprint listing "Comstock's suggestion" (See instructor's guide.)

Supplies — tomorrow:

- ✓ Determined by students as they design the experiment.

Supplies — several days later:

- ✓ Part B of "My Notes" (page 24)
- ✓ *The Scientific Gazette* for each student

Steps — today:

1. Point out Kilimanjaro, Tanzania, on a map.
2. Share highlights of Dr. Symphorose Tarimo Nesbitt's life.
3. Begin the SHOO, FLY, DON'T BOTHER ME Experiment. (See instructor's guide.)

Steps — tomorrow:

1. Determined by students in their lists of PROCEDURES. ("My Notes," Part A)
2. Assist students in clean-up.

Steps — several days later:

1. Observe experiment results.
2. Complete Part B of "My Notes."
3. Add Dr. Nesbitt's name and a memento to the map.
4. Distribute *The Scientific Gazette*.

For next time:

- Announce the next scientist.

Bibliography:

Arnett, Jr., Dr. Ross H. and Dr. Richard L. Jacques, Jr. **Guide to Insects**.

Comstock, Anna Botsford. **Handbook of Nature Study**.

Hemingway, Ernest. **The Snows of Kilimanjaro**.

Nature Series: **Kilimanjaro**, Produced and Directed by Ian Bodenham. Editor, Chris Fraser.

Nesbitt, Symphorose A. **Curriculum Vitae**.

Nesbitt, Symphorose A. **Telephone Interview**, November 29, 1994.

Souza, D. M. **Insects Around the House**.

Biography of
DR. SYMPHOROSE A. TARIMO NESBITT
b. 1952

"Usikate tamaa." (Never give up.)
— **Dr. Symphorose A. Tarimo Nesbitt**

Mt. Kilimanjaro is the highest mountain on the continent of Africa. It is a volcano that rises 3 miles in altitude and is visible from more than 100 miles away. Its snow-capped western peak is Kibo; its jagged eastern summit, Mawensi. In Chaga legend, Kibo was the elder brother of the younger Mawensi whose crater Kibo blew off when the younger brother asked once too often for a light to rekindle his pipe. To the pastoral Masai who call the western summit, "The House of God," Mt. Kilimanjaro brings rain for their cattle; to the agricultural Chaga, Mt. Kilimanjaro brings rain for their fields.

"One of the greatest challenges"

Dr. Symphorose (Rose) A. Tarimo Nesbitt was born in Kilimanjaro, Tanzania. Her family had a small farm where they raised four acres of coffee and some bananas. Dr. Nesbitt believes that her childhood was "one of the greatest challenges I have had." Her father died when she was two years old leaving her mother with eight children. We "usually ate only one meal a day. We often went hungry."

"She did not listen"

Crossing the educational barrier was very challenging. "Back home, it was like a taboo to send a woman to school. She was suppose to stay at home and have children, and to take care of the husband. In a way, a woman was looked upon as a commodity." The clan and some friends advised Rose's mother not to send her daughters to school. "But she did not listen," Dr. Nesbitt explains. "She did not have any formal education but she supported her children. She was an exception to the rule."

Rose enjoyed attending school. Education was free and when you passed the exams, you went on to the next grade. She decided that the best gift she could give her mother was good grades.

Malaria

When Rose was about nine years old, she contracted malaria, a deadly disease common in Tanzania. Her mother did not understand how her daughter had gotten the disease. She only knew that the mosquitoes gave people this sickness. Rose was intrigued: "I was determined to find out how a small thing like a mosquito could give you a deadly fever." In high school, she enjoyed biology but still wanted to learn something about malaria.

After high school, Tarimo attended Dar-es-Salaam University where her parasitology professor answered most of her questions about mosquitoes and malaria. Having learned this, Rose wanted to know about other insect-caused diseases. She wanted to become a doctor but took the wrong courses ("I didn't do my homework on what courses I needed") and couldn't attend medical school. After earning her B.Sc. in zoology and botany, Tarimo went to work at the Tanga Tsetse Research Institute in Tanzania.

"More dangerous than the mosquito"

More dangerous than the mosquito in Africa is the tsetse fly. Unlike malaria, which is only transmitted by the female mosquito, both the male and female tsetse fly transmit "the sleeping sickness" — a disease that can destroy herds of cattle and be fatal to humans. At the Tanga Tsetse Research Institute, Tarimo reared sterile tsetse flies for an insect release program. Once released, these flies would compete with others and, hopefully, reduce the number of tsetse flies in the area. Although "we watched the population go down systematically," this pilot project was not really a success because "to be successful you need to have an effective barrier. Wild animals crossed the physical barrier that we made and these animals had tsetse flies on them."

-40 degrees

In 1977 Tarimo left Africa to study at West Virginia University. "Leaving home was hard," she says. "Temperatures in West Virginia were -40 degrees sometimes. I bundled up so much." She earned a M.Sc. in entomology/parasitology (1979) and then returned to Kenya as a Graduate Research Scholar.

ICIPE

ICIPE is the International Center for Insect Physiology and Ecology in Nairobi, Kenya. From January 1980 through March 1988, Tarimo studied tsetse fly infection rates, conducted field work to evaluate the barriers to infection, attended the University of Alberta in Edmonton, Canada, to study tsetse genetics, and planned tsetse control strategies. A 98% reduction was achieved in one of the tsetse control groups aimed at using simple technology and community participation. In 1983 Tarimo earned her Ph.D. in Entomology/Parasitology from West Virginia University.

From January 1989 to the present, Dr. Rose Tarimo Nesbitt has been a lecturer in the Biology Department at Howard University, Washington, D.C. She has taught courses in animal diversity, parasitology, and general biology.

Future hopes

"My challenge at the moment," Dr. Nesbitt explains, "is to be able to give back to Africa." Having married a U.S. citizen, Nesbitt feels guilty about remaining in the United States when "Africa needs me more." Her hope for the future is a job that would take her to Africa from time to time. She tells herself, "Usikate tamaa."

Copy these steps on newsprint to use with activity described on next page:

SHOO, FLY, DON'T BOTHER ME
Experiment

From **Handbook of Nature Study** by Anna Botsford Comstock:

- Pour newly dissolved unflavored gelatin onto a clean plate.
- Allow gelatin to cool.
- Let a housefly walk over the gelatin.
- Cover the plate and leave for 3 or 4 days.
- Examine the gelatin to "see if you can tell where the fly walked."

Caution. **Boiling water** can cause severe burns. The instructor should do this part of the experiment.

Caution. **Flies transmit disease**. Do not touch fly with hands. Wash hands thoroughly before going on to other activities.

Caution. **Bacteria and molds** that grow on food can cause illness. Do not touch the gelatin after the experiment has begun. Wash hands thoroughly before going on to other activities and dispose of completed experiment in a safe manner.

Instructor's Guide:

SHOO, FLY, DON'T BOTHER ME
Experiment

Background Information:

Anna Botsford Comstock, founder and first head of the Department of Nature Study at Cornell University, believed "that we should know first and best the things closest to us." Her **Handbook of Nature Study** (originally published in 1911) was written for elementary school teachers who wanted a nature-study curriculum. The **Handbook**'s 859 pages are "informal and chatty" communications filled with information about animals, plants, geography, and astronomy. From "How to Make an Aquarium for Insects" to "Weather Proverbs," Comstock shares scientific data, personal observations, experiments, and legends.

Comstock's suggestion for an experiment with the common housefly gives students the opportunity:
- to study nature,
- to learn about a common disease-transmitting insect, and
- to sharpen their skills at designing and conducting experiments.

Determine the way you wish the experiment to be conducted i.e. as teams (2-6 students), as individuals, or as a classroom-created experiment.

Instructions:

Today

1. Distribute Part A of "My Notes."

> **Ask ...**
>
> *What do you know about houseflies?* [Discuss information and experiences. Be alert to references about the fly "being dirty" or "carrying disease."]

> **Explain ...**
>
> *About 80 years ago, a woman named Anna Botsford Comstock encouraged teachers and students to study nature. One of her lessons dealt with the housefly. The common housefly has two compound red-brown eyes made up of thousands of tiny six-sided lenses. Its wings beat more than 200 times a second. The fly uses its antennae to locate food but has no jaws. All solid food is changed by the fly into a liquid before the fly can suck the juice through its tubular mouth. Comstock described how its feet have hairy little pads that make it possible for it to walk on the ceiling. These hairs collect disease-causing microbes. To prove this, Comstock suggested the experiment we will be using during this discovery unit.*

2. Display the sheet featuring Comstock's suggestion. (Copied from page 21.)
3. Students are to use "My Notes" Part A to design the SHOO, FLY, DON'T BOTHER ME Experiment using Comstock's suggestion.
4. Circulate to answer questions.
5. After students have completed Part A, verify the supplies needed, writing these on the chalkboard as a reminder.

Tomorrow

1. Conduct experiment(s).
2. Assist students in clean-up.

Several Days Later

1. Observe experiment results.
2. Complete Part B of "My Notes."

Part A

Based on "Comstock's suggestion," What QUESTION do we want to answer?

What is our HYPOTHESIS? (Write an If . . . , then . . . statement.)

What EXPERIMENT can we conduct that will test that hypothesis?
The SHOO, FLY, DON'T BOTHER ME EXPERIMENT

What are the PROCEDURES? (List the steps sequentially.)

What SUPPLIES are needed?

Assignments with deadlines: (**who** does **what** and **when.**)

My Notes *by*_____*Date*_____

Part B

From our experiment I learned:_____

_____

_____

_____

_____

_____

_____

This is what we observed after the fly walked across the gelatin:

Illustration

The Scientific Gazette

Challenges in childhood lead to scientific career

Dr. Symphorose (Rose) Tarimo Nesbitt was born in 1952 in Kilimanjaro, Tanzania. She believes that her childhood was "one of the greatest challenges I have had." Her father died when she was two years old leaving her mother with eight children. We "usually ate only one meal a day. We often went hungry," Nesbitt explains.

When Rose was 9 years old, she contracted malaria, a disease transmitted by mosquitoes. Rose became determined to discover how a small insect can spread such a disease. Although she studied biology in high school, her questions about malaria remained unanswered.

After high school Rose attended Dar-es-Salaam University where her parasitology professor explained how mosquitoes transmit malaria. Rose decided to study other insect-caused diseases. She wanted to become a medical doctor but took the wrong courses and, consequently, could not attend medical school. Instead, she earned a doctoral degree in entomology /parasitology and worked to reduce tsetse fly infection rates.

Dr. Rose Tarimo Nesbitt, entomologist, is now a lecturer in the Biology Department at Howard University, Washington, D.C.

In Swahili "usikate tamaa" means _____.

Why do you think this is one of Dr. Nesbitt's favorite sayings?

Enrichment Activities:

◆ Conduct an insect inventory around your school or home.

◆ Create an aquarium housing insects of the "brook or pond," Anna Botsford Comstock's **Handbook of Nature Study** provides directions for an aquarium plus 857 pages of information, observations, and suggestions. This is a great resource for school, home, and overland trips.

◆ Collect poems and stories featuring flies and other insects.

◆ Find a recipe for Shoofly Pie and prepare this rich molasses dessert popular among the Pennsylvania Dutch.

Fun Facts:

On Mt. Kilimanjaro:
◆ Rats have short tails.
◆ The giant grandsel plant, a member of the daisy family, grows 20' high.
◆ School children learn agricultural practices by growing cabbages.

— **Kilimanjaro**, A Nature Series video produced/ directed by Ian Bodenham. Editor is Chris Fraser.

"It is never too early to set goals. The mistake I made was not to do my homework on what was necessary to achieve the goals. You must do this homework. Stay in school. Remember that some kids elsewhere do not have the privilege of going to school."

— **Dr. Symphorose Tarismo Nesbitt**

A flea can jump 200 times its length.
　　What is your height?
　　What is 200 times your height?
　　Can you jump that far?

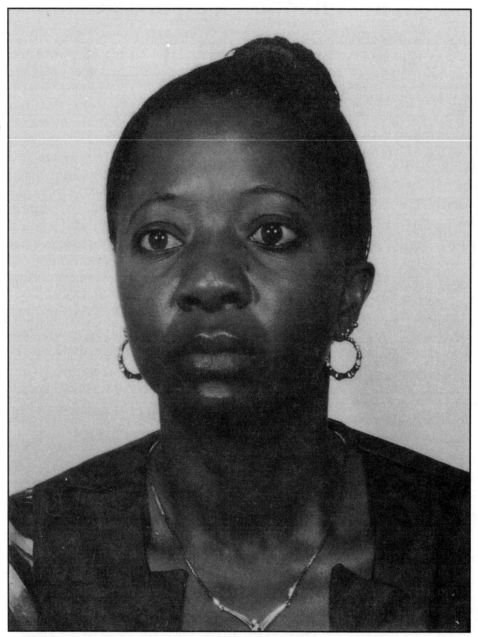

Agriculturist Grace Ngemukong Tima teaches new agricultural practices to village extension workers in Cameroon, Africa.

Discovery Unit No. 4

Grace Ngemukong Tima
Agriculture

SEARCH and SPROUT Experiment

Time-line:
- 1954 Grace Ngemukong Tima is born in Cameroon.
- 1960 - Cameroon becomes an independent nation
- In 1974, 23.2% of the U.S. Department of Agriculture's permanent employees are women.
- Late 1970s - Dr. Wafaa El Sadeek, Egyptologist, becomes the first woman in Egypt to head an archeological team on a major dig, the Temple of Karnak.
- 1985 - In Africa 60 - 80% of the cultivation of foodstuffs relate to labor by women.

Key points:
☛ In Cameroon, Africa, Grace Ngemukong Tima is an agriculturist, a scientist who studies soil, crops, and livestock.

☛ Tima's job in Agricultural Extension includes coordinating the activities of agricultural engineers, teaching new agricultural practices to village Extension workers, and supervising the activities of field technicians.

☛ In the SEARCH and SPROUT Experiment students search for seeds in their home and school environments, and attempt to sprout their discoveries. Activity includes classification, prediction, and observation.

Supplies:
✓ Seeds that students have collected
✓ Paper cups or rinsed milk cartons
✓ Permanent markers for labeling
✓ Good soil or potting soil
✓ Spoons or trowels
✓ Newspapers (to make clean-up quicker)
✓ Spray bottle and water
✓ "My Notes" for each student (pages 30-32)
✓ *The Scientific Gazette* for each student

Steps — prior to day 1:
1. SEARCH and COLLECT. (See instructor's guide.)

Steps — day 1:
1. Point out Bamenda, Cameroon, on a map.
2. Share highlights of Grace N. Tima's life.
3. CLASSIFY and PLANT. (See instructor's guide.)
4. Spread newspapers.
5. Distribute seeds and supplies.
6. Complete Day 1 of "My Notes."
7. Assist students in clean-up.

Steps — day 3 to day 9:
1. WAIT and OBSERVE. (See instructor's guide.)
2. Examine seed pots (and plants) and enter observations in "Notes and Illustrations."
3. Share observations with other scientists.

Steps — day 10:
1. Examine seed pots and plants.
2. Complete Day 10 of "My Notes."
3. Decide the future of the plants (See instructor's guide).
4. Assist students in clean-up.
5. Distribute *The Scientific Gazette*.
6. Add Grace N. Tima's name and a memento to the world map.

For next time:
- Announce the next scientist.

Bibliography:
Althouse, Rosemary. **Investigating Science with Young Children**.

Tima, Grace Ngemukong. **Letter**, October 26, 1994.

Biography of
GRACE NGEMUKONG TIMA
b. 1954

"Do not try to change the world, but try to change yourself. Those around you may imitate and so would the world be changed."

— **Grace Ngemukong Tima**

Family has always been important to Ms. Tima. She grew up in a sharecropper/market-oriented family in Bamenda, Cameroon, where she spent time farming and selling farm produce. Her parents did not receive a formal education but encouraged their children to attend school. Her sister became a trained teacher and her brothers are a vice-principal of a college, an architect, and a banker. Two other siblings are studying in the United States. Ms. Tima is the mother of three sons.

From housewife to scientist

When Grace Tima entered Saint Augustine's College of the North-West Province of Cameroon, she was planning to finish her secondary education and get married. However, her mother, neighbors, teachers, and church elders encouraged Grace to "make good use of her brains." The idea of becoming a scientist came from one of the lecturers in the Regional College of Agriculture. He told Grace about the requirements for and benefits of becoming an agriculturist. She changed her major from "housewife to agriculturist."

Agricultural extension

After graduating from the Regional College of Agriculture with a diploma in General Agriculture, Grace traveled to the United States where she received her B.Sc. from California State University at Pomona. She went to Canada to earn her M.Sc. in Agricultural Extension at the University of Guelph in Guelph, Ontario. Upon returning to Cameroon, Ms. Tima became the Chief of Extension and Training with the Ministry of Agriculture at the Provincial Delegation of Agriculture in the Northwest Province, Bamenda.

Tima's job includes coordinating the activities of eight subject-matter specialists all of whom are agricultural engineers, training 159 village Extension workers about new agricultural practices, conducting workshops and seminars, and supervising 232 field technicians.

Her greatest challenge

Looking back at her career, Tima believes that her greatest professional challenge was being nominated to a duty post because the person doing the nominating believed he could manipulate her for his benefit — not for the benefit of the program or its beneficiaries. Tima's solution to this challenge was to "keep working hard with a clear conscience." She believes that "what is yours can only be delayed, not withheld."

Active scientist & citizen

Grace Tima's participation in associations reflects her commitment to agriculture as well as to the advancement of women. In addition to being a member of the Canadian Society of Extension (CSE) and secretary of an advisory committee that supervises and coordinates technical, financial, and administrative activities, Tima is:

- Founder of the Cameroon Association of University Women,
- Founder of the Cameroon College of Arts, Science and Technology Bambili Day Care Centre,
- Foundation member of the Sustainable Livestock Foundation,
- Member of the Association of Women in Science (AWIS), and
- Stakeholder of a Winrock International Program on African Women Leaders in Agriculture and the Environment (AWLAE).

Advice

Through her work and activities, Grace Ngemukong Tima believes that "God never created anybody without a purpose. All we need to do is to find out what each person has the aptitude for, and develop it."

Instructor's Guide:

The SEARCH and SPROUT Experiment

Instructions:

SEARCH and COLLECT

The SEARCH portion of this experiment enhances a student's understanding of where seeds can be found. Seed packets and the outdoors are two obvious sources but the kitchen and grocery store offer seed-getting opportunities as well. Allow several days for the SEARCH. Label seeds as students COLLECT them; discuss other seed sources i.e. "the grapefruit you had for breakfast"; and trek to the local grocery store where the produce section, the spice racks, and the food bins contain a variety of seeds (coconut, potato, walnut, sesame seeds, poppy seeds, fennel, 13-bean soup . . . even bird seed).

Enjoy a seed safari around the school. Discuss how seeds travel by **wind** ("Ever notice how a dandelion or thistle seed looks like a parachute?"), by **water** (rivers carry seed-bearing twigs downstream, rain may wash seeds downhill), and by **animals** (burrs in dog/cat fur, nuts carried and dropped by squirrels and crows, seeds eaten and eliminated by birds).

CLASSIFY and PLANT

Scientists have grouped plants and animals according to traits they have in common. This organization is called classification.

CLASSIFY the seeds. Name these classifications such as "large round seeds," "hair-like seeds," and "ragged-edged seeds."

Distribute supplies. PLANT seeds. Keep soil moist, but not soaked.

> To help the students understand the germination of the seeds in the soil, set aside some of the beans, fill a glass jar with scrunched damp paper towels, place the beans between the towels and the sides of the jar, and watch them germinate. Observe how the seed coats "open" to allow the roots, shoot, and leaves to emerge; note how the roots grow down; and imagine how this process is being duplicated in the moist darkness of the soil.

WAIT and OBSERVE

OBSERVE for 10 days or longer. From Day 3 through 9:

- **Build**. . .a common vocabulary together i.e. germinate, seed coat, roots, stem, and seed leaves (the first leaves to emerge) — plant leaves come later.

- **Discuss** how scientists write down and illustrate (or photograph) their observations.

- **Decide** what observations might be helpful: *[Do all seed leaves look alike? Do big seeds have big seed leaves and small seeds, small seed leaves? Compare the shape of the seed leaves with the plant leaves.]*

This portion of the experiment may be short- or long-term. Transplant young plants to larger containers or to an outdoor garden or yard. The plants can become subjects for experiments testing fertilizers (commercial products vs. compost), light (natural vs. artificial), water (drip-water method vs. hydroponics), and/or climate (indoors vs. outdoors).

Add notes here:

My Notes by _____ Date _____

Day 1:

List the seed classifications you planted. Predict which seeds will germinate.

Kind of seed planted	I predict that it **will** germinate	I predict that it **will not** germinate
_____	☐	☐
_____	☐	☐
_____	☐	☐
_____	☐	☐

Day 3: Notes and Illustration

_____

_____

_____

_____

_____

_____

Day 4: Notes and Illustration

_____

_____

_____

_____

_____

_____

Day 5: Notes and Illustration

_____

_____

_____

_____

_____

_____

My Notes by _____Date _____

Day 6: Notes and Illustration

_____

_____

_____

_____

_____

_____

Day 7: Notes and Illustration

_____

_____

_____

_____

_____

_____

Day 8: Notes and Illustration

_____

_____

_____

_____

_____

_____

Day 9: Notes and Illustration

_____

_____

_____

_____

_____

_____

Day 10:

Complete this chart.

Kind of seed planted	Did germinate	Did not germinate
_____	☐	☐
_____	☐	☐
_____	☐	☐
_____	☐	☐

Reread the predictions you made on Day 1. How accurate were your predictions?

_____

_____

_____

Two of the seeds that germinated looked like these:

After today the plants will _____

_____

_____

"The object of planting any seed should be to rear a plant which shall fulfill its whole duty and produce other seed." — Anna Botsford Comstock

The Scientific Gazette

Agriculturist in Cameroon

"Do not try to change the world, but try to change yourself. Those around you may imitate and so would the world be changed."

— Grace Ngemukong Tima, agriculturist

In Cameroon, Africa, Grace Ngemukong Tima is an agriculturist, a scientist who studies soil, crops, and livestock. Her official title is the Chief of Extension and Training. She coordinates the activities of 8 subject-matter specialists, trains 159 village Extension workers about new agricultural practices, conducts workshops, and supervises 232 field technicians.

The advancement of women is also a concern to Tima. She is a member of the Association of Women in Science and the founder of the Cameroon Association of University Women. She founded a day care center at the Cameroon College of Arts, Science and Technology, and is active in AWLAE, African Women Leaders in Agriculture and the Environment.

Grace Tima believes that "God never created anybody without a purpose. All we need to do is to find out what each person has the aptitude for, and develop it."

Some facts about seeds

Some plants make new plants by means of seeds. We not only eat seeds but plant them for future crops (agriculture) and convert them into products (industry) such as soaps, varnishes, medicines, perfumes, and even plastics.

Seeds travel by wind, water, and animals.

- Winds lift seeds to heights of 5,000 feet.
- River currents carry uprooted trees seaward.
- Scientist Charles Darwin extracted the seeds from a wad of mud carried on a bird's plumage and raised 82 separate plants! (Rachel Carson, **The Sea Around Us**.)

During The **SEARCH and SPROUT Experiment** we collected and germinated seeds. I discovered _____

_____

_____

..." the struggle of the little plant to get free from its seed coats may be a truly dramatic story."

— Anna Botsford Comstock

At Home:

- Visit a plant nursery.
- Design a garden.
- Germinate bird seed in a damp sponge.
- Purchase alfalfa seed and germinate your own sprouts.
- Explore your library to find the directions for **Mancala**, the "national game of Africa" and one of the five most widely played board games in the world. Although commercial game boards are available through catalogues and retail outlets, you can play the game with common household objects. After all, the game was originally played with seeds, or stones, and holes scooped in the earth!

"Perfectly Good Light"

Dr. Sara C. Beck — b. 1954

Astrophysicist Dr. Sara C. Beck lives in Israel and holds a tenured faculty job at Tel Aviv University. Her husband "does theoretical physics of particles, which are the smallest things around, and I do experimental physics of galaxies which are the largest things around."

"A devoted spectroscopist"

Light from these galaxies travels in waves invisible to the human eye. Infrared light is, "perfectly good light," Beck explains, "it's only our human eyes which are limited and can't see it." Spectroscopy, by converting light waves into a spectrum visible to the human eye, makes the detailed study of this light possible.

"A spectroscopist can measure the light of a star and tell how hot the star is, how much of every element it contains, and how the gas on the surface moves, or measure the light from Jupiter and see what chemicals are in its atmosphere, how deep they are, and the temperature. Spectroscopy is what turns astronomy into astrophysics. We can't go to another star or galaxy and take a sample to find what it's made out of, but spectroscopy is the next best thing to being there. So I became a devoted spectroscopist."

Sara Beck grew up in Virginia. Among her earliest childhood memories is "that of lying on the grass at night staring up at the stars in fascination. When I was somewhat older I would go to the library and work my way through every book . . . on the stars and planets. When the books contradicted each other . . . I found it exciting; it meant that there was something important and basic which wasn't known and I would daydream about being the one to find the right answer."

"A good mathematical foundation"

As a youth Dr. Beck did not consider a career in astronomy. The sciences in school were weak but she was "lucky enough to have superb math teachers." Beck believes that "if you have a good mathematical foundation, any other deficiencies in your education can be overcome."

Beck's family and math teachers encouraged her. When she attended Princeton University in New Jersey and, later, the University of California at Berkeley, Beck was the only woman in the lab. She was treated "with perfect fairness" and welcomed as a colleague. "It was a complete contrast to the discouragement of high school."

"The rest of my life"

In 1986 Dr. Beck and family left Boston, Massachusetts, to live in Israel, her husband's birthplace. The mother of three children, she believes Israel is a great place for children: ". . . it's a society which makes it easy to have both a family and a professional life."

Since astronomy is "a young field" in Israel, Beck has been involved in the beginning of many important projects: "I brought the first infrared instrument to the Israeli national observatory, I am working on the first Israeli astronomical satellite, and we are making plans for the first radio telescope in the country." Beck's enthusiasm for her work is, like the galaxies she studies, boundless: "I won't be surprised if I work on these problems for the rest of my life."

Enrichment Activity: Explore astrophysics through the eyes of author Madeleine L'Engle. She calls **A Wrinkle in Time, A Wind in the Door,** and **A Swiftly Tilting Planet** her Time Trilogy. Her book, **A Ring of Endless Light,** took months to research.

Bibliography:

Beck, Sara. **Letter**, June 6, 1994.

A N T A R C T I C A

Antarctica covers 10% of the earth's land surface. Almost 95% of this land surface is covered with ice — approximately 7.5 million cubic miles of ice. The weight of this ice crushes the continent's geographic features causing much of the land mass to lie below sea level. This ice sheet, formed between 25 to 42 million years ago affects the world's climate and the hemisphere's ozone depletion. The melting of this ice sheet would raise the world's ocean levels an estimated 130 feet to 250 feet.

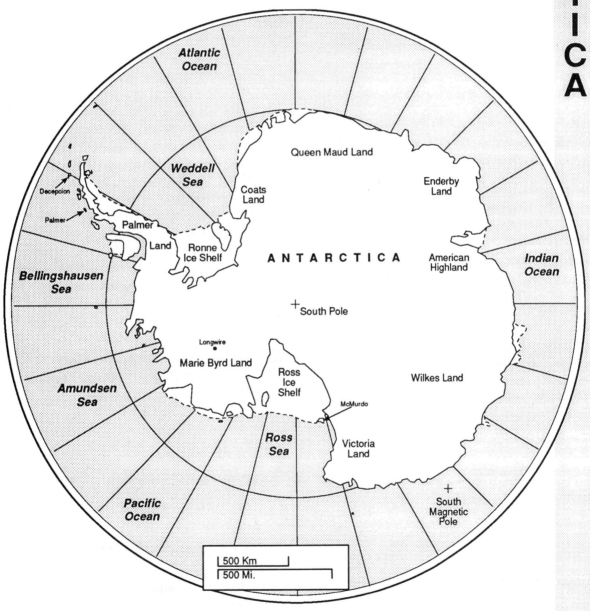

Antarctica and Science:

During the International Geophysical Year in 1957 and 1958, scientists from around the world worked together to answer basic questions about our earth. They explored and mapped uncharted land around the world including Antarctica. This coldest place on earth became a science laboratory with international scientists conducting research, exchanging information, and sharing equipment and supplies.

This arrangement worked so well that scientists persuaded their governments to sign the 30-year Antarctic Treaty of 1959. This treaty:

- prohibited military operations including weapons testing on the continent,
- erased national boundaries, and
- dedicated the continent exclusively to scientific research.

Twelve nations signed the Antarctic Treaty. They were: France, United Kingdom, New Zealand, Australia, Norway, Chile, Argentina, Belgium, Japan, South Africa, United States, and the Union of Soviet Socialist Republics (USSR). In 1961 Poland agreed to abide by this treaty followed by Czechoslovakia (1962), Denmark (1965), the Netherlands (1967), Romania (1971) East Germany (1974), Brazil (1975), Bulgaria (1978) West Germany in 1979, and Uruguay (1980). These nations established over 40 international research stations.

Scientists from these stations have conducted thousands of experiments. They have:

- detected a hole in the ozone layer over the continent,
- scaled mountains to collect fossil spores and pollen,
- lowered microphones into arctic waters to monitor the "voices" of seals,
- discovered a natural antifreeze that prevents Antarctic fish from freezing to death,
- grown vegetables without using soil,
- studied how six months of darkness can affect human behavior, and
- uncovered a fossil of a meat-eating dinosaur that lived on Antarctica about 200 million years ago when this now-arctic continent had a climate like that of today's Pacific Northwest.

For many years the only scientists working in Antarctica were men.

In 1956 the USSR became the first government to send a woman scientist into this remote region. She was Dr. Marie Vasilievna Klenova whose work in Marine Geology earns her the honor of being the first woman scientist to work in Antarctica. See Discovery Unit No. 16 which features Klenova's life and work.

Argentina dispatched four women scientists in the summer of 1968-69. The first women to join the US and New Zealand research programs on the continent stepped ashore in 1969. By the 1970s, almost 150 years after the first explorer went ashore in 1821, women were finally accepted as equal partners in science. Three of these women scientists will be spotlighted in this unit. They are **Dr. Mary Alice McWhinnie, Dr. Roseli Ocampo-Friedmann,** and **Dr. Irene Carswell Peden.**

Bibliography:

Bickel, Lennard. **Mawson's Will: The Greatest Survival Story Ever Written.**

Brewster, Barney. **Antarctica: Wilderness at Risk.**

Cameron, Ian. **Antarctica, The Last Continent.**

Caras, Roger A. **Antarctica, Land of Frozen Time.**

Land, Barbara. **The New Explorers: Women in Antarctica.**

Continental Facts:

- "Antarctic" is a shortening of "anti-Arctic" since this continent rests opposite the Arctic region.

- Antarctica is the only continent without national borders.

- In its dry valleys snow evaporates before it hits the ground.

- This continent is a cold desert.

- Its largest land animal is a wingless mosquito.

Continental Curiosities:

- Lake Vanda, 17 miles from the sea, is salty but fed by freshwater glaciers.

- Several interior valleys are free of ice and snow year-round.

Exploration Questions:

- Why do scientists consider Antarctica a cold desert?

- Was the 30-year Antarctica Treaty of 1959 renewed?

Enrichment Activities:

- Take a globe or map, and draw a line (or use straight pins and string) from Antarctica to each of the countries agreeing to the Antarctic Treaty of 1959.

- Older students could research the names and locations of research stations, and then draw lines connecting the stations and their respective countries i.e. from Decepcion on the Antarctic Peninsula to Argentina.

Add information and ideas here:

Biologists Dr. Mary Alice McWhinnie (right) and Sister Mary Odile Cahoon (left) collect samples for their study of krill. They were the first women to spend the winter in Antarctica engaged in scientific research.

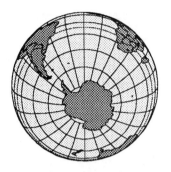

Discovery Unit No. 5

Dr. Mary Alice McWhinnie
Biology

EARTHWORM EXPERT Activity

Time-line
- 1927 - 1980 Dr. Mary Alice McWhinnie
- 1935 - Caroline Mikkelsen from Norway becomes the first woman to step on the Antarctic shore.
- 1956 - Professor Marie V. Klenova (USSR) maps areas of the Antarctic coast.
- 1978 - 1979 - Meteorist Dr. Ursula Marvin collects meteorites in Antarctica.

Key points
☛ Dr. Mary Alice McWhinnie, biologist, was the first woman to serve as a scientific leader at a research station in Antarctica.

☛ Dr. McWhinnie was an international authority on krill, shrimplike creatures that are the "main course" of the Antarctic food web.

☛ To honor her contributions to science and her work in Antarctica, the biology center at Palmer Station was renamed the Mary Alice McWhinnie Biology Center.

☛ Substituting earthworms for krill, students in the EARTHWORM EXPERT Activity will plan and conduct experiments that will increase their knowledge of earthworms.

Supplies — today
✓ Sheets of newsprint and a felt marker
✓ A waterproof container (a 32 oz. yogurt container works well) for every 3 to 4 students
✓ Soil (damp, but not soaked) to fill containers three-quarters full
✓ 1 to 4 earthworms in each container
✓ Compost i.e. fruit and vegetable scraps mixed gently into the soil
✓ A cool dark place to store earthworms for several days
✓ "My Notes" Parts A, B, & C, for each student (pages 43-44)

✓ A magnifying glass, ruler, pencil, a clock with a second hand, and a damp paper towel for each student or group of 3 to 4 students
✓ A library or resource person with information about earthworms

Supplies — several days later
✓ Determined by experiment(s) that students decide to conduct
✓ "My Notes" Part D, for each student (page 44)
✓ *The Scientific Gazette* for each student

Steps — today
1. Point out McMurdo and Palmer Stations on a map or globe. (page 42)
2. Share highlights of Dr. McWhinnie's life.
3. Begin the EARTHWORM EXPERT Activity. (See instructor's guide, pages 41&42.)
4. Complete "My Notes" Parts A, B, & C.
5. Determine future experiment(s).

Steps — several days later
1. Conduct experiment(s).
2. Complete "My Notes" Part D.
3. Return earthworms to outdoor soil.
4. Add Dr. Mary Alice McWhinnie's name and a memento to the world map.
5. Distribute *The Scientific Gazette* .

For next time
- Introduce the next scientist.

Bibliography
Brewster, Barney. **Antarctica: Wilderness at Risk**.

Burton, Robert. **Animals of the Antarctic**.

Land, Barbara. **The New Explorers: Women in Antarctica**.

Lawlor, Elizabeth P. **Discover Nature Close to Home: Things to Know and Things to Do**.

Biography of
DR. MARY ALICE McWHINNIE
1927 - 1980

For biologist Dr. Mary Alice McWhinnie, her curiosity was the link between crayfish in Chicago, Illinois, and krill in Antarctica. In the summer of 1958, while teaching at DePaul University in Chicago, Dr. McWhinnie conducted experiments with crayfish, fresh-water crustaceans that look like lobsters. She observed how crayfish grow and molt (shed their outer shells).

During the following winter, Dr. McWhinnie repeated some of the experiments but the crayfish did not grow or molt. Being a scientist, she needed to know why the same experiments produced different results. She discovered the variable to be the temperature of the tap water holding the crayfish. In winter the temperature of the water fell to 2 degrees above freezing. When transferred to warmer water, the crayfish resumed growing and molting.

To study krill

Krill are shrimp-like crustaceans that live in Antarctic waters. Dr. McWhinnie wondered how krill could live in colder waters than their relatives, the crayfish. The best way to answer this question, she decided, was to go to Antarctica and study krill. In 1959 she sent her proposal to the National Science Foundation (NSF), an agency that evaluated Antarctic research projects proposed by U.S. scientists.

Although the NSF approved McWhinnie's proposed study, a major obstacle remained. Only the U.S. Navy provided transportation for American scientists to Antarctica and, since 1948, the Navy had refused to transport women. However, the NSF offered a scientific "cruise" through Antarctic waters aboard a new research ship, the *Eltanin*. Dr. McWhinnie jumped at the opportunity.

First woman leader

Between 1962 and 1972 Dr. McWhinnie made six trips on the *Eltanin* . By 1972 she was the *Eltanin*'s chief scientist. Two years later the U.S. Navy had changed its policy and transported Dr. McWhinnie to McMurdo, a U.S. research station on the continent, where she became the first woman to serve as the station's scientific leader.

Dr. McWhinnie's work with krill continued. She studied how the austral winter affects these crustaceans whom she considered the "main course" for whales, seals, and penguins. In 1975 she traveled to the Palmer Station on the Antarctic Peninsula and designed a large aquarium with circulating sea water so krill could survive in the lab. Krill, she concluded, was a key species in the Antarctic food chain.

Rich in protein and vitamins, krill were being caught in the early 1970s by fishing fleets from many countries, and marketed as a shrimp substitute or manufactured into krill meal, animal feed for cows and salmon. In 1976 the demand for these small crustaceans soared. Dr. McWhinnie, now regarded as an international authority on krill, wondered if the supply were sufficient to meet global demands. A reduced supply of krill could hurt, or even destroy, Antarctic animal populations.

Proposal saves krill

In 1977 at an international meeting of scientists from the fifteen Antarctic Treaty nations, Dr. McWhinnie proposed a study of the biology of krill and advocated an international effort to conserve this important food source.

The study led to a management program for the entire Southern Ocean. In May 1980, the Antarctic Treaty nations and representatives from international organizations and commissions agreed to a Convention on the Conservation of Antarctic Marine Living Resources. This agreement proved a landmark in international law.

Dr. McWhinnie did not live to see the signing of the Convention. In the fall of 1979, she became ill with a condition that left her partially paralyzed and unable to speak. She died in March 1980. To honor her contributions to science and her work in Antarctica, the biology center at Palmer Station was renamed the Mary Alice McWhinnie Biology Center.

Instructor's Guide:

EARTHWORM EXPERT Activity

Background Information:

Scientists ask many questions. Answers to their questions may come from other scientists involved in similar work, additional resources including publications, or from scientific experiments. This activity is intended to help students understand how scientists, like biologist Dr. Mary Alice McWhinnie, become experts.

Instructions:

Today

1. Post newsprint.
2. Set out supplies needed today.
3. Distribute "My Notes" Part A, B, & C, to each student.

> **Explain . . .**
>
> *Scientists ask many questions. To become an expert on krill, Dr. Mary Alice McWhinnie began by asking questions. She asked, "How long do krill live?" "What are they made of?" "How do they see?" "How do they live in the Antarctic winter when sea waters are covered with ice?"*
>
> *Since krill live in Antarctic waters, we cannot study them firsthand. Instead, we will study earthworms.*
>
> **Ask . . .**
>
> *What do you know about earthworms?* [Listen to responses.] *What questions do you have about earthworms?* [Are all earthworms the same size? Do they have eyes? Do they have mouths? What do they eat? What animals eat earthworms? How do they move? Do they like light? Where do they live?]

4. Record all questions on newsprint.
5. Determine which questions can be answered by using the "supplies needed today for this unit" (the earthworm, magnifying glass etc.).

6. Divide the questions so each discovery group of 3 to 4 students receives one or two questions.
7. Give students time to complete Part A of "My Notes."

> **Explain . . .**
>
> *Dr. McWhinnie shared her scientific findings and opinions with other scientists.*

8. Invite groups to share their answers while other students record these "scientific findings" in Part B of "My Notes."

> **Explain . . .**
>
> *Dr. McWhinnie conducted experiments to learn some of the answers to her questions about krill. In one of her laboratories, she designed a large aquarium with sea water flowing through it. This invention made it possible for her to keep krill alive in the laboratory so she could observe them firsthand. She learned that krill live more than two years, grow new exoskeletons regularly, and eat each other if their food, plankton, is unavailable.*

9. Return to the original list of questions. Decide which ones could be answered by conducting experiments. Have each group select a question. Allow time for gathering information, forming a hypothesis, and planning the experiment. Circulate to answer questions and to allow time for students to complete Part C of "My Notes."
10. Assist students in clean-up.
11. Explore resources on earthworms.
12. Begin experiments.

Several days later

1. Discovery groups share the results of or conduct their experiments.

2. Allow time for students to complete Part D of "My Notes."

3. Assist students in clean-up.

4. Return earthworms to outdoor soil.

5. Add Dr. Mary Alice McWhinnie's name and a memento to the world map.

6. Distribute *The Scientific Gazette*.

Enrichment Activity:

Food webs illustrate links between plants, fish, insects, and animals. A food web shows who is the predator (the eating animal) and who is the prey (the eaten animal). In Antarctic waters, a killer whale (predator) eats leopard seals (prey), crabeater seals, and blue whales; leopard seals (predator) eat Emperor penguins (prey) who eat squid and small fish who eat krill; crabeater seals eat krill; and blue whales eat krill. The leopard seal is prey to the killer whale but the predator to Emperor penguins.

1. What animals eat earthworms?

2. What do earthworms eat?

Create a food web that includes earthworms.

3. How does this food web compare with the one for krill?

Add notes here:

Map Study No. 1:

Palmer Station is located on an island off the Antarctic Peninsula. The Antarctic Peninsula extends north towards the tip of which continent? On a globe, or world map, locate Argentina, Drake passage, South Shetland Islands, the Falkland Islands, Tierra del Fuego, and the Straits of Magellan.

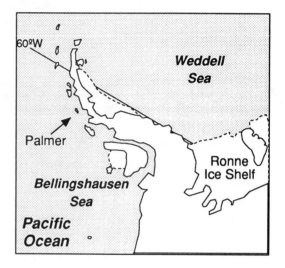

Map Study No. 2:

McMurdo Station is located on an island at the edge of the Ross Ice Shelf. McMurdo Station is always one day behind Palmer Station. Why is this? What is an ice shelf? Who was Ross? Who was Victoria? Have students find the answers to these questions, sharing their resources with each other.

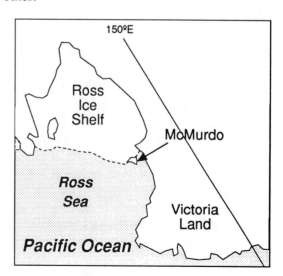

My Notes *by* _____ *Date* _____

Part A

OUR QUESTIONS	OUR ANSWERS
1.	1.
2.	2.

Part B

From other scientists I learned that earthworms:

_____

_____

_____

_____

_____

_____

_____

My Notes by _____ Date _____

OUR EARTHWORM EXPERIMENT

What QUESTION do we want to answer? _____

_____

What INFORMATION will help us form a hypothesis? _____

_____

What is our HYPOTHESIS? _____

_____

What EXPERIMENT can we conduct that will test that hypothesis? _____

_____

What are the PROCEDURES?   What SUPPLIES are needed?

_____   _____

_____   _____

_____   _____

ASSIGNMENTS: _____

_____

_____ DEADLINE: _____

Part D

From our experiment I learned:

_____

_____

_____

From other scientists I learned:

_____

_____

_____

_____

The Scientific Gazette

Biology   **Dr. Mary Alice McWhinnie**

Interest in krill draws scientist to Antarctica

How do krill live in Antarctic waters when crayfish, a distant fresh-water cousin, grow only in warmer waters. To find the answer to this question, biologist Dr. Mary Alice McWhinnie left Chicago, Illinois, and sailed through Antarctic waters aboard the *Eltanin*, a science research ship. Between 1962 and 1972, she made six trips to Antartica. By 1972 she was the ship's chief scientist

Two years later the U.S. Navy transported Dr. McWhinnie to McMurdo, a U.S. research station on the Antarctic continent, where she became the first woman to serve as the station's scientific leader.

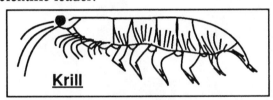

Krill

Her work with krill continued. She learned that these small crustaceans:

- live more than two years,
- grow new exoskeletons regularly,
- eat small animals and plants called plankton,
- eat each other if plankton is unavailable,
- light up at night, like fireflies,
- travel together in "aggregations," and
- are the "main course" for whales, seals, and penguins.

Dr. Mary Alice McWhinnie, Biologist

In 1977 at an international meeting of scientists, Dr. McWhinnie proposed a biological study of krill and conservation of this important food source. In May 1980 the Antarctic Treaty nations approved the Convention on the Conservation of Antarctic Marine Living Resources.

Dr. McWhinnie did not live to see this landmark in international law. This biologist, whose love of nature began as a girl helping her father in the family garden, died in March 1980. The Mary Alice McWhinnie Biology Center at Palmer Station on the Antarctic Peninsula honors her contributions to science and her work in the world's southernmost continent.

To become an expert on krill, Dr. McWhinnie asked questions, conducted experiments, and shared her information and opinions with other scientists. During our EARTHWORM EXPERT Activity, we asked questions, conducted experiments, and shared information and opinions. I learned:

- Earthworms live _____
- Earthworms eat _____
- Earthworms move _____

Fun Fact: In Norwegian, "krill" means "small fry."

Fun Fiction: How to Eat Fried Worms by Thomas Rockwell

Fun Books: Compare your earthworm experiments with those featured in **Animals: Spectacular Science Projects** by Janice Van Cleave, **Backyard Scientists, Series Three** by Jane Hoffman, and **The Amazing Earthworm** by Lilo Hess.

Dr. Irene Carswell Peden was the first woman to receive a Ph.D. in electrical engineering from Stanford University.

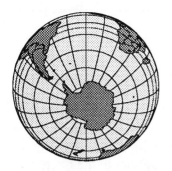

Discovery Unit No. 6

Dr. Irene Carswell Peden
Electrical Engineering

INVISIBLE FORCES Experiment

Time-line:

- 1925 - Dr. Irene Carswell Peden is born in Topeka, Kansas.
- 1942 - Westinghouse Electric hires mathematician Mildred Bennett to work as an electrical engineer.
- 1959 - Photographs of the bottom of Antarctica's Ross Sea show varied animal life including sponges, starfish, and fish.
- 1978 - Dr. Michele Raney becomes the first woman physician to spend a winter at the South Pole.

Key points:

- ☛ Dr. Peden was the first woman to receive a Ph.D. in electrical engineering from Stanford University; the first to teach in the College of Engineering at the University of Washington; and the first U.S. woman engineer/scientist to conduct field work in the interior of Antarctica.
- ☛ Electromagnetism occurs when an electric current, or field, produces a magnetic field.
- ☛ Students will observe electromagnetism in the INVISIBLE FORCES Experiment.

Supplies:

- ✓ A 9V alkaline battery
- ✓ Electrical tape
- ✓ 4-foot length of single strand insulated wire
- ✓ Cable "stripper" (optional)
- ✓ Sharp scissors
- ✓ Piece of wood aproximately 3-inch x 1-inch
- ✓ Two thumbtacks
- ✓ One paper clip

- ✓ One 4" long nail
- ✓ A small (1") nail
- ✓ "My Notes" sheets for each student (pages 51 & 52)
- ✓ *The Scientific Gazette* for each student

Steps:

1. Point out Byrd Station on a map or globe.
2. Share highlights of Dr. Irene C. Peden's life.
3. Conduct the INVISIBLE FORCES Experiment.
4. Assist students in clean-up.
5. Add Dr. Irene C. Peden's name and a memento to the world map.
6. Distribute *The Scientific Gazette* .

For next time:

- Announce the next scientist.

Bibliography:

America Online, **Compton's Encyclopedia, Online Edition** (downloaded November 9, 1994).

Buban, Peter, and others, editors. **Understanding Electricity and Electronics**, Fifth Edition

Cash, Terry. **Electricity and Magnets.**

Dobbs, E. R. **Electricity and Magnetism.**

Land, Barbara. **The New Explorers: Women in Antarctica.**

Peden, Irene C. **Telephone Interviews**, October 25 and November 10, 1994.

Biography of
DR. IRENE CARSWELL PEDEN
b. 1925

In high school Irene C. Peden put off science until her senior year. Then, she took chemistry because everyone said physics was too hard. When chemistry finally "clicked" at the end of her senior year, Peden decided to study chemistry in college.

At Kansas City Junior College, Peden's chemistry professor explained that a good chemist must take physics. Peden reluctantly agreed and took a course called engineering physics. She liked it: "I found answers to questions that I had as a child. Questions like 'Why is the sky blue?' I settled upon engineering as a four-year curriculum."

The University of Colorado

This decision provided an "upward-mobility path" for Peden. After junior college, she entered the engineering program at the University of Colorado at Boulder. The year was 1944. Men were off to war so more women than usual were attending college. At the University of Colorado twelve women were enrolled in the engineering program. There had never been that many before the 1940s nor would there be again until the 1970s.

The challenge

After earning a degree in electrical engineering, Peden faced the challenge of getting a job. Since World War II was over, industries were no longer eager to hire women. She was grateful when she accepted a fairly low-paying job making long-range planning calculations for a power and light company.

Stanford University

Two years later Peden moved to Palo Alto, California, so her husband could attend Stanford University. Hired by the Stanford Research Institute (SRI), she worked with antennas for aircraft and missiles and learned how to use a Freden calculator. "I wanted to learn more but didn't have the background."

Now divorced, Peden, in her characteristic if-you-want-to-do-something-then-do-it pattern, entered the electrical engineering program at Stanford. She planned to get a master's degree but became fascinated with the subject. She was appointed a research assistant in the microwave lab. Although school was "terribly hard and took all of my time," Peden succeeded and in 1961 became the first woman to receive a Ph.D. in electrical engineering from Stanford.

Another "first"

Finding employment was again difficult. People refused to interview her because she was a woman. However, a colleague from SRI convinced the University of Washington to interview Peden. They hired her and in 1962 Dr. Irene C. Peden became the first woman to teach in the College of Engineering at the University of Washington.

At the university she worked with microwaves and antennas, and created lab-scaled models for an Antarctic electrical engineering project. She became one of the principal investigators on the project and, in line with National Science Foundation policy, was required to conduct scientific research in Antarctica.

"Antarctica is like nothing else . . ."

In 1970 Dr. Peden became the first U.S. woman engineer/scientist to conduct field work in the interior of Antarctica. Being an electrical engineer, Peden's specific interest was the electromagnetic (electric and magnetic) properties of polar ice and how these properties affect radio waves.

Following her two-month stay in Antarctica, Peden returned to the University of Washington. "Antarctica is like nothing else," she recounts twenty-four years later. The interior of Antarctica is "fantastic. Beautiful in its own way . . . very silent . . . no birds . . . a very unique experience."

◆ ◆ ◆

Instructor's Guide:

The INVISIBLE FORCES Experiment

Background Information:

In 1820 Hans Christian Oersted, a Danish scientist, observed that the needle of a compass moved when electricity flowed through a wire placed near the compass. Why is this significant? A compass needle responds to a magnetic field. If an electric current causes a compass needle to swing away from the North-South direction, then there is some relationship between electric fields and magnetic fields. In studying *electromagnetism* scientists explore these links between electricity and magnetism.

Electricity can create magnetic fields. In the INVISIBLE FORCES Experiment students observe how an electric current can transform an ordinary nail into an *electromagnet*. This will be done in two stages:

1. Assembling an electrical circuit, and
2. Using this circuit to create an electromagnet.

Instructions:

1. Show that the large nails cannot pick up the smaller ones.
2. Cut wire so one strand is 3' long and the second strand measures 1'.

   Wind the center of the long wire tightly — at least 20 times — around the 4" nail.

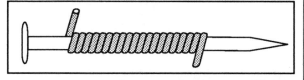

   Use a cable stripper or sharp scissors to remove 1" of the plastic insulation from both ends of the two strands of wire.

   Wrap one end of each wire strand to battery caps. Secure with electrical tape.
3. Stabilize battery by taping to a table top or piece of wood.
4. Partially press the thumbtacks (about 1 1/2" apart) into the wood.

Wrap remaining wire ends under thumbtack heads.

Open paperclip and insert **only** one end under one of the thumbtack heads. (Inserting both ends turns on the electric current.)

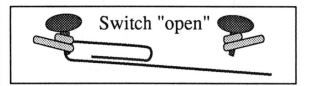

5. Distribute "My Notes" sheet (Part A) and give students time to illustrate the layout of the experiment.

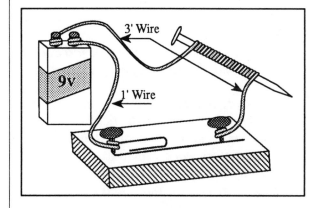

6. Switch on the electric current by inserting the other end of the paperclip under the thumbtack head. (There will be a little spark!)

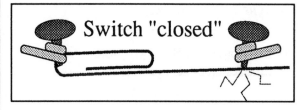

7. Wait 3 minutes. (Feel the battery. If it is warm, then the switch has turned on the current.)

Continued on next page

Explain . . .

The word "electricity" comes from "electrons"— negatively charged particles in atoms. Free electrons race through the wires in the form of an electrical current. As these electrons race through the wire, they create a magnetic field. When we wind a wire around a nail, we concentrate the magnetic field into a small area. The nail becomes a magnet, an **electromagnet,** *since we use electricity to create a magnet.*

8. Show that the large nail can pick up the smaller ones. Compare with a large nail that was not magnetized.

9. Switch off the electricity. Test to see if the nail remains magnetized.

Ask . . .

What do you think are the invisible forces in this experiment? [electricity and magnetism]

Electromagnetism *occurs when an electric current produces a magnetic field. Electromagnetism explains how doorbells and electric generators work. It also explains how electricity and magnetism combine to create radio waves. In Antarctica Dr. Peden used radio waves to learn the electromagnetic properties of polar ice. She hypothesized that if radio waves changed when they passed through the polar ice, then the ice contained electromagnetic forces (or properties) that interacted with the electromagnetic radio waves.*

10. Distribute Part B of "My Notes" and allow time for students to complete.

Map Study:

Peden's field laboratory was inland at 80ºS and 120ºW. Its formal name was Byrd VLF Substation, but was referred to as "Longwire" because it had a 21-mile-long radio antenna. Longwire was located 15 miles from the older and larger Byrd station.

Who was Admiral Richard E. Byrd?

There were a total of five bases named for Admiral Byrd. On a map of Antarctica locate these bases.

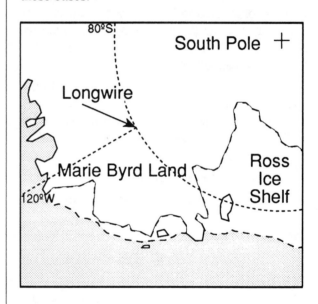

Expanded Discussion:

Scientists use symbols to express ideas. Scientists who study electromagnetism use the symbol "I" for electric current, "E" for voltage, and "R" for resistance. Symbols help scientists communicate with each other.

What symbols do we use to express ideas?

Have students draw symbols they can think of on the chalkboard. As they are identified, write the word(s) next to the symbol. (Example: # = pound.)

The INVISIBLE FORCES Experiment

Part A

This is my drawing of the layout of the experiment:

The INVISIBLE FORCES Experiment

Part B

To conduct the experiment, the long wire was coiled around the nail. The nailed looked like this:

During the experiment, the electric current created a magnetic field and the nail became an

_____

If the nail is made of iron, it will be magnetized only as long as the electric current is switched on. If the nail is made of steel, it will remain magnetized after the electric current is switched off. The nail we used was made of

_____

The Scientific Gazette

Arctic conditions just another challenge to engineer

Dr. Irene Carswell Peden was:

- the first woman to receive a Ph.D. in electrical engineering from Stanford University;
- the first to teach in the College of Engineering at the University of Washington; and
- the first U.S. woman engineer/scientist to conduct field work in the interior of Antarctica.

In Antarctica, near the Byrd VLF Substation, she and assistant Al Chandler concentrated a month-long project into a week's time since missing equipment delayed the experiment. When a substitute frequency synthesizer was located, Peden and Chandler drove 16 miles in near whiteout conditions to retrieve this piece of equipment from a 40-foot-deep hole.

Working 24-hour shifts, they sent signals from a transmitter. At varying distances from the transmitter, they received the signals from an antenna mounted on a mobile sled. By learning how these signals changed, Peden discovered many things including the electromagnetic properties of polar ice.

Throughout her career in electrical engi-

Dr. Irene Carswell Peden

neering, Dr. Peden has received many awards including:

- 1973 Achievement Award of the Society of Women Engineers,
- U.S. Army's Outstanding Civilian Service Medal in 1987,
- National Science Foundation's 1993 Engineer of the Year, and
- An honorary Doctor of Engineering degree from Michigan State University, December 10, 1994.

An inspiration

Lena Anderson Carswell was a mathematics major at a teachers college; taught math in rural schools; and, during World War II, worked as a loftsman at a bomber plant in Kansas City, Kansas. A loftsman took the blueprints of the planes and translated them into extremely accurate metal templates from which the parts of the plane were cut. She often told her daughter, "If you want to do something, then do it." Lena Carswell was quite an inspiration to her daughter, Dr. Irene Carswell Peden.

"Assess your own interests as honestly as you can and go with it. You decide what you like, and what you do well." — **Dr. Irene C. Peden**

In the INVISIBLE FORCES Experiment, we learned how an electric current can produce a magnetic field. The nail became an **electromagnet.** Electromagnets and electromagnetic waves are everywhere.

Some examples are:

_____

_____.

Without electromagnetism, there would be no television, no computers, and no communication satellites.

Microbiologist Dr. Roseli Ocampo-Friedmann studies microorganisms that live in Antarctic desert rocks.

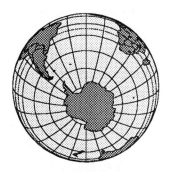

Discovery Unit No. 7

Dr. Roseli Ocampo-Friedmann
Microbiology

A SLICE OF MICROBES Experiment

Time-line:
- 1937 - Dr. Roseli Ocampo-Friedmann is born in Manila, Philippines.
- 1956 - Jennie Darlington's *My Antarctic Honeymoon: A Year at the Bottom of the World* describes her visit to Antarctica in 1947 - '48.
- 1975 - U.S. launches Viking 1 and Viking 2 space probes.

Key points:
- ☛ Microbiologist Dr. Roseli Ocampo-Friedmann studies microbes, living organisms too small to see without a microscope.
- ☛ There are more microbes, or microorganisms, on earth than any other life form. They live in water, air, soil, food, animals, plants, and, as Dr. Ocampo-Friedmann learned, microbes even live in rocks.
- ☛ Dr. Ocampo-Friedmann studies microbes that live in Antarctic desert rocks. These microbes are "endolithic" or "within stones".
- ☛ In A SLICE OF MICROBES Experiment, students will see how yeast, a microbe in the fungi kingdom, makes bread rise.

Supplies:
- ✔ 2 loaf pans (9"x5"x3"), greased
- ✔ 2 mixing bowls and 2 mixing spoons
- ✔ measuring cups and spoons
- ✔ 1 1/2 cups water
- ✔ one Tablespoon active dry yeast
- ✔ 2 Tablespoons sugar
- ✔ 4 Tablespoons oil
- ✔ 2 teaspoons salt
- ✔ 4 cups white flour
- ✔ 2 clean dishtowels
- ✔ oven for baking
- ✔ a serrated knife for slicing bread loaves

✔ A "My Notes" sheet for each student
✔ *The Scientific Gazette* for each student

Steps:
1. Point out McMurdo Station on a map or globe.
2. Share highlights of Dr. Roseli Ocampo-Friedmann's life.
3. Enjoy A SLICE OF MICROBES Experiment.
4. Assist students in clean-up.
5. Add Dr. Ocampo-Friedmann's name and a memento to the world map.
6. Distribute *The Scientific Gazette* .

For next time:
- Announce the next scientist.

Bibliography:
America Online, **Compton's Encyclopedia, Online Edition** (downloaded November 29, 1994).

Friedmann, E. Imre, and Roseli Ocampo-Friedmann. "Endolithic Microorganisms in Extreme Dry Environments: Analysis of a Lithobiontic Microbial Habitat," **Current Perspectives in Microbial Ecology**, 1984.

Friedmann, E. Imre, and Roseli Ocampo. "Endolithic Blue-Green Algae in the Dry Valleys: Primary Producers in the Antarctic Desert Ecosystem," **Science** Magazine, September, 1976.

Land, Barbara. **The New Explorers: Women in Antarctica**.

Ocampo-Friedmann, Roseli. **Curriculum Vitae**, 1994.

Ocampo-Friedmann, Roseli. **Telephone Interview**, November 22, 1994.

Sagan, Dorion, and Lynn Margulis. **Garden of Microbial Delights: A Practical Guide to the Subvisible World**.

Biography of
DR. ROSELI OCAMPO-FRIEDMANN
b. 1937

"When you work with something unusual, you are likely to discover things. I find it very rewarding to discover something that no one else has discovered."

— Dr. Roseli Ocampo-Friedmann

Dry valleys dot Antarctica's ice-covered landscape. They are deserts — cold deserts. Precipitation is low. When snow does fall — which is rarely — the flakes evaporate before they hit the ground or are "blown away by wind without melting." To the untrained eye, the rock-strewn landscape appears lifeless. To microbiologist Dr. Ocampo-Friedmann, these dry valleys are home to billions of creatures.

As a microbiologist, Dr. Ocampo-Friedmann studies microbes (or microorganisms), living organisms that are too small for the human eye to see without a microscope. The billions of creatures that she and co-researcher Dr. Imre Friedmann discovered in these dry valleys live inside rocks or are "endolithic" ("within stones"). Without a microscope these endolithic microorganisms appear as black, white, and green stripe zones just under a broken rock's surface. The black and white zones are colonies of lichen, and the wider green zone is primarily green algae. These microbial communities may also include bacteria, fungi, and yeasts.

Not all rocks contain microorganisms so the Friedmann team must first locate the light-colored rocks that contain the black, white, and green stripe zones. Once found, they put the rock pieces into sterile plastic bags for transport to the McMurdo Research Station.

At McMurdo Dr. Ocampo-Friedmann adds a sterilized culture medium and dry ice to preserve the microbes during transport to Tallahassee, Florida. At the laboratory in the U.S., she "feeds" the microbes and keeps them in a refrigerator. The Friedmanns conduct experiments to learn how the microorganisms respond to changes in temperature and light. They are learning how microorganisms have adapted to the harsh Antarctic environment where no organisms live on the rock surfaces. Instead, microorganisms live under rock crusts secure from freezing wind gusts and warmed by solar radiation.

For over 30 years Dr. Ocampo-Friedmann has studied endolithic algae. Back in 1963 when Ocampo was a graduate student from the Philippines studying at The Hebrew University of Jerusalem, she decided to write her master's thesis on the endolithic blue-green algae that Professor Imre Friedmann had found in Israel's Negev Desert. Roseli took these samples and successfully grew the algae in the laboratory.

After earning her master's degree in biology, Roseli Ocampo returned home to Manila. Her work at the National Institute of Science and Technology centered on pond algae but lacked the excitement of endolithic microbial research. She decided to join her mentor, Professor Friedmann — now at Florida State University, to resume her work on endolithic desert algae as well as earn a Ph.D. in biology. In 1973 she received her Ph.D.

About this time, Ocampo and Friedmann received Antarctic dry-valley rock samples collected by a colleague. They discovered a greenish stripe similar to that found in hot desert rocks. Dr. Roseli Ocampo successfully grew some of these microbial samples in culture dishes thereby confirming the existence of microbial life in cold-desert rocks.

By 1976 Roseli Ocampo and Imre Friedmann were a wife-and-husband research team. They followed with interest the U.S. Viking 1 and 2 space probes that collected soil samples from Mars. In the September 1976 issue of *Science* Magazine, they suggested that scientists exploring the possibility of life on Mars should look for endolithic microbes in the samples collected by space probes.

In 1978 Dr. Ocampo-Friedmann visited Antarctica for the first time. Sixteen years later she has made six trips. On each occasion she has flown by helicopter into dry valleys to collect microorganisms the study of which may unlock secrets to "pioneer life forms" on earth and other planets. Her work is unusual; her rewards are unique.

Instructor's Guide:

A SLICE OF MICROBES Experiment

Background Information:

Living organisms can be divided into five kingdoms: Animal, Plant, Protozoa (or Protoctists), Bacteria, and Fungi. To say that all living organisms are either "plant" or "animal" is impossible. Some green microorganisms move like animals but photosynthesize like plants, and others are "gas eaters" using inorganic chemical reactions to survive. Microbial life includes the Protozoa, Bacteria, and Fungi kingdoms. Dr. Ocampo-Friedmann's blue-green algae are bacteria: the yeast in A SLICE OF MICROBES are fungi.

Instructions:

1. Distribute a "My Notes" sheet to each student.
2. Select students to prepare Recipe A and Recipe B.

Recipe A

- Pour 3/4 c. warm water into the bowl.

Recipe B

- Pour 3/4 c. warm water into the bowl.
- Add 1 Tablespoon yeast in the water. Stir gently to dissolve.

Explain . . .
The water must be warm, not hot or cold. Hot water kills yeast and cold water slows its growth.

Recipe A (continued)

- Add 1 T. sugar. Stir to dissolve.
- Add 2 T. oil.
- Add 1 tsp. salt.
- Add 1 cup flour. Stir well to mix.
- Add remaining cup of flour. Mix well.

Recipe B (continued)

- Add 1 T. sugar. Stir to dissolve.
- Add 2 T. oil.
- Add 1 tsp. salt.

- Add 1 cup flour. Stir well to mix.
- Add remaining cup of flour. Mix well.

Ask . . .
*In an experiment, one condition, or **independent variable**, is changed. What is the independent variable in this experiment?*
[The yeast]

Explain . . .
Yeast are microbes. In one Tablespoon, there are millions of yeast cells.

---

3. Cover each mixing bowl with a dishtowel. Label bowl containing Recipe A.
4. Allow batters to set for 30 - 40 minutes.
5. Remove dishtowels and observe Recipes A and B.
6. Give students time to complete question #1 in "My Notes."
7. Stir both batters for 50 strokes.
8. Spoon batters into greased loaf pans. Cover each loaf pan with a dishtowel. Label the loaf pan containing Recipe A.
9. Give students time to complete question #2 in "My Notes."
10. Allow batters to set for 30 - 40 minutes.
11. Remove dishtowels and observe Recipes A and B.
12. Preheat oven to 375°F.

 Caution. **Hot bakeware** can burn. Use hot pads and other precautions to assure safety with this part of the experiment.

---

11. Give students time to complete questions #3 and #4 in "My Notes."
12. Bake loaves for 45 minutes.
13. Remove loaves from pans immediately; place loaves across pans to cool.
14. Give students time to answer question #5 in "My Notes."

Continued on next page

---

15. Discuss observations/answers as a class.

> **Ask . . .**
> *What do you think is the question this experiment answers?* [What does yeast do?]
>
> **Explain . . .**
> *Yeasts are microbes that are inactive when they are dry but become quite active when given warm water and food i.e. sugar and starch (in the form of flour). As these millions of microbes digest the sugar and starch, they release alcohol and carbon dioxide. The bubbles are carbon dioxide.*

> **Ask . . .**
> *How can we use the information that hot water kills yeast to understand why yeast breads stop "growing" in the oven?"* [The oven heat kills the yeast.]
>
> **Explain . . .**
> *Also during baking, the alcohol in the batter evaporates. The holes in the bread are from the carbon dioxide.*

16. Enjoy a slice of microbes. Slice both loaves; compare taste and texture.

17. Assist students in clean-up.

◆ ◆ ◆

Enrichment Activity:

Tour a bakery that specializes in bread-making. Explore the history of making and baking bread. Collect recipes; create loaves from different eras and cultures; compare tastes and textures.

Add information and ideas here:

A SLICE OF MICROBES Experiment — Page 1

Recipe A	**Recipe B**
3/4 cup water	3/4 cup water
1 Tablespoon sugar	1 Tablespoon active dry yeast
1 Tablespoon oil	1 Tablespoon sugar
1 teaspoon salt	1 Tablespoon oil
2 cups white flour	1 teaspoon salt
	2 cups white flour

Prepare Recipes A and B. Wait 30 minutes.

1.   The batter in Recipe A is now _____.

It looks like this:

The batter in Recipe B is now _____.

It looks like this:

A SLICE OF MICROBES Experiment — Page 2

Spoon batter into loaf pans.

2. I think that 30 minutes from now, the batter in Recipe A will be ————————————

   _____ .

   and the batter in Recipe B will be _____

   _____ .

(This answer is your **hypothesis**.)

Wait 30 minutes.

3. My hypothesis was _____ because _____
   accurate/inaccurate

   _____ .

4. I think that in the oven the loaf in Recipe A will _____ ,

   and the loaf in Recipe B will _____ .

(This answer is your **hypothesis**.)

Bake bread for 45 minutes.

5. My hypothesis was _____
   accurate/inaccurate

   because _____

   _____

   _____ .

The Scientific Gazette

From Manila to Mars

"When you work with something unusual, you are likely to discover things. I find it very rewarding to discover something that no one else has discovered."

— Dr. Roseli Ocampo-Friedmann

Dr. Roseli Ocampo-Friedmann, microbiologist, was born on November 23, 1937, in Manila, Philippines. Her mother and father were teachers. She was "always attracted to science" and in 1958 earned a Bachelor of Science degree from the University of the Philippines. For her master's degree, she traveled to Israel and studied endolithic blue-green algae in hot desert rocks. She earned her master's degree in biology from the Herbrew University of Jerusalem and her Ph.D. (biology) from Florida State University.

Ocampo-Friedmann has traveled to Antarctica six times. She and her colleague, husband Dr. Imre Friedmann, have discovered endolithic microorganisms in Antarctic dry valley rocks. These valleys are cold deserts. They are more like Mars than any other place on earth. These microorganisms may unlock secrets to "pioneer life forms" on earth and other planets.

A microbiologist studies microbes. "Micro" means "small," and "bio" means "life." A microbiologist studies "small life."

There are more microbes, or microorganisms, on earth than any other life form. They exert both positive and negative influences: they purify water, create oxygen for animals, fertilize the soil, cause disease, cure disease, and even "consume" oil spills. Colonies of different microbes — or microbial gardens — surround us. In one square centimeter on your skin, 100,000 microbes live.

Become a microbiologist. Collect or grow microbes and study them with a magnifying glass or microscope ("scope" means "to look at").

Ideas include:

◆ collect pond water, compost, or garden soil
◆ grow bread mold, fruit mold, or compost

Unscramble these syllables to make words that a microbiologist would understand:

* cro - scope - mi   _____
* fau - cro - mi - na _____
* bi - cro - gy - o - ol - mi _____
* flo - mi - ra - cro _____
* e - crom - ter - mi _____

The Scientist With a Sense of Wonder

Rachel Louise Carson — 1907 - 1964

Rachel Carson grew up on a farm in Pennsylvania and learned to love nature from her mother who believed that each living creature has value. Rachel spent her childhood exploring wildlife, writing stories, and drawing animals and flowers. Her favorite author was Beatrix Potter.

Science in high school proved dull. But Miss Mary Skinker's biology class at Pennsylvania College for Women convinced Carson to seek a career that combined science and writing.

Stunned the world

As a marine biologist, she wrote **Under the Sea-Wind**, **The Sea Around Us**, and **The Edge of the Sea**. In 1962 her **Silent Spring**, a book about the popular use of pesticides, became "the history-making bestseller that stunned the world

Our hometown:

Springdale, Pennsylvania

Both scientist Rachel Carson and sculptor William Accorsi were born in Springdale, Pennsylvania. Accorsi fulfilled a long-held dream when he wrote and illustrated **Rachel Carson**. Published in 1993 by Holiday House (New York), his children's book blends an easy-to-read account of Carson's life with colorful illustrations that enhance the text and delight the eye.

More than a runny nose and sneezing

Chemicals are widespread. Their use may improve life for many but cause discomfort to others. Allergic reactions to chemicals in common household/industrial products like air fresheners, carpets, office machines, and window screens, may range from skin rashes and fatigue to respiratory problems and serious nervous disorders.

with its terrifying revelations about our contaminated planet." (Fawcett Publications)

A fragile balance

Rachel Carson denounced the most popular pesticide, DDT (an abbreviation for dichloro-diphenyl-trichloroethane), urged restriction and supervision of pesticide use, and introduced the idea that plants and animals, air and water, are linked together in an ecological web that encircles the world. Her sense of wonder, nurtured on a farm and carried into science, compelled her to discover how pesticides were destroying the planet's fragile balance of nature.

Enrichment Activities:

♦ Rachel Carson kept a microscope in her living room. Imitate this tradition in the classroom and encourage students to bring leaves, petals, insects etc. to examine under the microscope.

♦ Check your home for indoor air pollution. Contact state or local environmental groups to obtain information on the health hazards of mold, mildew, pesticides, household cleaners, and radon gas.

♦ Contact a lawn care/landscape service to learn what chemicals they use. To obtain information about these chemicals, contact a local chemist, extension agent, or environmental agency.

Bibliography:

Carson, Rachel. **Silent Spring**.
Harlan, Judith. **Sounding the Alarm: A Biography of Rachel Carson**.
Kudlinski, Kathleen V. **Rachel Carson: Pioneer of Ecology**.
Stwertka, Eve. **Rachel Carson**.

Asia is the world's largest continent covering 33% of the earth's land surface. To travel the perimeter of Asia, you would: trek the length of the Ural Mountains in Russia south to the Caspian Sea and west to the Black Sea; sail through the Bosporus Strait south to the Suez Canal cutting through to the Red Sea; circle around the Arabian Peninsula, India, Burma, and Malaysia; tour through Indonesia, New Guinea, and the Philippines; and explore the shoreline of the East China Sea, and the Seas of Japan and Okhotsk before crossing through the Bering Strait to skirt the Arctic Ocean west to the Kara River.

When finished, you would have encircled 16,992,000 square miles, passed through deserts and arctic tundra, and caught glimpses of camels, monkeys, snakes, and bears — as well as reindeer, yak, and tiger.

Asia and Science:

Asia's contributions to science and technology include wheeled vehicles, kiln-fired bricks, writing, the potter's wheel, silk, candles, tea, the wheelbarrow, and even paper. By observing that a carved piece of iron ore (lodestone) always pointed in the same direction, the Chinese constructed a compass. They developed movable type four centuries before Europeans and invented gunpowder to fuel weapons and fireworks.

Mesopotamia

From Mesopotamia come the multiplication tables and a series of measurements based on the number 60 e.g. 60 minutes in an hour and 360º in a circle. The Sumerians of Mesopotamia designed a calendar based on the phases of the moon and the Babylonians created the zodiac, a diagonal strip across the sky through which the sun, moon, and planets appeared to travel. Both Sumerians and Babylonians used fractions.

India

To India goes credit for the spinning wheel, cotton, the decimal system, and the idea that from nine different numeric symbols any number, no matter how large, could be written.

Islamic contributions to science

Transporting ideas and inventions between these cultures were Arab caravans connecting Baghdad with China and India. These travelers preserved the science of ancient civilizations and built centers of learning. Islamic mathematicians developed *aljabr*, or modern-day algebra; their scientists explained the refraction of light, as shown by rainbows; and their physicians used antiseptics, made sutures from animal intestines and silk, and understood how blood circulated throughout the body. By conducting experiments and making careful measurements, Islamic scientists modernized the scientific method.

Alchemists

Women supervised the perfume industry in Mesopotamia. These perfumers were early chemists who developed the techniques of distillation and extraction to create aromatic substances used in cosmetics, religious ceremonies, and medicines. From the second millenium BC comes the name of **Tapputi-Belatekallim**, a woman chemist who was the female overseer of the palace. **Keng Hsien-Seng,** ninth century A.D., and **Li Shao-Yum,** 12th century, were Chinese alchemists whose elixirs earned them widespread reputations including a summons to Keng to appear before the emperor.

Empress Zoe of Byzantium (d. 1050) converted her residence into a chemistry laboratory where she developed ointments and perfumes.

Women Scientists

Healers: From 4,600 B.C. to 2,000 B.C. in lower Mesopotamia, there were no restrictions on women's participation in the healing arts. During the Middle Ages, women studied at the medical school in Baghdad. Royal women **Julia Anicia** and the **Empresses Eudocia** and **Pulcheria** studied medicine and natural sciences with scholars at court. Women practiced medicine in 16th-, 17th-, and 18th-century Turkey. Called *hekime* , the list of women physicians includes **Mevlana Ramazan, Sinan Yahudi,** and **Kari Hakime.** In late 19th century Japan, medicine became the first professional field open to women. During the early 1900s, **Drs. Saneya Haboub** and **Adma Abu Shadid** were the first women doctors practising in Lebanon. One-third of the physicians practicing in present-day Turkey are women.

Women continue to play important roles in science in Asia. This unit will feature **Dr. Aslihan Yener** (Turkey), **Zdenka Samish** (Israel), **Dr. Pham Thi Tran Chau** (Vietnam), and the **Mullick family** (India).

Continental Facts:

- Mt. Everest (29,023') in the Himalayas is the highest peak in the world.
- The shore of the Dead Sea (-1,310') between Israel and Jordan is the lowest place on dry land in the world.
- In China over 300 million people live in the Yangtze River basin.
- The Republic of the Philippines is a group of 7,107 islands.
- Indonesia has 167 active volcanoes.
- Over 600,000 domestic camels roam the Gobi in Mongolia.

Continental Curiosities:

- The musk deer of eastern Asia grows a pair of curved tusks.
- The giant panda is a strict vegetarian.
- Olive trees can live longer than 1,000 years.
- Siberia's Lake Baikal holds 20% of all the fresh water on earth. Its hydrothermal vents and mysterious tides support unique life forms including translucent shrimps and snails, large mushroom-shaped sponges, and the nerpa — the only fresh-water seal on earth.

Exploration Questions:

- How many countries are there in Asia?
- How many time zones does Russia have?

Enrichment Activities:

- Construct an *abacus* and use this device to add, subtract, multiply, and divide — or to calculate square roots.
- Invite a spinner to demonstrate how a spinning wheel works.

Add notes here:

Bibliography:

Alic, Margaret. **Hypatia's Heritage**.

America Online, **Compton's Encyclopedia, Online Edition** (downloaded February 2, 1995).

Beshore, George. **Science in Ancient China**.

Beshore, George. **Science in Early Islamic Culture**.

Graham-Brown, Sarah. **Images of Women: The Portrayal of Women in Photography of the Middle East 1860-1950**.

Lebra, Joyce, Joy Paulson, and Elizabeth Powers, editors. **Women in Changing Japan**.

Lye, Keith. **Take A Trip to Indonesia**.

Major, John S. **The Land and People of Mongolia**.

Matthiessen, Peter. **Baikal: Sacred Sea of Siberia**.

Moss, Carol. **Science in Ancient Mesopotamia**.

Taskiran, Tezer. **Women in Turkey**.

Tope, Lily Rose R. **Philippines**.

Wong, How Man. **Exploring the Yangtze: China's Longest River**.

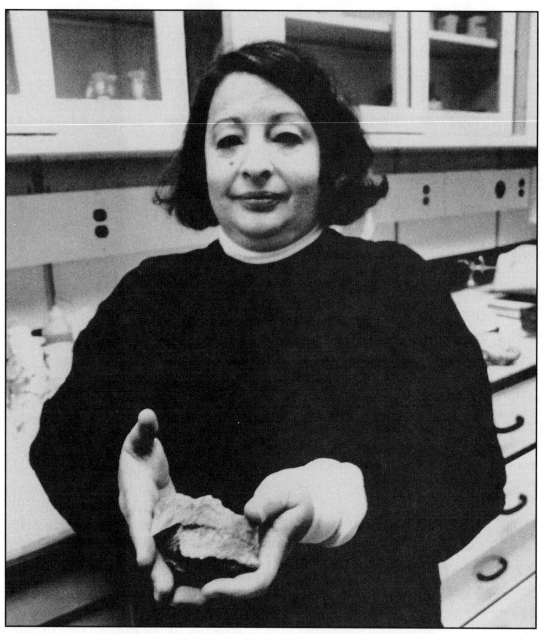

Archaeologist Dr. Aslihan Yener discovered a Bronze Age tin mine and ancient mining village in southern Turkey.

Discovery Unit No. 8

Dr. Aslihan Yener
Archaeology

DIGGING UP HISTORY Project

Time-line:
- 1946 - Dr. Aslihan Yener is born in Turkey.
- 1952 - Dame Kathleen Mary Kenyon excavates the biblical site of Jericho.
- 1969 - Archaeologist Dorothy A. E. Garrod dies. Her field work included sites in England, Palestine, Bulgaria, and Lebanon.
- 1983 - Hannah Marie Wormington receives the Distinguished Service Award of the Society for American Archaeology.

Key points:
- ☛ An archaeologist makes careful observations at an excavation site, writes exact descriptions of all artifacts, and creates a theory that explains all findings.
- ☛ In 1989 archaeologist Dr. Aslihan Yener discovered a Bronze Age tin mine and ancient mining village in southern Turkey.
- ☛ Her discoveries prove that tin mining was a well-developed industry in that location.
- ☛ In the DIGGING UP HISTORY Project students will use archaeological techniques to conduct a dig.

Supplies:
- ✓ A "dig" for each crew — prepared in advance (See instructor's guide.)
- ✓ Archaeological tools — toothpicks, brushes, measuring tape or ruler, spoons, string, and tape for each group of archaeologists.
- ✓ "Dump site" with sieve, colander, or framed wire mesh
- ✓ Grid Map instruction sheet and blank paper for each crew
- ✓ Daily Field Report Form for each student — one for each day dig is conducted (page 71)
- ✓ Sacks to store artifacts
- ✓ Final Site Report for each student (page 72)

✓ *The Scientific Gazette* for each student

Steps — in advance:
1. Prepare digs. (See instructor's Guide.)

Steps — today:
1. Point out southern Turkey on a map or globe.
2. Share highlights of Dr. Aslihan Yener's life and work.
3. Begin the DIGGING UP HISTORY Project.
4. Write Daily Field Report.
5. Clean-up dig site.

Steps — other dig days:
1. Continue the DIGGING UP HISTORY Project.
2. Write Daily Field Report.
3. Clean-up dig site.

Steps — final dig day:
1. Write Final Site Report.
2. Add Dr. Aslihan Yener's name and a memento to the world map.
3. Distribute *The Scientific Gazette*.

For next time:
- Introduce the next scientist.

Bibliography:
Avi-Yonah, Michael. **Dig This!: How Archaeologists Uncover Our Past.**

Bass, Thomas. "Land of Bronze," **Discover**, December 1991.

Harms, William. "The University of Chicago NEWS," January 4, 1994.

McMillon, Bill. **The Archaeology Handbook: A Field Manual and Resource Guide.**

Wilford, John Noble. "Enduring Mystery Solved as Tin Is Found in Turkey," **The New York Times**, January 4, 1994.

Biography of
DR. ASLIHAN YENER
b. 1946
Born in Turkey

Becoming an archaeologist was not Aslihan Yener's childhood dream. An American of Turkish descent, she was born in 1946 in Turkey. Her family moved to New Rochelle, New York, when Aslihan was six months old. In 1964 she entered Adelphi College in Garden City, New York, planning to be a chemistry major but transferred to Robert College, renamed Bosporus University, in Istanbul, Turkey, to study art history. Roman ruins along Turkey's coastline fascinated Yener as well as the buried pre-Roman structures and artifacts. She returned to New York to complete a doctorate in archaeology at Columbia University.

The Bronze Age and Anatolia

By 1980 Dr. Yener was back in Turkey and was a member of the faculty of Bosporus University. The Bronze Age (about 3000 BC to 1100 BC) captured Yener's imagination. During this era, bronze, an alloy stronger than its elements — copper and tin, was used in the production of tools, weapons, and numerous objects ranging from hair pins to swords and statues. Copper was mined in the Middle East but tin, according to clay tablets left by the neighboring Assyrians, was imported from mines in Afghanistan 1,000 miles away. Dr. Yener set out to explore potential mining sites in ancient Anatolia, present-day Turkey, to learn if tin had been mined in the region and not imported from Afghanistan.

850 mines

Dr. Yener began her research in the mines of the snow-capped Taurus Mountains of southern Turkey. She scaled peaks, discovered ancient mine shafts, and unearthed bronze-age treasures. In one 6-square-mile area, Yener and her colleagues discovered 850 mines. Silver in these mines was evident but tin was not.

In 1987 a friend suggested that Dr. Yener take her search to Kestel, 60 miles north of Tarsus. The mines at Kestel measured more than two miles with shafts about 2' wide — too narrow for most adults to enter. Children ages 12 to 15 years old may have worked in these mines.

The ancient mining village

For four summers Yener and her colleagues excavated these 4,500-year-old mines. They discovered little tin. But in 1989 one of her students discovered some stones on a hill opposite the mine. Yener investigated the site and discovered 50,000 tools scattered over a small area. In 1990 she returned to the site to excavate what proved to be an ancient miners' village. Called Goltepe, the slag found in crucibles, the vessels used to melt ores or metals, contained such a high percentage of tin that Dr. Yener concluded it was mined and smelted (melted) locally.

Further tests revealed that Goltepe was occupied from 3290 B.C. to 1840 B.C. Several hundred people lived at the site. While the mine at Kestel produced about 5,000 tons of ore during its 1,000 years of operation, the neighboring mining village of Goltepe smelted that tin at relatively low temperatures. Tin mining was apparently a well developed industry in the area at the beginning of the bronze age (about 3000 BC).

Rewriting history

The mine at Kestel and the crucibles at Goltepe have forced archaeologists to rethink old theories. Anatolians were not merely importers of tin but providers of this element necessary for the production of bronze. This new information changes the economic, political, and social picture of the Bronze Age in the Middle East.

Instructor's Guide:

The DIGGING-UP HISTORY Project

Background Information:

In excavating their "digs," students use archaeological techniques: the use of the tools calls for patience and measuring skills; the grid map (page 70) encourages careful observations; the Daily Field Report (page 71) requires exact descriptions; and the site report (72) allows students to create a hypothesis that explains their findings. The length of time spent on this project may be from an hour to several weeks. Distribute a new daily field report for each day spent on this project.

The metric system for measurement is being used in this unit since it forms the basis for nearly all scientific observation and is the standard for archaeological measurement.

Instructions:

In Advance

Prepare dig sites.

✓ The "dig" site, into which objects are buried, may be a sandbox, a section of garden, a produce or cardboard box, or a book box. Size of each dig should be at least 20 centimeters square.

✓ Objects in each "dig" should have some relationship to each other. Possibilities are:

• A broken flower pot whose pieces are excavated and reassembled by student archaeologists. (Omit a piece or two.)

• A broken coffee mug, crumbled paper, whittled-down pencil . . .

• Fish bone, broken stick, orange peels, egg shells, pieces of burnt wood, crushed tin can . . .

• Styrofoam plate, pieces of plastic fork, paper wrapper, drinking straw . . .

• Used candle, broken pair of scissors, ripped garment or shreds of cloth, a bead, chipped button, rusty zipper . . .

✓ Compact the dirt or mix with water allowing time for the soil to harden before student archaeologists patiently tackle the dig with "picks and mini-shovels." Feel free to add pine needles, leaves, petals etc. to the dirt.

✓ Give students the opportunity to make a "dig" for the instructor.

Conducting the Dig

1. Distribute "digs" and archaeological tools to individuals or groups.

2. Establish a "dump site" where archaeologists bring the dirt from their digs and sift it to insure that no item goes undetected.

3. Instruct each group to select a "dig" name.

4. Distribute the Grid Map Instruction Sheet and blank paper. The grid pattern is a set of 5 cm. squares (30 cm squares if the dig is a sandbox or garden plot). Students select and mark their **base line** on their dig. From the far left of this line, measure the squares and stretch pieces of string across the "dig." Use tape to secure string ends to the sides of the dig's container. If using a sandbox or garden plot, use sticks to mark the grid and connect markers with string.

5. Place a stick securely into the ground at the beginning of the base line. This is the **datum stake** and will be used to calculate depth (level) of the artifact. Each level is 5 cm deep (30 cm in the large dig)

6. Distribute a new Daily Field Report each day of the dig. Students remove one level of dirt, one grid at a time, across the entire surface of the dig. This method of excavation is called **vertical-face**. Any finding (even if it is a tip of something) is recorded on this field report with its location and level recorded. After the first level is removed, students should proceed to the 2nd level, and so on until the excavation is completed. (The method for measuring depth is shown on the Grid Map Instruction Sheet.)

7. Students label all artifacts (dig name, grid unit, and level) and store in sacks.

8. Clean-up after each dig session.

Final Dig Day

1. Prepare Final Site Report.

Grid Map Instruction Sheet

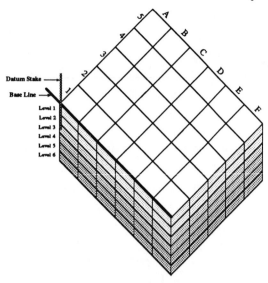

A grid map, like a travel map, tells you your location. Archaeologists create a grid map of an excavation site so they can work together ("Let's excavate unit E2 on level 3 today."), share information ("The bone needle was found at B5 Level 5 but the bone button at B3 Level 2."), and accurately record their findings.

The diagram to the left shows an excavation site measuring 30 cm. long x 25 cm. wide x 30 cm. deep. Each cube is 5 cm. long x 5 cm. wide x 5 cm. deep. The bottom line is the **base line** for the dig. The left corner of this line becomes the **datum point** from which you measure the squares. The **datum stake** is pounded in here.

To determine the depth of an artifact, choose a place on the datum stake. This will be the zero point for measuring. Measure the distance on the Datum Stake from the zero point to the ground level. This is measurement A. After finding an artifact, stretch a string attached at the zero point and level to the ground. Measure the distance from the string to the artifact. This is measurement B.

B - A = depth of artifact

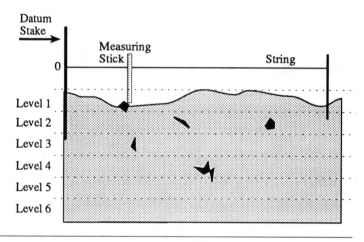

Each crew should draw its own grid maps — one for each level — marking the location of various finds. Excavating should be done one level at a time.

Below a garden plot dig has been staked out. To the right is a grid drawn on paper. The crew should draw a grid for each level of the dig. Be sure to mark the scale of the grid and indicate the level.

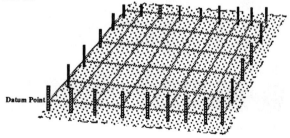

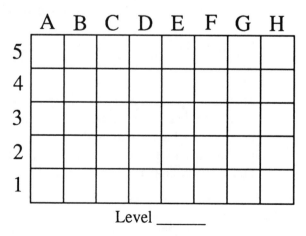

Daily Field Report Form

Dig name: ———————————————————————————————

Date: —————————————

Names of archaeologists: ———————————————————

———————————————————————————————————————

———————————————————————————————————————

Grid units worked: ————————————————————————

Description of artifact
(List each artifact. Descriptions include color, texture, special markings, etc.)

Location found
(For example, A3 level 2)

———————————————————   ———————————

———————————————————   ———————————

———————————————————   ———————————

———————————————————   ———————————

———————————————————   ———————————

———————————————————   ———————————

———————————————————   ———————————

———————————————————   ———————————

———————————————————   ———————————

Additional notes and observations: ————————————

———————————————————————————————————————

———————————————————————————————————————

Final Site Report

Dig name: _____

Date: _____

Names of archaeologists: _____

_____

_____

After reading the daily field reports and examining the artifacts, we have created a hypothesis to explain our findings.

Our Hypothesis: _____

_____

_____

_____

_____

_____

_____

_____

_____

_____

_____

_____

The Scientific Gazette

Dr. Aslihan Yener

Discovery leads to re-examining Bronze Age history

An American of Turkish descent, Aslihan Yener was born in 1946 in Turkey.

Imagine you are an archaeologist. You look carefully through mud, dirt, and sand, explore caves, or search underwater for objects called "artifacts" that tell you what life was like hundreds, if not thousands, of years ago. You are not a treasure hunter but a scientist who makes careful observations at an excavation site, writes exact descriptions of all artifacts, and creates a theory that explains all of the findings. The artifacts you discover may support an existing theory or may, like Dr. Yener's discoveries, rewrite history.

In the early 1980s Dr. Yener decided to explore mining sites in Turkey (called Anatolia in ancient times) to learn if tin had been mined in the region during the bronze age. She:

- scaled peaks,
- squeezed through mine shafts,
- unearthed treasures, and
- discovered a Bronze Age tin mine and an ancient mining village in southern Turkey.

Tests conducted on the slag found in the crucibles from the mining village have proven than tin mining was a well developed industry in Anatolia. This new information changes archaeological theories about the Bronze Age in the Middle East.

Meanwhile, Dr. Yener tackles new questions.

- Did children work in the tin mines?
- Whose job was it to smelt the tin?
- Who first thought of making bronze?

Fun Facts:

- Metal workers in ancient times used iron from fallen meteorites to make weapons and tools.

- In Israel archaeologists discovered a 12,000-year-old skeleton wearing a seashell headband.

- In the 1960s an archaeological crew excavated a submerged sailing vessel in waters off the coast of southern Turkey and determined it was a 3,000-year-old shipwreck.

> ## April 23 is
> ## **Children's Day**
> ## in Turkey.

Fun to do at school:

Find **The Terra Cotta Army of Emperor Qin** by Caroline Lazo and read about the colossal discovery of seventy-five hundred 2,000-year-old life-size clay figures buried at Emperor Qin's tomb site.

> The Turkish alphabet has 29 letters.

Fun to Read:

The Archaeology Handbook: A Field Manual and Resource Guide by Bill McMillon provides a comprehensive introduction to archaeology including travel agencies specializing in archaeological tours, archaeological sites and museums, field schools, and organizations that assist in placing volunteers. Who knows — your next family vacation may be spent excavating a cave in France.

Zdenka Samish, a researcher in Food Technology, helped develop Israel's food industry.

Discovery Unit No. 9

Zdenka Samish
Food Technology

AFTER THE HARVEST Experiment

Time-line:

- 1904 - Zdenka Samish is born in what is now the Czech Republic.
- 1925 - Clarence Birdseye develops methods for freezing foods in small quantities
- 1935 - The United States produces about 8 billion cans of fruits, vegetables, fish, and meat annually.
- 1947 - Microwave oven is invented.
- 1971 - Dr. Chloe Tal, an immunologist at Hadassah-Hebrew University Medical Center, develops test for early detection of cancer.

Key points:

- ☞ For 35 years, Zdenka Samish worked as a researcher in Food Technology, the science of food preservation.
- ☞ Working in Israel, Samish improved methods of preserving olives, extracted oils from fruit peels, and developed regional products like peanut butter, grape juice, raisins, picked cucumbers, tomato paste, jams, and dried citrus fruits.
- ☞ Food preservation allows produce to be eaten beyond their growing season.
- ☞ In AFTER THE HARVEST Experiment, students use banana slices to conduct experiments testing two methods of food preservation.

Supplies — today:

- ✓ 4 ripe bananas
- ✓ "My Notes" for each student
- ✓ One sharp knife
- ✓ Oven and cookie sheet - or - cheesecloth and rack - or a food dryer (see instructor's guide)
- ✓ Access to a freezer

Supplies — several days later:

- ✓ Experiment results

- ✓ "My Notes" for each student.
- ✓ *The Scientific Gazette* for each student.

Steps — today:

1. Point out Rehovot, Israel, on a map.
2. Share highlights of Zdenka Samish's life.
3. Begin the AFTER THE HARVEST Experiment.
4. Assist students in cleanup.

Steps — several days later:

1. Observe experiment results.
2. Prepare and present reports.
3. Complete "My Notes."
4. Assist students in cleanup.
5. Add Zdenka Samish's name and a memento to the world map.
6. Distribute *The Scientific Gazette*.

For next time:

- Announce the next scientist.

Bibliography:

Kedem, Aliya. "Zdenka Samish Senior Founding Member of the Rehovot Club of Israel Reaches 88," **The Link** (A European Soroptimist monthly publication), May 1993.

Levin, Beatrice. **Women and Medicine: Pioneers Meeting the Challenge!**

Manchester, Richard B. **Mammoth Book of Fascinating Information.**

Ontario Science Center. **Foodworks.**

Oregon State University Extension Service. **Drying Fruits & Vegetables.**

Samish, Zdenka. **Curriculum Vitae.**

Samish, Zdenka. **Letters,** June 30, 1994 and October 6, 1994.

Samish, Zdenka. **List of Scientific Publications.**

Biography of
ZDENKA SAMISH
b. 1904

When Zdenka was a girl growing up in Prague, Czechoslovakia, her favorite subjects in school were the natural sciences: "I excelled in mathematics and did not enjoy languages and history." She lived among houses "glued one to the other with walled-in backyards." At age 17 she joined the Zionist youth movement and found herself happily occupied with hiking and camping.

A dream that changes

In 1924 Zdenka and her husband Rudolf moved to Palestine where they were members of an agricultural settlement. Their dream was to study horticulture, the science of growing fruits, flowers, and vegetables. To make this dream come true, they moved to the United States in 1927 and enrolled in the University of California's College of Agriculture. According to Zdenka Samish, the dream changed: "...as the only woman student among some 80 men, the professor found that climbing ladders was not suitable for women. Therefore I switched to food technology, since the preservation of horticultural crops still kept us close to our ideal."

Becomes head of the department

Samish earned her Bachelor of Science degree in Food Technology in 1931 and her Masters degree two years later. Rudolf earned his degree in Horticulture. Upon their return to Palestine, Zdenka Samish worked for a short time as a technologist and chemist in a fruit factory before she was invited to join her husband's department at the Agricultural Research Station in Rehovot, Israel. Soon she became Head of her own department, the Department of Fruit and Vegetable Technology. Her first laboratory was housed in a shop adjacent to the police station.

For the next 35 years, Zdenka Samish was a researcher in Food Technology, the science of food preservation. Since foods will not remain fresh for long periods of time, food technology conducts experiments to determine the best way to keep fresh foods from spoiling i.e. through freezing, canning, and drying.

The mystery of the spoiled olives

Samish's first task was to determine why green olives at a particular agricultural settlement were spoiling. She discovered that the farmers were rinsing the olives too often. These frequent rinsings removed the sugars necessary for fermentation. Her research results were published and accepted in Israel and Spain. In 1950 Samish traveled to Greece and Turkey to study their olive industries.

From orange peels to green tomatoes

When World War II halted the export of Jaffa oranges, Samish extracted oils from the fruit peels to use in the production of soaps and perfumes. She is also responsible for the regional development of peanut butter, grape juice, pomegranate juice, raisins, pickled cucumbers, tomato paste, jams, and dried citrus fruits.

Her professional organizations and committees included: the Olive Planning Committee and Grape and Wine Committee in the Ministry of Agriculture; International Institute of Freezing and Cold Storage; American Society for Microbiology; American Chemical Society; and the Israeli Society of Food and Nutrition Sciences. Her list of scientific publications includes 83 articles ranging from the dehydration of bananas to the fermentation of green tomatoes.

Instructor's Guide:

AFTER THE HARVEST Experiment

Background Information:

Food preservation allows produce, crops, and meat to be eaten beyond their growing season, their time of harvest, or day of slaughter. Careful food preservation discourages the growth of microorganisms that cause spoilage and illness.

Ancient people sun-dried fruits and vegetables, and the Sumerians, as long ago as 3500 BC, used salt to preserve meat. Modern preservation methods are more varied. At home we pickle, can, freeze, and dry (dehydrate) foodstuffs. Methods requiring more sophisticated technology include freeze-drying, a processing method that combines freezing and drying. Freeze-dried foods, popular with astronauts and outdoor enthusiasts, must be reconstituted with water.

The method of preservation varies according to the type of produce used. In the AFTER THE HARVEST Experiment, two methods of preservation are explored: drying and freezing (not freeze-dried!). The directions for oven- and sun-drying follow. If you have a food dryer or dehydrator, follow the manufacturer's directions.

Drying methods for bananas:

Sun-Dried Bananas
Approximate time: 4 days

1. To make a drying rack, cover a wire rack or wooden frame with cheesecloth. Stretch the cloth tightly and secure by lacing with strings on the underside.

2. Peel bananas, cut into 1/8" slices, and arrange slices in a single layer on the rack.

3. To keep insects off the food, cover slices with cheesecloth. Placing small paper drinking cups at each corner will keep the cheesecloth cover from touching the food. Place rack in a sunny window.

4. Turn banana slices once or twice a day.

5. When slices are two-thirds dry, move rack into the shade and continue drying until slices are tough and leathery. Do not allow the sun to scorch or burn the food.

6. Let slices cool. Store in a plastic bag with air extracted. To extract air, insert a straw into the bag opening; grip the bag opening around the straw; suck out the air; remove the straw (keep the bag closed!); and fasten with a twist tie.

Oven-Dried Bananas
Approximate time: 5 hours

1. Preheat oven to 140ºF. If this setting is too low for your oven, place oven rack in its highest position. (Bananas are to be oven-dried, not cooked!)

2. Peel bananas, cut into 1/8" slices, and arrange slices in a single layer on a cookie sheet.

3. Place in oven.

4. Turn slices every 30 minutes for 5 hours, or until tough and leathery.

5. Let slices cool. Store in a plastic bag with air extracted.

Instructions:

Today

1. Discuss food preservation methods.

> **Ask . . .**
> *What fruits and vegetables have you eaten that have been dried, canned, frozen, or pickled?*

2. Bring out the bananas.

> **Ask . . .**
> *What is the best method for preserving bananas?* [Unless you are equipped to explore other options, experiment only with drying and freezing.]
>
> Note: Discussion should lead to two hypotheses: (1) If we freeze the banana, then it should be preserved for eating at a later date. (2) If we dry the banana, then it should be preserved for eating at a later date.

3. Divide into four teams.

- Appoint a technology assistant for each team. This student is responsible for the hands-on preparation of the food. Hands should be thoroughly washed and the working surface clean.

- Appoint a manager for each team. This student supervises the experiment making sure that each team member is contributing with suggestions and tasks.

4. Give each team a banana and each student a "My Notes" sheet.

   - Team A will conduct the experiment using a drying method.

   - Teams B, C, and D will conduct experiments using freezing methods.

5. Give Team A the information on drying. Instruct them to complete numbers 1, 2, and 3 on the "My Notes" sheet, then conduct the experiment. Assignments will need to be made to monitor the drying process.

6. Facilitate a combined discussion with **Teams B, C, and D** to help them come up with at least three different methods to test their hypothesis. Use the chalkboard to list suggestions for ways to prepare a banana for freezing. [Note: suggestions could include peeled, in skin, wrapped in plastic wrap, cut, whole, etc.] When three different methods have been established, each team selects one method.

   Instruct **Teams B, C, and D** to consider the final form the banana should take after freezing i.e. thawed? frozen? mashed? Discuss how they want it to be eaten i.e. frozen like a popsicle, sliced on cereal, etc.

7. Instruct **Teams B, C, and D** to meet separately, and to complete numbers 1, 2, and 3 on the "My Notes" sheet, then conduct the experiment.

8. Team managers supervise cleanup.

Several days later

1. Bring the teams together to evaluate their experiments. Have students fill out numbers 4 and 5 on their "My Notes" sheets. [Note: the best evaluations will be in tasting.] Teams B, C, and D can safely sample their experiment while it is frozen, and as soon as it has reached room temperature. It should not be eaten after this point. The team managers should supervise final cleanup.

2. Each team is to prepare and present an oral report illustrated with samples or drawings. This finale should be a fun exchange of information and opinion. Encourage questions.

3. Following the reports, students complete numbers 6 and 7 on their "My Notes" sheets.

 Caution: Anytime you are working with food, and cooking or baking, you need to follow healthy and safe practices.

Reinforcement Activity:

Now that students have an understanding of food preservation methods, take them on a field trip to a supermarket. Here they will learn other methods for extending the shelflife of foods.

Prior to trip list the departments of interest and questions pertaining to the food items in that department.

Example: **Produce department**.

- Examine available produce.

- Where was it grown?

- What short-term preservation methods are being used?

- What happens to discarded produce, etc.?

Other departments include meat, bakery, and dairy products.

How many ways are apples sold? [fresh, juice, sauce, canned, leather] Are there differences in costs?

The Supermarket Detecting Sheet on page 80 can be used in this activity.

Students can share the information from this activity by designing a bulletin board showing short-term and long-term food preservation methods. Many supermarkets have consumer handouts explaining methods to ensure fresh produce and foods. Incorporate these handouts in your display.

My Notes by _____ *Date* _____

The AFTER THE HARVEST Experiment

Team A B C D (Circle One)

1. What is the best method to use in preserving bananas? _____
   Write this question and answer as a hypothesis statement.

   _____

   _____

2. How will we test the hypothesis? _____

   _____

3. How will the results be evaluated? _____

   _____

Conduct Experiment.

4. How do the results compare with my expectations?

   _____

   _____

5. This is what I learned from my team's experiment:

   _____

   _____

6. This is what I learned from the other team's experiments:

   _____

   _____

7. The preservation method I liked best was:

   _____

   _____

Supermarket Detecting Sheet

List four fresh items:

_____   _____

_____   _____

List four fresh items that are also sold as canned and frozen products:

_____   _____

_____   _____

List four fresh items that have gone through a short-term preservation process:

_____   _____

_____   _____

What do the butchers do to meat to extend its shelf life?

_____

_____

How long does it take for meat to spoil?

_____

_____

How can you tell the freshest dairy products?

_____

_____

_____ ? _____

_____

_____ ? _____

_____

_____

The Scientific Gazette

Israel benefits from expertise

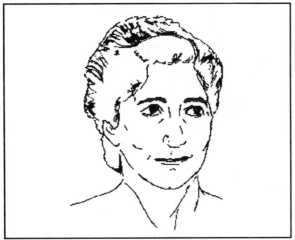

Zdenka Samish

As a girl growing up in Prague, Czechoslovakia, Zdenka Samish was not particularly happy until she joined the Zionist youth movement and was introduced to hiking and camping. "Closeness to nature, swimming and reading" remain favorite activities for Samish, a 91-year old retired food technologist living in Rehovot, Israel.

Zdenka Samish was a researcher in Food Technology, the science of food preservation. As Head of the Department of Fruit and Vegetable Technology at the Agricultural Research Station in Rehovot, Israel, Samish:

- determined how to prevent green olives from spoiling,
- extracted oils from fruit peels to use in soaps and perfumes, and
- developed regional peanut butter, grape juice, raisins, picked cucumbers, tomato paste, jams, and dried citrus fruits.

During her 35 years of research, Zdenka Samish "gladly advised and assisted the newly developing food industry in my adopted country - Israel."

Fun Fact:

The Chinese fermented vegetables as early as the third century BC.

The AFTER THE HARVEST Experiment

Our class conducted experiments to determine the best food processing method to use in preserving bananas. We formed four teams. One team used the _____ method to dry banana slices. The other teams experimented with freezing methods.

- The results tasted _____

- The method I feel works best is _____

- The reason I choose this method is _____

Food preparation methods vary:

Food preservation helps us to eat foods after the growing season is over. There are many ways of preserving food. Some methods used in the home include canning, pickling, freezing, and drying (dehydration). Pickling cucumbers to make "pickles" is common but one can pickle beets, beans, zucchini, and even watermelon rind. Smoking is a method used to preserve bacon, hams, and salmon. _____ is another food preservation method that is popular with astronauts.

> *"Since women have no longer to devote most of their productive years to the time-demanding task of housewives and mothers, they are free to select suitable professions for the fulfillment of their life and to improve their social and financial status."* — **Zdenka Samish**

At Home:

- Create a snack using foods Samish developed at the Agricultural Research Station in Rehovot, Israel.
- Play **Scrabble**, a favorite game of Zdenka Samish's. Double the score when a word relates to food or food preservation.

Dr. Pham Thi Tran Chau is the Head of the Department of Biochemistry in the Faculty of Biology at Hanoi University.

Discovery Unit No. 10

Dr. Pham Thi Tran Chau
Biochemistry

ENZYME ACTION Test

Time-line:

1938 - Dr. Pham Thi Tran Chau is born.

1968 - Gertrud Woker, Swiss biochemist interested in enzymes, dies.

1974 - AWIS (Assn. for Women in Science) establishes an Educational Foundation whose monetary awards fund predoctoral students in science and engineering.

1981 - Society for Canadian Women in Science and Technology is founded.

1993 - EWISH (European Women in Science and Humanities) is organized.

1993 - AWSA (Assn. of Women in Science in Africa) is established.

1995 - The Fourth World Conference on Women is scheduled for September 1995 in Beijing, China.

Key points:

☛ Dr. Pham Thi Tran Chau is the Head of the Department of Biochemistry in the Faculty of Biology at Hanoi University, Vietnam.

☛ Her research of proteinase and proteinase inhibitors has led to the development of a more nutritious powder for infants.

☛ In 1988 Dr. Chau received the Kovalevskaia Prize, and Vietnam conferred upon her the title of "Elite Teacher."

☛ In order to help women establish careers in science, Dr. Chau founded a women's club at Hanoi University.

☛ In the ENZYME ACTION Test, students will experiment with various foods to determine which ones have enzymes that catalyze the protein in gelatin.

Supplies:

✓ Unflavored gelatin (1 or more envelopes)

✓ Water (cold and boiling)

✓ Measuring cups

✓ Mixing spoon

✓ Mixing bowl

✓ Jar lids (one per each chunk of fruit)

✓ Chunks of FRESH fruit:
- pineapple (essential)
- orange
- kiwi (essential)
- apple
- banana
- strawberry

✓ Meat tenderizer (optional experiment) and Liquid Detergent (optional experiment)

✓ "My Notes" Part A and B for each student

Steps:

1. Point out Hanoi, Vietnam, on a map.
2. Share highlights of Dr. Chau's life.
3. Conduct the ENZYME ACTION Test.
4. Assist students in clean-up.
5. Add Dr. Chau's name and a memento to the world map.

For next time:

• Announce the next scientist.

Bibliography:

American Online. **Compton's Encyclopedia, Online Edition** (downloaded May 7, 1995).

AWIS Magazines: March/April 1993; November/December 1993; March/April 1994; and May/June 1994.

Borst, Richard A. "Enzymes: An Introduction to Biotechnology," **Science Scope,** Vol. 14, No. 7.

Chau, Pham Thi Tran Chau. **Letter,** May 16, 1995.

Kass-Simon, G., and Patricia Farnes. **Women of Science: Righting the Record.**

Schlesinger, Sondra. "Women Scientists in Vietnam," **AWIS Magazine,** Vol. 23, No. 1 January/February 1994.

Biography of
DR. PHAM THI TRAN CHAU
b. 1938

I found the living phenomena around me more and more fascinating. Why did uncoloured leaves of germinating seeds turn green when brought from darkness into light? Why is blood red? ...Why does bovine meat when cooked with pineapple, gradually become ground down? Those and other questions interested me.

— Dr. Pham Thi Tran Chau

"Very good biology teacher"

Dr. Chau, the Head of the Department of Biochemistry in the Faculty of Biology at Hanoi University, Vietnam, was fortunate to have a "very good biology teacher" in her last year of secondary school. She decided to study biology in college. While at Hanoi University in her native Vietnam, she discovered that Biochemistry, the chemistry of living organisms, provided answers to her questions about "living systems" and gave her "practical knowledge that could benefit people's lives."

Proteinase

Professor Chau's major area of research became proteinase and proteinase inhibitors. Proteinase is any enzyme that promotes a chemical change in proteins. For example, bromelin in fresh pineapple breaks down the proteins in meat. "I was able to isolate bromelin from the waste of pineapple fruit and identify uses for it in medical and food processing practices." Her research has led to the development of a more nutritious powder for infants.

Responsibilities and awards

In addition to her responsibilities at Hanoi University, Dr. Chau is a member of the State Consultative Council for Science-Technology Policies, executive member of the Vietnam General Associates of Biologists, and a member of the Vietnam Association of Biochemists and the Editorial Board of the "Journal of Biology" (in Vietnamese).

In 1988 Dr. Chau received the Kovalevskaia Prize whose monetary awards provide support for scientific research conducted by women in the developing countries of Vietnam, Nicaragua, and El Salvador. The $2,000 prize money is to be used for the purchase of scientific literature and equipment. That same year Vietnam conferred upon Professor Chau the title of "Elite Teacher."

Husband helps with family chores

Dr. Chau's husband, Professor and Vice Rector of Hanoi University Nguyen Huu Xi, has always helped with the family chores, particularly in caring for their daughter. Eager "to see women progress further in the fields of science," Dr. Chau admits that "it is especially difficult for them." To enjoy both happy family lives and scientific careers, "women must learn to organize their time well. Private and professional lives can be fitted together so that both benefit from one another and neither suffers from lack of attention."

"At times sacrifices have to be made in order to give enough time to science. Even though you may be the perfect wife and mother, there are times when family life does not bring personal satisfaction, but science will always be fulfilling if you are devoted to it."

A women's club

To assist women who are establishing careers in science, Professor Chau founded a women's club at Hanoi University. Women faculty and students meet to discuss problems faced by women who are pursuing careers in science. They also discuss scientific topics and interests. Dr. Chau's advice to all girls and women aspiring to enter science reflects the challenge of reality and the power of faith:

"You should work hard and have patience as a scientific career is not an easy path to choose. Things rarely go smoothly and there are often difficulties to overcome but be diligent, have faith in yourself and don't give up."

Instructor's Guide:

ENZYME ACTION Test

Background Information:

Biochemistry is the branch of science which deals with the chemistry of living organisms. A biochemist investigates the processes of life at a cellular level and can also study related subjects such as growth, reproduction, and heredity. The biochemist, also studies living matter at the molecular level. Proteins, nucleic acids, enzymes and DNA are some of the chemical compounds of living organisms that are studied and analyzed.

Proteins are made of **amino acids**, small units necessary for growth and tissue repair. **Enzymes** are proteins that catalyze (speed up) organic reactions.

Animals use enzymes in their digestive systems to break down foods into simpler components so that the body can readily absorb them. Plants use enzymes in photosynthesis, the process by which plants obtain their food from sunlight. Enzymes also help plants and animals get energy from food.

In the ENZYME ACTION Test students will experiment with various foods to determine which foods have enzymes that act as a catalyst to the protein contained in gelatin.

Instructions:

Earlier in the Day

1. Mix unflavored gelatin and pour into jar lids. You will want as many lids as you have foods to experiment with.

   [Note: 1 envelope unflavored gelatin holds 1/4 oz. of powered gelatin. This envelope will make 1 cup of gelatin solution.]

   Recipe for gelatin solution: In bowl sprinkle 1 envelope powdered gelatin on top of 1/4 cup water. Let stand 1 minute. Add 3/4 cup *boiling water* and stir to dissolve. Pour solution into jar lids. Double recipe if needed.

    Caution. **Boiling water** can cause severe burns. The instructor should do this part of the experiment.

2. Store in a cool place to "set-up", then allow to return to room temperature.

3. Cut fruit into pieces (about 1/2-inch cubes) and store in a plastic bag or container. There should be one piece per lid.

Experiment

1. Set lids (with gelatin mixture) on a table. Place a roll of masking tape and a marking pen beside them.

> **Explain . . .**
> *This is a solution made of gelatin. Gelatin has a high concentration of protein. Proteins are essential for growth, repair, and maintenance of body tissue. They help our bodies fight off diseases.*
>
> **Ask . . .**
> *What animal and plant foods can you name that are rich in protein?* [meat, fish, poultry, milk, eggs, beans, peas, nuts, grains]

2. Distribute "My Notes" sheets.

3. Discuss proteins, amino acids, and enzymes (see Background Information).

4. Instruct students to fill in Part A on their "My Notes." They may need help with answers.

5. Set out bag with fruit chunks. With students helping, place a different piece of fruit on each jar lid containing the gelatin mixture. Using the masking tape and marking pen number each lid. Wait 10 to 15 minutes.

> **Explain . . .**
> *One of the first enzymes discovered in the latter part of the 18th century was named pepsin. This enzyme breaks down protein. The pepsin enzyme papain is found in some fruits.*
>
> **Ask . . .**
> *What do you think will happen to the gelatin when a fruit with papain is placed on it?* [Let students share their ideas.]

6. Instruct students to list the numbers of the lids and write the type of fruit used on each gelatin mixture on Part B of "My Notes."

7. Examine the gelatin mixtures. Carefully remove each chunk of fruit. Observe the surface of the gelatin. The surface beneath a fruit with the enzyme papain should show a slight indentation in the shape of the fruit chunk. The surface will also have liquified. The surface beneath the other fruit will usually stay dry and sometimes the fruit will stick to it.

   [Note: fresh pineapple and kiwi both contain papain.]

> **Ask . . .**
> *Why does the gelatin package caution against using fresh pineapple in preparation of gelatin-based salads and desserts?* [The papain in the pineapple will prevent the gelatin from setting by breaking down the protein.]

8. Ask students to complete the rest of Part B on "My Notes."

9. Assist students in clean up — or — conduct further experiments.

Further Experiments

1. In a small cup mix a spoonful of water with a pinch of unseasoned meat tenderizer. Place 2 or 3 drops in one of the gelatin-filled lids that previously supported a chunk of fruit that did not contain papain.

2. In another gelatin-filled lid squirt a drop of liquid detergent.

3. Wait 10-15 minutes. Observe what happens to the surface of the gelatin. [Both should have the same results as the pineapple and kiwi.]

> **Ask . . .**
> *How do the enzymes in the meat tenderizer work?* [The enzymes in the meat tenderizer break down the proteins in meats making them more "tender."]

> **Ask . . .**
> *How do the enzymes in the detergent work?* [Most stains on clothing are from foods and plants. The enzymes help break up the proteins in these stains.]

4. Assist students with clean-up.

Add notes here:

My Notes by _____ Date _____

ENZYME ACTION Test

Part A

Proteins are made of _____, small units necessary for growth and tissue repair. They also help our bodies fight off _____.

Proteins are found in these foods: _____

_____

_____

Enzymes are _____ that catalyze organic reactions.

Catalyze means _____ .

Why do animals need enzymes in their digestive systems? _____

_____

_____

Plants use enzymes in photosynthesis. What is meant by photosynthesis? _____

_____

_____

Gelatin has a high concentration of _____.

Our next step is to determine what fruits contain an enzyme that acts as a catalyst with the gelatin.

ENZYME ACTION Test

Part B

These are the fruits we are using to test for the enzyme papain:

Number	Fruit Type	Reaction
<u>**1**</u>	_____	_____
<u>**2**</u>	_____	_____
____	_____	_____
____	_____	_____
____	_____	_____
____	_____	_____
____	_____	_____
____	_____	_____
____	_____	_____
____	_____	_____
____	_____	_____
____	_____	_____

These are the fruits we have identified as containing the enzyme papain:

_____

_____

This is how the gelatin mixture looked:

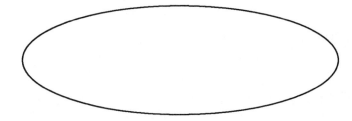

The Scientific Gazette

Biochemistry　　　　　　　　　　　**Dr. Pham Thi Tran Chau**

Award-winning Vietnamese Scientist

Women hold the key to the social framework and the passing on of knowledge and influence. Thus, it appears to me that if you teach a man, you teach an individual, but if you teach a woman, you teach a generation. — **Dr. Pham Thi Tran Chau**

Dr. Pham Thi Tran Chau is the Head of the Department of Biochemistry in the Faculty of Biology at Hanoi University, Vietnam. Her research of proteinase and proteinase inhibitors has led to the development of a more nutritious powder for infants.

In addition to her many responsibilities, Dr. Chau is coordinating a five-year government-funded research project "Producing Protein Proteinase Inhibitors and the Utilization of These in Practice." She has published 60 papers in scientific journals and written **Biochemistry**, a 250-page book published by Vietnam Educational Publishing House.

In 1988 Dr. Chau received the Kovalevskaia Prize. The Kovalevskaia Fund was established by American professor of mathematics Dr. Ann Koblitz with royalties earned from her book on Russian mathematician Sofia Kovalevskaia (1850 - 1891). The Prize now assists scientific research done by women in Nicaragua, El Salvador, and Vietnam.

Since 1985 the Vietnam Kovalevskaia Prize Committee has annually selected two Vietnamese women scientists and awarded each $2,000. This prize money purchases scientific literature and equipment from the Western world.

The Vietnamese recipient must meet several qualifications. I have put down my ideas on how Dr. Chau meets each one.

◆ Be a researcher in the natural sciences:

_____

◆ Completed research projects recognized at home and abroad:

_____

◆ Credited with good social and family relations:

_____

◆ Contributed to the Vietnamese women's movement:

_____

◆ Contributed significantly to her own institution:

_____

Gelatin + Pineapple = _____

To understand Dr. Chau's research with enzymes that catalyze organic reactions in proteins, we conducted the ENZYME ACTION Test.

Unscramble

tnsproei　smyneze　yactalst　nappia

At Home:

◆ Find and prepare a recipe that includes beef and pineapple. Prepare the recipe again but omit the pineapple. Compare taste and texture.

◆ Dr. Chau appreciates the biodiversity of Vietnam. Discover this biodiversity through books, travel brochures, or conversations with individuals who have lived in or visited the country.

Dr. Parul Mullick (seated third from the left) is a resident physician planning to be an anesthesiologist; Dr. Adarsh Bala Minocha (standing first from the right) practices obstetrics/gynecology; Dr. Sarojini Mullick (to the left of Dr. Minocha) is a pediatrician; and, Dr. Vandana Chakarvarty, behind the two women holding children) works as a general practitioner.

Discovery Unit No. 11

Mullick Family
Medicine

INTEREST TREE Activity

Time-line:

- 1947 - Prem Mullick leaves Pakistan to live in India.

- 1950 - Her Excellency Raj. Kumari Amrit Kaur, the first woman to serve as India's Minister of Health, is elected president of the Third World Health Assembly at Geneva. Upon accepting this responsibility, she says: *"Though we live in different countries, speak different languages, and belong to different races, the language of the heart is one and human nature is the same the world over . . .On those who have been called to the noblest of all professions, the art of healing, lies a special responsibility. They are in charge not only of physical but also of mental health — if confidence is to replace fear it can only be done through love and service."* [1]

- 1953 - Ludhiana Christian Medical College becomes coeducational.

- 1954 - Of 61,000 physicians in India, 4,452 are women.

Key points:

☞ In New Delhi, India, several women in the Mullick Family are physicians.

☞ These women "chose medicine because they wanted independence." Their specialties include anesthesia, obstetrics/gynecology, pediatrics, and general practice.

☞ Many members of the Mullick Family share an interest in science and mathematics while others prefer the arts. Patterns of interests and occupations often run in families.

☞ Through the INTEREST TREE Activity, students will learn what patterns of interest exist in their families and among their close friends.

Supplies:

✓ Paper for each student to list their family members and friends

✓ Copy of Trunk and Branch pattern on page 95 for each student OR a sheet of paper and dark-colored construction paper

✓ Copy of Leaf and Blossom pattern on page 94 for each student OR Green and light-colored construction paper

✓ Scissors for each student

✓ Information sheet on **Women Physicians** for each student (page 96)

✓ *The Scientific Gazette* for each student

Steps:

1. Point out New Delhi, India, and Portland, Oregon, on a map.

2. Share "A Family Photo," the story of the Mullick Family.

3. Enjoy the INTEREST TREE Activity.

4. Assist students in clean-up.

5. Display and discuss students' Interest Trees.

6. Distribute information sheet on **Women Physicians**.

7. Distribute *The Scientific Gazette*

For next time:

- Announce the next scientist.

Bibliography:

Lovejoy, Esther Pohl. **Women Doctors of the World.**

[1] Esther Pohl Lovejoy, **Women Doctors of the World** (New York, 1957), p. 230.

A Family Photo

In spring 1995 Meera Mullick Batra and her sixth-grade daughter Ayesha participated in a "Mother-Daughter Choices" program led by author Rebecca Lowe Warren. While discussing the need for girls to develop careers, Meera, a Parent Educator with a degree in Educational Psychology, mentioned that several women in her family in India are physicians. When asked if these women physicians could be included in "Women Scientists from The Seven Continents," Meera not only agreed but collected information and a Mullick Family photograph taken in New Delhi, India.

These women "chose medicine because they wanted independence," Meera explains. "Independent, headstrong and determined" are traits characteristic of these women who have pursued careers in a field considered "very respectable" in India:

Dr. Parul Mullick (seated third from the left) is a resident physician at Safdarjung Hospital in New Delhi. Educated at New Delhi Medical College, Dr. Mullick works in the Department of Anesthesia and plans to be an anesthesiologist. Her husband is an eye surgeon.

Dr. Adarsh Bala Minocha (standing first from the right) was born in Harbanspura, Pakistan, and educated at R. G. Kar Hospital in Calcutta, India. Her specialty is obstetrics/gynecology and she works as a specialist with the Central Government Health Scheme (CGHS) in New Delhi. She is married to Dr. Surinder Mullick, an internist.

To the left of Dr. Minocha is pediatrician **Dr. Sarojini Mullick**. Also born in Pakistan, Dr. Mullick was educated at the Medical College in Ludhiana, India, and is a children's specialist at the Kalavati Saran Hospital in New Delhi. Her husband was also a pediatrician and they practiced together until his death five years ago.

Dr. Vandana Chakarvarty (behind the two women holding children) is a General Practitioner working with the Central Government Health Scheme (CGHS). Born in Ambala Haryana, India, Dr. Chakarvarty was educated at the Bhopal Medical College in Bhopal, India. She is married to an eye surgeon.

Not pictured in the family photograph is **Dr. Indra Mullick** who holds two Ph.D. degrees — one in microbiology and another in biochemistry. She teaches microbiology at the University of Delhi.

These women are on Meera's father's side of the family. Although most of the women on her mother's side "are all writers and romantics," Meera's mother, Prem Mullick, is an exception. She was in medical school in 1947 when the country of Pakistan came into existence. Pakistan covers the parts of the former Indian Empire with a predominately Moslem population. Since her family was Hindi, they left Pakistan to live in India where Prem did not continue in medicine but studied mathematics.

Despite the thousands of miles that separate Prem Mullick from her family in Portland, Oregon, she "faxes" correspondence including mathematical puzzles to her granddaughter Ayesha who shares her grandmother's interest in and talent for mathematics.

Instructor's Guide:

INTEREST TREE Activity

Background Information:

The Mullick family photo brings together women with a common interest in healing. These women are from the father's side of Meera Mullick Batra's mother's family. Although Meera's mother also was educated in the sciences and mathematics, many of her mother's relatives from her grandmother's side had stronger interests in the arts. Patterns of interests and occupations often run in families. This exercise encourages students to view interests of family members (and the close friends of their families) to determine what patterns exist. These interests can be captured in a "family tree" format in which the student is the trunk and the branches and the family members and friends are the leaves and blossoms. Those closest to the student are placed closest to the trunk, those the student interacts with less frequently should be placed towards the ends of the branches.

A completed INTEREST TREE might look like this:

Instructions for the student:

1. Write your name and interest at the top of a sheet of paper.

2. List those family members and friends that are closest to you. (Those that you see most often and thus have the most influence on you.) This is list number 1.

3. Identify each person's occupation or major interest (medicine, art, piano, teacher).

4. List other family members and friends. What are their interests? This is list number 2.

5. Place a * by each person who has an interest similar to yours.

6. Draw the trunk of the tree and the branches. You may choose to cut this out of brown or dark colored-construction paper, or use the model on page 95.

7. Draw blossoms on the tree for every person with an interest the same as yours. (You marked these with a star.) You may cut blossoms from light colored construction paper. Write each person's name and interest on one of the blossoms. Those names from list 1 should be closest to the trunk: those from list 2 further out on the branches.

8. Draw leaves on the tree for every other person on your lists. You may cut these from green construction paper. Write a name and interest on each leaf. Place those from list 1 closest to the trunk, from list 2, further out on the branches.

What to do with your tree:

If your tree has lots of blossoms, you are in luck. These are the people who can help you develop your talents and interests. If you don't have any blossoms, then look around and find some people who share your interests and will be there to encourage your explorations in this area. Where do you find these people? Share this tree with your family and ask them to suggest people or groups to contact.

---

9. Distribute information sheet on women physicians. Allow time for students to read it silently. Use these questions as discussion points:

   • Why do you think many women from Asia studied at women's medical colleges in the United States? Canada? Europe?

   • Who was the first woman physician in your country? State or province? County? City?

   • Why did these women enter medicine?

   • What challenges did they overcome?

10. Assist students in clean-up.

A Classroom Interest Tree:

1. Make the trunk and branches for the Classroom Interest Tree by drawing on newsprint or cutting-out construction paper and attaching to a bulletin board. These indicate the classroom or group.

2. Ask students to write one important interest on a piece of paper

3. Collect all interest sheets, and with the class assemble sheets into general categories (science, math, music, finance, engineering, etc.).

4. Assign a color to each category.

5. Give each student a sheet of construction paper in the color assigned to his/her category. The student then cuts a leaf from the paper, writes his/her name on the leaf with a marking pen, and attaches the leaf to the tree.

The Classroom Interest Tree gives a visual depiction of the diversity of interests in your classroom. It also helps students identify others who share similar interests.

In the future: Call together students of similar interests and assign an exploration of occupations based on that interest category. The student reports should be given in a creative and interesting way such as through song, a poem, art work, skit, etc.

◆ ◆ ◆

Leaf & Blossom Patterns:

Trunk & Branch Pattern:

Women Physicians Throughout Asia

Japan

According to Dr. Tomo Inouye in her 1931 article in the *Medical Women's International Journal*, **Dr. O. Nakanishi** of Tokyo and **Dr. T. Naka** of Osaka in 1822 had "attained a wide reputation as efficient physicians." In the 1830s **Dr. H. Morizaki** of Tokyo was not only an experienced physician but, in Dr. Inouye's words, "a scholar and author of obstetrical works." In 1902 **Dr. Yayoi Yoshioka** and her husband founded the Tokyo Women's Medical College.

China

Dr. Ya Mei Kin from Honolulu, Hawaii, became the first Chinese woman to receive a doctor of medicine degree in the U.S. when she graduated head of her class from the Women's Medical College of the New York Infirmary in 1885. She established a hospital for women and children in North China at Tientsin. In the early 1900s **Dr. Ah Mae Wong** began her medical studies at Toronto University when she was 37 years old. Following graduation, she worked in a Nanking hospital before returning to Shanghai where she became one of the city's leading women physicians.

Korea

In 1900 **Dr. Esther Kim Pak** graduated from the Woman's Medical College of Baltimore and became the first Korean physician to practice Western medicine in Korea. By 1950 more than 400 women in Korea had qualified as physicians.

The Philippines

Dr. Honoria Acosta-Sison graduated from the Woman's Medical College of Pennsylvania in 1909. Her specialty was obstetrics and gynecology and in 1940 she became head of the Department of Obstetrics at the University of the Philippines College of Medicine. **Dr. Marie Paz Mendoza** was the first woman to receive a medical degree in the Philippines. She graduated from the University of the Philippines College of Medicine in 1912. She was professor of pathology at the medical school for many years. To honor her husband's memory, she built the Gauzon Operating Pavilion of the Philippine General Hospital.

Thailand (Siam)

Dr. Pierra Hoon (Vejjabul) decided to become a physician when she was 11 years old and watched a French physician save her mother's life. In 1932 she graduated from the medical school of the University of Paris and returned to Siam in 1937. "Vejjabul" is a title which means "great woman doctor." Dr. Pierra Hoon Vejjabul not only practiced medicine but opened a hospital for women and children at Bangkok, published a monthly magazine, organized the National Association of University Women, and adopted 45 orphans. In 1953 she organized a national association of women physicians.

* * *

Bibliography:

Lovejoy, Esther Pohl. **Women Doctors of the World.**

The Scientific Gazette

A Family Photo

In the Mullick Family in New Delhi, India, several women are physicians. Although they work in different branches of medicine, they share an interest in the science and art of healing. Draw lines to connect the physician and her field of medical specialty:

Dr. Parul Mullick   pediatrics
Dr. Adarsh Bala Minocha   general practice
Dr. Sarojini Mullick   obstetrics
                                  /gynecology
Dr. Vandana Chakarvarty   anesthesia

My Interest Tree

An Interest Tree for the Mullick Family would include science, mathematics, and art. Patterns of interests and occupations often run in families. From the INTEREST TREE Activity I discovered:

_____

_____

_____

First woman physician in India . . .

Dr. Anandibai Joshee was born at Poona in 1865. She graduated from the Woman's Medical College of Pennsylvania in 1886 and returned to India to head the woman's division of the new hospital at Kolhapur. Shortly after her arrival home, she contracted tuberculosis and died a month before her twenty-second birthday.

Medicine is more than healing

While physicians use their medical knowledge to heal patients, they also help prevent disease by practicing preventative medicine. Immunizations are preventative medicine. Many diseases once common in childhood are nearly non-existent in areas where children are vaccinated. According to information from the National Immunization Campaign, diseases prevented through immunizations include:

➡ measles, mumps, and rubella

➡ polio

➡ diphtheria, tetanus (lockjaw), and pertussis (whooping cough)

➡ Haemophilus influenze type b (a major cause of meningitis)

➡ Heptatis B (liver infection)

The following suggestions will help the student learn more about disease prevention.

• Locate your immunization record.

• Research one of the diseases on the record and discover who developed the vaccine.

• At school: create a bulletin board that displays your research, public health literature, and historical information.

During the 18th century approximately 60 million people died from smallpox. Each year 45,000 people died in the British Isles. When Lady Mary Wortley Montague visited Turkey in 1717, she observed "innoculations" against smallpox, a procedure that had been common practice for centuries in parts of the Middle East, China, and India. Lady Montague carried the practice back to England where it spread to Europe and North America.

About 1200 years ago the Government of Japan bestowed upon some 50 women 15 to 30 years of age the title of Doctresses.

"Feel Free to Explore"

Christine Graves — b. 1951

Born in Maryland, Christine Graves has lived in California, conducted field work in Mexico, studied in Spain, and worked in Peru and Italy.

While Graves's life has bridged three continents, her work as a science writer links a background in literature, an interest in nature, and a desire "to contribute to improving the welfare of rural people throughout the developing world."

Nature and literature

Her mother is Cuban. Her father was a Commander (pilot) in the Navy so the family moved many times during Christine's early years. "The common denominators in all those travels, as far as my interests, were nature - from insects and animals to forests and oceans - and literature." She enjoyed all subjects in school, "perhaps with a special liking for literature and math."

In college Christine "was drawn to the social sciences, particularly to the field of cultural anthropology." Her BA degree is in anthropology. After an independent European study-tour, Graves studied Iberian literature and Latin American literature. "I studied for one year in Spain and then returned to San Diego where I studied and taught at the university until I received my MA in Latin American literature."

International Potato Center

Graves then traveled to Peru where she wanted to meet the poet who had been the subject of her master's thesis and to "gain some first-hand experience in South America." The country intrigued her and she "decided to stay indefinitely." Years later she became a writer/editor at the International Potato Center (CIP)—a venture that "brought together many of my interests and talents, . . ."

Challenged "with learning about a wide range of activities in agriculture - from biotechnological methods of plant improvement, to planting systems, to marketing and consumption trends," and communicating these "activities and concepts" to the general public, Graves's work at CIP bridged her new interest in the agricultural sciences and her background in literature and writing.

Preparing speeches, writing general information publications, and working with scientists on "numerous technical articles for outside journals," were her primary tasks. She became Senior Editor and was responsible for all of the Center's publications. After eight years at CIP, Graves left Peru in 1993 and moved to Rome, Italy.

Rome, Italy

Her work in Rome at the Food and Agriculture Organization (FAO) of the United Nations "is in many ways similar to that in Peru" although FAO is much larger. Graves has recently researched, written, and prepared for production the FAO Annual Review. The Information Materials Production Division "includes a full team of graphic artists, editors, photographers, photography editors and audio-visual specialists." Most of Graves's day is spent writing.

An "open mind" helped Christine Graves link her loves of literature and nature in a way she did not originally imagine. She advises students to develop "their skills in their areas of interest, even if they are not sure how they may apply them." She credits her career in science writing to her "good background of writing skills . . . and training in critical thinking and analysis," and encourages students "to follow their instincts and interests, and above all to feel free to explore."

Enrichment Activity:

◆ Prepare a group publication on the history, varieties, and uses of the potato.

◆ Create a Potato Recipe Book.

◆ Grow potatoes.

Bibliography:

Graves, Christine. **Letter,** Sept. 28, 1994.

A
U
S
T
R
A
L
I
A

With an area of 2,966,153 square miles (including the island of Tasmania), Australia is the world's smallest continent and the only country in the world to occupy an entire continent. Australia is also considered the "flattest" continent with its highest point being Mount Kosciusko at 7,316 feet.

Next to Antarctica, Australia is the driest continent. Desert and semidesert cover almost 66% of the land. Sunshine and drought are common with summer temperatures daily exceeding 100ºF in most places. In the continent's interior rain may not fall for months or even years.

Women Scientists from Australia and New Zealand:

"Science is as creative as art or music or literature."

— **Dr. Philippa Marion Wiggins**
Physical Chemist
Auckland School of Medicine

From New Zealand and Australia women entered a variety of scientific fields during the Depression and World War II. Their reasons were almost as varied as their choice of disciplines. Some came to science by accident and some by sheer will. Others spent years acquiring a formal education while a handful succeeded with few or no formal courses to their credit.

- During World War II botanist Joan Marjorie Dingley applied her knowledge of mycology (fungi) to "mould-proof" military tents and radio equipment.

- Before Dr. Helen Newton Turner became an animal geneticist, she was an architect and a secretary. Her study of mathematical statistics and its application to inherited characteristics of sheep increased Australia's output and quality of wool.

- Self-taught vertebrate paleontologist Joan Wiffen uncovered fossils that proved the existence of dinosaurs in New Zealand 65 to 70 million years ago.

- Physicist Dr. Rachel Makinson forewent a probable career in nuclear physics in England to move to Australia where she worked in textile physics. She discovered the properties of wool fiber and wrote a book that remains "the standard reference" on the subject.

- One genus and five species of marine animals, and a coral reef, have been named in honor of marine biologist **Dr. Isobel Bennett**. (See Discovery Unit 13.)

- Dr. Philippa Marion Wiggins, physical chemist, believes intuition and imagination are key to scientific discoveries. In 1986 Dr. Wiggins was promoted to professor at the Auckland School of Medicine, New Zealand.

- One of **Dr. Joan Freeman**'s purposes in writing her autobiography, **A Passion for Physics: The Story of a Woman Physicist**, was to encourage young women to plan careers in science. (See Discovery Unit 12.)

- In 1993 botanist Nancy Mary Adams finished the text and illustrations on her book featuring New Zealand seaweeds. This award-winning scientist is a research associate at Dominion Museum, New Zealand.

For decades the work and contributions of these women scientists went unnoticed outside of their disciplines. Through articles written by Nessy Allen, a senior lecturer in the School of Science and Technology Studies at the University of New South Wales in Sydney, Australia, and Paula Martin's book, **Lives with Science: Profiles of Senior New Zealand Women in Science**, the lives of these women scientists are being celebrated.

Bibliography:

America Online, **Compton's Encyclopedia,** Online Edition (downloaded December 15, 1994).

Learmonth, A.T.A. & A.M. **Encyclopaedia of Australia.**

Marvin, Rob. "Coriolis Force Responsible for Appearance of Moving Curve," **The Oregonian**, March 16, 1994.

Newman, Steve. "Earthweek: A Diary of the Planet," **The Oregonian**, Mary 7, 1994.

Whitaker, Donald P., and others. **Area Handbook for Australia.**

Continental Facts:

Australia's geographic isolation has created unique forms of vegetation and animal life:

- Over 13,000 plant species are native to Australia.

- The native wildlife includes 230 species of mammals and 520 of birds including the emu and cassowary, neither of which can fly.

- Of the 230 mammal species, almost 50% are marsupials whose young are born in very early stages of development and are "matured" in the mother's pouch.

- Two species of monotremes (egg-laying mammals) also live in Australia. They are the duckbilled platypus and the spiny ant-eater.

Continental Curiosities:

- Lake Eyre is a salt "lake" covering 3,600 square miles in Australia's arid interior.

- In December 1994 the Royal Botanic Gardens in Sydney announced the discovery of living conifers that paleobotanists thought had become extinct 50 million years ago. Thirty-nine of these trees were found growing in Wollemi National Park west of Sydney.

- Weather patterns move clockwise in the Southern Hemisphere; they move counter-clockwise in the Northern Hemisphere.

- In March 1994 small fish were found "flapping around in parking lots and on roads" south of Darwin after rainstorms in Australia's desert interior. According to zoologist Beryle Morris, the heavy rains might have caused dry fish eggs to hatch and the high winds carried the "newborns considerable distances."

Exploration Questions:

- Who developed the "boomerang"?
- Why is the pouch of the long-nosed bandicoot unique?

Enrichment Activities:

- What was the supercontinent of Gondwana?

- Tektites are small pieces of volcanic glass — possible debris from a "comet swarm" — discovered in 9 or 10 locations around the world. Called "emu stones" and "button stones" by Australians, 2,000,000 tektites are estimated to have fallen over southern Australia. Where were the other sites? What were the stones called? How was their appearance explained?

Add notes here:

In 1976 physicist Dr. Joan Freeman became the first woman to receive the Rutherford Medal.

Discovery Unit No. 12

Dr. Joan Freeman
Physics

PHYSICS and PHONES Activity

Time-line:

1918 - Dr. Joan Freeman is born in Perth, Australia.

1934 - Dr. Marie Sklodowska Curie, the only woman to receive two Nobel Prizes, dies.

1935 - Dr. Irene Joliot-Curie and her husband share the Nobel Prize in Chemistry.

1964 - Dr. Dorothy Crowfoot Hodgkin receives the Nobel Prize in Chemistry.

1966 - Dr. Lise Meitner becomes the first woman to receive the U.S. Atomic Energy Commission's Enrico Fermi Award.

1976 - Dr. Joan Freeman is the first woman to be awarded the Rutherford Medal.

Key points:

☞ As a young girl Joan Freeman explored scientific topics on her own.

☞ After learning about an error in a science textbook, Freeman decided that being a scientist could be very exciting.

☞ Upon her arrival in England, Freeman learned to ride a bike, saw her first snowflake, and decided to work in nuclear physics.

☞ In 1976 Dr. Joan Freeman became the first woman to receive the Rutherford Medal.

☞ In the PHYSICS and PHONES Activity, students will recreate "the telephone project" that Joan Freeman conducted when she was a young girl growing up in Sydney, Australia.

Supplies:

✓ Paper cups

✓ Paper clips

✓ Tin cans with only one end removed

✓ String and wire

✓ Hammer and nail

Steps:

1. Point out Perth, Australia, on a map.

2. Share highlights of Dr. Joan Freeman's life.

3. Conduct the PHYSICS and PHONES Activity.

4. Conduct other experiments. (Optional—See instructor's guide, page 106, Holding a Physics Fair.)

5. Assist students in clean-up.

6. Add Dr. Joan Freeman's name and a memento to the world map.

7. Distribute *The Scientific Gazette.*

For next time:

• Announce the next scientist.

Bibliography:

Allen, Nessy. "Australian Women in Science - A Comparative Study of Two Physicists." **Metascience,** August 1990.

Ardley, Neil. **The Science Book of Sound.**

Freeman, Joan. **A Passion for Physics: The Story of a Woman Physicist.**

Jennings, Terry. **Sound and Light.**

Newman, Frederick R. **Zounds! The Kid's Guide to Sound Making.**

Biography of
DR. JOAN FREEMAN
b. 1918

At the Sydney Church of England Girls' Grammar School (SCEGGS), math was Joan's favorite subject. Since her school offered few science courses, Joan explored scientific topics on her own. Her ten volumes of **The Children's Encyclopedia** by Arthur Mee included chapters on natural history, astronomy, and geology. Under the chapter heading of "Wonder" were questions like "What makes a rainbow?" and "Why does smoke go up the chimney?" The easy-to-understand answers heightened Joan's appreciation of the physical sciences.

Textbook error

After learning from a science textbook that the atom was the "smallest quantity of any element; *it cannot be divided,*" 14-year-old Joan was surprised to read the following headline in the Sydney Morning Herald: SPLITTING THE ATOM AT THE CAVENDISH LABORATORY. How could someone split the atom — the "smallest quantity," especially if the textbook had said an atom could not be divided?

But the atom had indeed been split and the textbook was in error. Joan realized that scientific textbooks are not always accurate because new scientific discoveries may destroy existing beliefs. She concluded that being a scientist could be very exciting! Even though SCEGGS offered no further chemistry courses and "had scarcely even heard of physics," Joan decided to study science at Sydney University. Her mother encouraged her.

"That subject is more suitable for a girl"

Together they visited the Sydney Technical College to learn if Joan could enroll in science courses to prepare for the exams leading to "high school" graduation. The Head of the Chemistry Department encouraged Joan to return to domestic science (home economics) since "that subject is more suitable for a girl." Mrs. Freeman was furious. She immediately took Joan to interview the Head of the Physics Department who admired Joan's spirit and granted her permission to become the first female student in his physics classes. Two years later, Joan earned "top of the class" in the final exam at Sydney Technical College.

From chemistry to physics

Awarded scholarships to Sydney University, Joan enrolled with intentions to specialize in chemistry. Her plans changed for several reasons: she was encouraged to study physics by a professor who had recently conducted radiowave experiments in Europe; she was moved by another professor's tribute to experimental physicist Lord Rutherford and his work in radioactivity at the Cavendish Laboratory in Cambridge, England; and she was enjoying her courses in physics more than her work in chemistry. Joan Freeman changed her specialty to physics. She graduated from Sydney University in 1939 and immediately began work on her M.Sc. degree.

Learns to ride a bike

By 1941 Freeman was working at the Radiophysics Laboratory up the road from Sydney University. Freeman calls this time "The Radar Years." After World War II she won a scholarship to the Cavendish Laboratory in England. Shortly after her arrival, she learned to ride a bike, saw her first snowflake, and decided to pursue nuclear physics instead of radio astronomy, the use of radio waves to gather information about the universe.

Granted her Ph.D. in December 1949, Freeman wanted to return to Australia but accepted the opportunity "to investigate atomic energy in all its aspects —" at Harwell, an atomic energy research facility. She worked as a Senior Scientific Officer in the Van de Graaff Accelerator Group of Harwell's Nuclear Physics Division.

In the United States

In 1958, following her marriage to radio astronomer John Jelley, Freeman received a Research Fellowship at M.I.T.'s (Massachusetts Institute of Technology) High Voltage Lab in the United States. Her study of nuclear reactions continued. As her time in the U.S. was drawing to a close, Dr. Freeman was offered the position of Group Leader at Harwell's newest acquisition — a tandem accelerator. She accepted and, upon her return to England, began experiments on select radioactive nuclei whose half lives were a second or less.*

First woman to win the Rutherford Medal

Acknowledging that she was an experimental physicist, Freeman collaborated with a theoretical physicist from Oxford, Professor Roger Blin-Stoyle. Their collaborative work earned them the Rutherford Medal, a prestigious award in physics, in 1976. Dr. Joan Freeman was the first woman and the second Australian to receive this award.

"Physics is a delight, and physics is fun."

Since her official retirement from Harwell at age 60, Dr. Freeman has traveled, consulted with scientists worldwide, and taken up sailing. She has also written her autobiography entitled **A Passion for Physics: The Story of a Woman Physicist.** In writing this book, she realized her good fortune at fulfilling her dream of studying science, and of working in a profession that exposed her to the "beauty and mystery of the physical world." The last line in her autobiography sums up Dr. Joan Freeman's philosophy in these words: "physics is a delight, and physics is fun."

◆ ◆ ◆

* Half Lives:

Radioactive elements are ones that spontaneously "decay" or change into other elements by emitting charged particles.

The time it takes for 1/2 of the atoms in a sample to decay is called the element's half life. Half lives range from the 4.5 billion years of Radium 226 to millionths of a second for artificially produced elements. An important feature of half life is that only 1/2 of the remainder decays in the second half life and, of what is left, only 1/2 decays in the next half life.

For this reason, scientists can use this principle of half life decay to date material after they have determined the amount of radioactive materials in a particular specimen.

Add notes here:

Instructor's Guide:

PHYSICS and PHONES Activity

Background Information:

While exploring science topics on her own, the young Joan Freeman "rejoiced" in the conducting of "scientific" experiments. She learned how to:

- make a siphon,
- detect the rotation of the earth,
- observe atmosphere,
- make water rise inside an inverted glass,
- power a paper boat using pieces of camphor, and
- test the acidic and alkaline properties of vinegar, soda, and other "domestic substances."

She also conducted experiments involving sound waves. Today we will recreate Joan Freeman's "telephone project."

Instructions:

1. Talk about some of the fun experiments Dr. Freeman conducted as a young girl (Background Information). Tell students they will be recreating the telephone project.

Explain . . .
Sound begins as a vibration. The vibrations of speech begin in the larynx of the throat. You can feel this vibration by lightly touching your throat and humming or singing musical notes.
[Have students do this.]
These waves of sound travel across the molecules in the air, enter our ears, and vibrate against our eardrums. These impulses are carried to our brains where the sounds are identified.

Ask . . .
What other things can be used to conduct sound waves? [Possible responses: water, wire.]

---

2. Ask students to lay their heads down on their desks with one ear pressed to the surface and to hold their other ear closed with their finger. Move your chair on the floor. What do they hear? Have them listen carefully, they might even hear voices or movements from another room.

Explain . . .
Sound also travels through objects. Although you don't see it happening, the molecules in solid surfaces and in water can respond to the vibrations of sound.

Ask . . .
What three things are needed for sound? [A vibrating source to start the sound waves, a medium to carry the sound waves, and a receiver to detect them — i.e. voice, air, ear.]

---

3. Form small groups. Provide students with paper cups, aluminum cans, string, wire, paper clips (to help hold string in place), hammer and nail (for punching a hole in an aluminum can).

4. Encourage them to create their own telephone systems. (Some may wish to add a "party-line.")

5. Ask students to share their inventions and determine the merits of each. ("This is easy to make." "This carries sound the farthest." etc.)

Optional Activity:

PHYSICS FAIR

Suggestions for conducting the Fair:

- Using activity and resource books from the library, help the students draw up a list of experiments and activities that would be fun to do.

- Have students sign up (or draw names for certain projects).

- Students can work alone or in teams.

- Give students time to learn how to conduct these experiments.

- Set a date for the Physics Fair. [Students will share their information/experiment.]

- Note: Some students may wish to present their information in the form of displays or posters, while others may wish to bring in an outside resource to explain how something is done. Creative thinking should be encouraged.

- Consider inviting other students to attend your Physics Fair.

"physics is a delight, and physics is fun" — Dr. Joan Freeman

Dr. Joan Freeman was born in 1918 in Perth, Australia. At age six she fancied a career in dance. One year later she developed her "lasting passion for reading." During this same year, she explored the wonders of the laws of motion after successfully pleading with her mother to buy her a "meccano" set complete with wheels, pulleys, hooks, handles, nuts, bolts, metal strips, and screwdrivers. Her childhood was spent exploring the "wild, unspoiled territory" behind the family home overlooking the Pacific Ocean in Sydney, Australia.

Since her school offered few science courses, Freeman explored scientific topics on her own. At age 14 she was surprised to learn that scientists had succeeded in splitting the atom since her textbook said an atom could not be divided. If new scientific discoveries destroyed existing beliefs, then being a scientist could be quite exciting. Joan decided to become a scientist and her mother encouraged her. She studied physics at Sydney University and graduated in 1939.

After World War II, Freeman won a scholarship to study in England. She decided to work on nuclear physics and earned her Ph.D. in 1949. At Harwell, an atomic energy research facility, she experimented on radioactive nuclei whose half lives are a second or less. In 1976 Dr. Joan Freeman became the first woman — and the second Australian — to receive the Rutherford Medal, a prestigious award in physics.

STUDY PHYSICS

Dr. Joan Freeman believes that girls should be encouraged to study physics since careers in physics are rewarding and varied. Also, a general knowledge of physics helps explain the functioning of "many mechanical, electrical, and electronic devices," expands our understanding of contemporary problems such as "environment, pollution, and energy sources," and enhances our appreciation of the physical world.

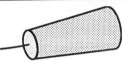
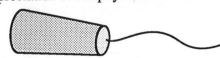

In class we recreated Dr. Joan Freeman's "Telephone Project" that she conducted as a young girl. This simple telephone works because _____

At Home:

◆ To explore issues and problems related to nuclear physics, Joan Freeman and co-workers began the *Nuclear Nit-Wits Clubs*. Organize a special interest club (kite-making, stamp collecting etc.) with family or friends.

◆ As a youngster Joan danced while her mother played the piano. She particularly enjoyed music composed by Chopin. Visit your local library and check out tapes/CDs featuring Chopin's Impromptus, Polonaises, and Scherzos. **Scherzo Opus 31** was one of Joan's favorites.

Marine Biologist Dr. Isobel Bennett is the author of ten books and an expert photographer.

Discovery Unit No. 13

Dr. Isobel Bennett
Marine Biology

SALTWATER PARFAIT Experiment

Time-line:

1909 - Dr. Isobel Bennett is born in Brisbane, Australia.

1918 - Physicist Dr. Joan Freeman is born in Perth, Australia.

1954 - Australian animal geneticist Dr. Helen Newton Turner begins her year-long study of sheep-breeding programs in Europe and the U.S.

1978 - Astrophysicist and cosmologist Dr. Beatrice Tinsley (born in England and raised in New Zealand) becomes professor of astronomy at Yale University.

1988 - Australia's Bicentennial Celebration

1991 - In her book **Valley of the Dragons: The Story of New Zealand's Dinosaur Woman**, vertebrate paleontologist Joan Wiffen describes her fossil discoveries including marine reptiles that inhabited the seas around New Zealand 65 to 70 million years ago.

Key points:

☞ Dr. Isobel Bennett's temporary job as a secretary/research assistant in the 1930s led to her becoming an internationally-known marine biologist.

☞ Bennett has written ten books including **The Fringe of the Sea** (1967) and the award-winning **The Great Barrier Reef** (1971).

☞ Bennett is an expert photographer whose photographs appear in her books.

☞ In the spring of 1995, the University of Sydney awarded Bennett an honorary Doctorate of Science degree.

☞ In the SALTWATER PARFAIT Experiment, students will observe a layering of water densities similar to conditions around the Great Barrier Reef.

Supplies:

✓ A large wide-mouth jar

✓ Table salt

✓ Yellow and blue food colorings

✓ Turkey baster

✓ Measuring cups

✓ Tap water

✓ "My Notes" sheets for each student.

✓ *The Scientific Gazette* for each student.

Steps:

1. Point out Brisbane and Sydney, Australia.
2. Share highlights of Dr. Isobel Bennett's life.
3. Conduct the SALTWATER PARFAIT Experiment.
4. Have students assist in clean-up.
5. Add Dr. Isobel Bennett's name and a memento to the world map.
6. Distribute *The Scientific Gazette*.

For next time:

• Announce the next scientist.

Bibliography:

Allen, Nessy. "Australian Women in Science: Two Unorthodox Careers," **Women's Studies International Forum**, Vol. 15. Nos. 5/6, 1992.

Allen, Nessy. "'The Sea has Many Voices': Profile of an Australian Woman Scientist," **Journal of Australian Studies,** No. 38, September 1993.

Bennett, Isobel. **The Great Barrier Reef.**

Simon, Seymour. **How To Be an Ocean Scientist in Your Own Home.**

Biography of
Dr. Isobel Bennett
b. 1909

As a young girl, Isobel Bennett had no intention of becoming a scientist. In fact, at age 16 family circumstances caused her to leave school and enroll in a business college. After completing the secretarial course, she worked at a patent attorney's office in Brisbane, Australia, until the family moved to Sydney.

In Sydney, Bennett worked four years at the Associated Board of the Royal Schools of Music until 1932 when the Depression forced the office to close. When Bennett was unable to find another job, she and her sister decided to take a five-day cruise.

Five-day cruise & a new career

The cruise destination was Norfolk Island — 1,035 miles northeast of Sydney. Fellow passengers included Professor W. J. Dakin, marine scientist, researcher, teacher, and chair of the Zoology Department, University of Sydney. Dakin and his wife befriended the Bennett sisters. Learning of Isobel's employment situation, he suggested that she check back with him if she could not find work.

Months later, Isobel Bennett went to work "under Dakin's direction" in the Zoology Department at the University. Although her appointment was to be temporary, she began in 1933 as a secretary/research assistant and retired in 1971 as a marine biologist of international repute. To Dakin's list of credentials, one must add the word "mentor" since "under his direction" Bennett:

- became a crew member of the University's research vessel,
- supervised the collection of plankton,
- learned microscope sectioning,
- enrolled in practical zoology classes,
- took over the Zoology Department's library,
- catalogued animal life along New South Wales' coastline, and
- prepared Dakin's **Australian Seashores** for publication.

Between 9 PM and 3 AM

Following Professor Dakin's retirement, Bennett's work in marine biology continued as well as her responsibilities with staff and students, including all field excursions. To this ambitious schedule, Bennett added the writing of a book. She used the hours between 9 PM and 3 AM to create **The Fringe of the Sea** (1967), a work that included her photographs. Nine other books followed — six of them written after her official retirement.

Bennett's **The Great Barrier Reef** (1971) was the first book to give comprehensive information and photographs about the Reef that stretches for 1,260 miles off the north-eastern coast of Australia. In 1982 the Royal Zoological Society of New South Wales conferred its Whitley Memorial Award for the Best Illustrated Book on the Natural History of Animals of the Australian Region on Isobel Bennett's **The Great Barrier Reef**. Her award-winning photographs confirm the reef's biodiversity, fragility, and beauty.

Travels

In 1955 Bennett visited research facilities and attended scientific meetings throughout the world. Her "ports of call" included Britain, Europe, Scandinavia, United States, Japan, New Zealand, and Australia. Between 1959 and 1968, Isobel Bennett made four voyages to Antarctica. In 1963 she sailed aboard Stanford University's research vessel to study the Indian Ocean.

Dr. Isobel Bennett

"Under Dakin's direction" Bennett took practical zoology classes in 1935 but earned no degree. In 1962 the University of Sydney awarded her an unprecedented honorary Master of Science degree, and in the spring of 1995, that same institution awarded her an honorary Doctorate of Science degree. Dr. Isobel Bennett, now in her 80s, continues to edit, consult, and enjoy the beauty and richness of the sea.

Instructor's Guide:

SALTWATER PARFAIT Experiment

Background Information:

The Great Barrier Reef is a vast complex of islands and reefs located off the northeastern coast of the Australian state of Queensland. The islands, made from the same materials as the continent, were separated from the mainland by geological events. The reefs, formed from the skeletons of marine animals called coral polyps, are extensive structures sometimes hundreds of feet thick.

Reef-building corals grow best in shallow tropical waters between 15 and 90 feet and in temperatures ranging from 20ºC to 30ºC. While some corals become highly specialized and sensitive to small temperature and salinity (salt content) fluctuations, other tolerate greater extremes. The reef organisms, however, exist in a delicately balanced environment. If one vital environmental factor exceeds its limit, the whole reef community may be in danger of extinction.

The ocean is so vast that one might assume that the temperature and salinity remain constant. This is not the case. In warmer climates the water is saltier. When fresh water from rivers and rainfall enters the currents, such as those around the Great Barrier Reef, the less salty (lighter) water flows along the surface, with the saltier (heavier, denser) water flowing independently beneath it. The SALTWATER PARFAIT Experiment will demonstrate the layering effect brought about by the varying densities of water around the Great Barrier Reef.

Instructions:

In Advance

The SALTWATER PARFAIT Experiment is to be conducted by the instructor because of the importance of transferring the solutions without agitating the liquid in the jar. You should practise this action in advance to get the "feel" for it.

Today

1. Set out supplies for the experiment. Place the large jar so it is eye level with your students.

2. On a map of Australia, point out the location of the Great Barrier Reef and share the background information with your students.

3. Distribute "My Notes" sheets.

> **Explain . . .**
> *Today I will show you how the saltier (denser) water lies near the bottom of the ocean while the less salty water stays on the surface.*

4. Fill the large wide-mouth jar about 1/4 full of tap water.

5. Solution #1 — Fill a water glass about 3/4 the way full with tap water. Stir 1/4 cup of salt into the water until dissolved. Put a drop of yellow food coloring into this water. [Note how the food coloring "floats" on the surface until it is mixed.]

6. Have students fill out Part A on "My Notes."

7. Squeeze the turkey baster bulb tightly, insert into the glass, relax your grip on the bulb allowing the tube to fill with the salty yellow solution.

8. Keeping the turkey baster perfectly vertical and your hand no longer squeezing the bulb, carefully lift the baster out of the glass and insert into the wide-mouth jar until the tip is touching the bottom of the jar. (If you have done this correctly, no water has dropped from the baster.)

10. S-l-o-w-l-y squeeze the bulb releasing the salty yellow solution at the very bottom of the jar. When the solution is released, don't relax your hold on the bulb, but lift it straight up and out of the jar.

11. Continue until most of the contents of the glass have been transferred to the bottom of the jar. If this has been done correctly, the yellow solution is at the bottom of the jar and the clear water has "risen" to the top. These bands of water have not mixed.

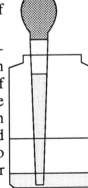

12. Ask students to complete Part B on "My Notes."

13. Solution #2 — Fill another glass about 3/4 full of water. Stir 1/2 cup of salt into the water. Depending on the amount of water in your glass, this salt may not completely dissolve. The reason is that the water is completely saturated. If some salt remains at the bottom of the glass, it will cause no difficulties.

14. Color this water with several drops of blue food coloring. Stir until color is even.

15. Ask students to complete Part C on "My Notes."

16. Using the turkey baster, c-a-r-e-f-u-l-l-y transfer the salty blue solution from the glass to the bottom of the jar. Do not stir the water in the jar while you are doing this. As the "heavy" water is transferred to the jar, the other "lighter" water moves up.

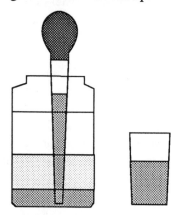

When you are through you will have a colorful SALTWATER PARFAIT.

17. Ask students to complete Part D on "My Notes." They may wish to color the results.

18. G-e-n-t-l-y move the jar to a shelf or a ledge by a window. See how long it takes for the layers to start blending.

19. Have students assist in clean-up.

Expanded Activity:

Brine shrimp are tiny relatives of crabs, lobsters, and prawns. When mature they are about 1/2 inch long. They live in salt water and their growth is affected by the water's salinity and temperature.

Brine shrimp eggs can be purchased at any pet store that sells tropical fish and aquarium equipment. The eggs may be packaged with sea salt.

To hatch your brine shrimp eggs, use a clean jar or bowl that has been rinsed thoroughly in running water. If you are using sea salts, follow the directions on the package (air pump and an aquarium heater are unnecessary). When using table salt add 6 level tablespoons to 1 gallon fresh tap water. Add a pinch of Epson salts. When all is dissolved, add a pinch of the tiny brine shrimp eggs to the top of the water. (The ones that sink are the ones that have the greatest chance of hatching.) Place the jar in a warm spot in your room (not on top of a radiator or heater). Shrimp will begin to hatch in a day or two.

Although brine shrimp will hatch using tap water and table salt, they will only live in it for about a week. You should make provisions to move them to water mixed with sea salt. You should feed your brine shrimp from a mixture of dry yeast and warm water. Place a few drops into the jar each day.

If you can keep the brine shrimp alive for three weeks, they should begin producing eggs of their own. You can remove a few of the brine shrimp and try different experiments with them:

• Test them for sensitivity to light.

• Observe how salinity and temperature variations affect their growing rate. (Their lifespan can be as long as two months.)

These tiny crustaceans will help demonstrate how fluctuations in the marine habitat can gravely affect the creatures living in that environment.

Observation Sheet

The SALTWATER PARFAIT Experiment

Part A

What do you think will happen when Solution #1 is added to the tap water?

_____

_____

_____

How will you be able to tell if your prediction is correct? (What will you see?)

_____

_____

_____

_____

Part B

This is what happened:

_____

_____

_____

_____

_____

How it looks.

This is the reason it happened:

_____

_____

_____

Observation Sheet

The SALTWATER PARFAIT Experiment

Part C

What do you think will happen when Solution #2 is added to the jar?

_____

_____

_____

_____

Part D

This is what happened: _____

_____

_____

_____

This is a picture of our "Saltwater Parfait."

Top _____

Middle _____

Bottom _____

It looks like this because _____

_____

_____ .

The Scientific Gazette

Secretary Becomes Eminent Marine Biologist

Born in Brisbane, Australia, in 1909, Isobel Bennett was the eldest of four children. Her mother died when she was 9 years old. Although her stepmother supported Isobel's enrollment in a respected girls' school, farmily circumstances forced Isobel to leave school at age 16 and enroll in a business college.

In 1933 the Zoology Department at the University of Sydney hired Isobel Bennett as a temporary secretary/research assistant. Thirty-eight years later, she retired from the University. Between 1933 and 1971, Bennett:
- enrolled in zoology classes,
- catalogued the marine animal life of intertidal zones,
- visited marine laboratories in Britain, the U.S., and Scandinavia,
- attended scientific meetings in Japan, Europe, and New Zealand,
- studied marine animals off Antarctica's Macquarie Island,
- wrote books,
- participated in a multi-nation study of the Indian Ocean, and
- received an honorary Master of Science degree from the University of Sydney.

In 1982 Dr. Bennett became the second woman to receive the Mueller Medal from the Australia and New Zealand Association for the Advancement of Science. Noted for her contributions to marine biology, Dr. Bennett was particularly pleased to receive this honor. In 1984 she received the Order of Australia. In the spring of 1995, the University of Sydney awarded an honorary Doctorate of Science (1995) to Isobel Bennett, eminent marine biologist.

Discover Bennett's Marine Interests

Dr. Bennett's career in marine biology has included many interests.

She studied plankton which are: _____

_____

She catalogued marine animals living in the intertidal zones off the States of New South Wales and Victoria, and the island of Tasmania. An intertidal zone is: _____

_____

She explored the Great Barrier Reef, a complex of islands and reefs stretching for 1200 miles off the northeastern coast of the Australian State of Queensland. This delicately balanced environment supports fish, worms, and crustaceans. The Great Barrier Reef is one of Australia's natural treasures.

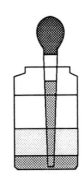

How does The SALTWATER PARFAIT Experiment explain what happens to water around the Great Barrier Reef?

_____

_____

_____

At Home:

Visit your local library and explore the life and work of Rachel Carson. Why do you think Carson is one of Dr. Isobel Bennett's favorite scientists?

A Medical Legacy for the World

Dr. Esther Clayson Pohl Lovejoy — 1869 - 1967

"Give up medical school and you can keep this job," warned the floorwalker at the department store where Esther Clayson was earning money for her medical school tuition. She went to work at a com-petitor's store. Earning her medical degree in 1894, Dr. Lovejoy became the second woman to graduate from the University of Oregon Medical School and the first to devote a lifetime to medicine.

The nation and the world

◆ From 1909 to 1912 she was the director of the Portland City Health Bureau and was the first woman in the U.S. to hold such a position. Under her direction the Bureau launched a campaign to rid the city of rats, began health inspections of city schools, and wrote a milk ordinance adopted by the city council.

◆ Dr. Lovejoy founded the American Medical Women's Association (AMWA) and served as its president. During World War I the AMWA established the American Women's Hospitals, "an international service," which Lovejoy directed for 48 years.

◆ After World War I Lovejoy traveled to France to investigate the plight of women and children, and to the Near East to assist refugees. Her books, **House of the Good Neighbor** (1919) and **Certain Samaritans** (1927) describe these relief efforts.

◆ Dr. Lovejoy helped establish the Medical Women's International Association and served as president from 1919 to 1924. This organization worked to obtain world-wide medical aid for many peoples, and to secure "recognition and status for women physicians in Asia and Europe." Dr. Lovejoy features these women in her books, **Women Physicians and Surgeons: National and International Organizations** (1939) and **Women Doctors of the World** (1957).

Honors

In appreciation and recognition of her services, Lovejoy received the:

◆ Gold Cross of the Legion of Honor of France,

◆ Gold Cross of the Order of King George I from Greece,

◆ Gold Cross of the Holy Sepulcher from Jerusalem,

◆ Gold Cross of Saint Savafrom Yugoslavia, and

◆ White Russian Red Cross of Constantinople.

A hall in the Philippine Medical Women's Association is named the "Esther P. Lovejoy Hall" and a bust of Dr. Lovejoy stands in the town square of Nikea, Greece.

Her honors, like her life and work, traversed national boundaries and encircled the globe.

Enrichment Activity:

Establish a "Distinguished Service Award" to honor school or community individuals who have distinguished themselves.
  ◆ Determine criteria;
  ◆ Create and name the award; and
  ◆ Schedule and organize an awards ceremony.

Bibliography:

Larsell, O. **The Doctor in Oregon.**

Lovejoy, Esther Pohl. "My Medical School, 1890 - 1894," **Oregon Historical Society Quarterly**, Vol. 75, March 1974.

Lovejoy, Esther Pohl. **Women Doctors of the World.**

Europe covers 7 % of the world's land surface. "Varied" best describes the geography of this continent that stretches from the Norwegian Svalbard Archipelago in the north to the Mediterranean and Black Seas in the south. Its westernmost point is Iceland at 25º West with the Ural Mountains in Russia providing an eastern boundary with Asia.

During the 2 1/2 million year-long Pleistocene Epoch (ending 10,000 to 15,000 years ago), glacial ice sheets covered all of northern Europe, the Alps, and the Pyrenees. These ice sheets scoured the terrain leaving rugged landscapes like the Norwegian fiords or deposited layers of soil creating some of Europe's most fertile farmland.

Europe and Science

In Russia, Germany, France, and England, laws prohibited the admission of women in universities and custom discouraged their participation in science. Women in Italy, from the late Middle Ages on, enrolled in the universities and excelled in the sciences.

"The universities which had been opened to them at the close of the Middle Ages, gladly conferred upon them the doctorate, and eagerly welcomed them to the chairs of some of their most important faculties."
— H. J. Mozans, **Woman in Science**

In medicine

In the 11th century at the University of Salerno, women physicians practiced medicine, gave lectures, and wrote medical treatises.

Trotula, a physician and medical writer, wrote treatises on a variety of medical problems including lice, toothaches, cancer, stress, and childbirth. For 500 years her **Diseases of Women** was a standard text for medical students.

Other "Ladies of Salerno" were Abella, Rebecca de Guarna, and Mercuriade. All wrote on medical subjects and Mercuriade was renown for her surgical skills.

At the University of Bologna (Bah-LOAN-nyah) in the early 1300s, Alessandra Giliani, an anatomist, invented the diagnostic technique of injecting blood vessels with dyes. In 1390 Dorotea Bocchi succeeded her father as professor of medicine at Bologna and taught for 40 years.

In mathematics

In the 17th and 18th centuries, Clelia Grillo Borromeo of Genoa excelled in mathematics, mechanics, and languages, and the medal honoring her bears the inscription the "glory of the Genoese." It was said of her that no problem in mathematics was beyond her comprehension.

Elena Cornaro Piscopia of Venice studied astronomy, mathematics, music, philosophy, and theology, and earned a doctorate of philosophy. And mathematician Diamante Medaglia wrote a dissertation on the value of including mathematics in the curriculum for girls.

Perhaps the most famous Italian woman mathematician was Maria Gaetana Agnesi, the eldest of 21 children. Her father was a mathematics professor and encouraged her studies. In 1738, at age 20 she began her **Analytical Institutions**. Completed in ten years, this mathematical treatise was so impressive that Pope Benedict XIV appointed her a chair of mathematics and natural philosophy at the University of Bologna.

In physics

A contemporary of Agnesi's was Laura Bassi (1711-1778). This mother of twelve gave lectures on experimental physics for 33 years at the University of Bologna. She was also a member of Bologna's Academy of Science.

And today . . .

The requirement that all high school students in Italy must take math and sciences ensures women's continued participation in the sciences. Girls are more likely to discover an interest in science in high school, pursue this interest in college, and select careers in scientific fields. Some 200 years after writing her dissertation on the importance of mathematics for women, Diamante Medaglia's words still ring true: "To mathematics, to mathematics, let women devote attention for mental discipline."

Continental Facts:

- Italy has 3,015 miles of coastline.
- 40% of present-day Netherlands would be underwater if it were not for the country's network of dams and dikes.
- 8,000 years after England was separated from the continent of Europe by the rising waters of what is now the English Channel, a 31.5 mile underwater rail tunnel reconnects England to its continent.
- The Rhone glacier in Switzerland is the source of the Rhone River, the largest river in France.
- The Bug River empties into the Black Sea.
- Some veins of salt in the Carpathian Mountains are 600' thick.
- At .17 square mile, Vatican City is Europe's smallest political unit.

Continental Curiosities:

- Stonehenge is a large circular arrangement of monolithic stones on Salisbury Plain in England. Archaeologists believe Stonehenge was constructed in the late Neolithic to early Bronze Age (1800-1400 BC). It has long been assumed that this curious circle of stones was used as a place of worship. Scientists now believe Stonehenge to be an early day "computer" used to calculate and predict astronomical events.
- In Scandinavia the Norway Lemming on rare occasions undertake a mysterious and frenzied migration that ends when they plunge into the sea and drown.

Exploration Questions:

- Why are there no volcanoes in the Alps?
- Why is the city of Venice sinking into a lagoon and what are the Venetians trying to do to save their city?

Add information and ideas here:

Bibliography:

Alic, Margaret. **Hypatia's Heritage.**
America Online. **Compton's Encyclopedia,** Online Edition (downloaded May 8, 1995).
Encyclopedia Britannica.
Flam, Faye. "Italy's Warm Climate for Women on the Mediterranean," **Science,** March 11, 1994.
Mozans, H. J. **Woman in Science.**
Ogilvie, Marilyn Bailey. **Women in Science: Antiquity through the Nineteenth Century.**
Osen, Lynn M. **Women in Mathematics.**
Strahler, Arthur N. **Physical Geography.**

Atomic physicist Dr. Lise Meitner and her nephew, Dr. Otto Frisch, coined the phrase "fission."

Discovery Unit No. 14

Dr. Lise Meitner
Atomic Physics

HARNESSING ENERGY Simulation

Time-line:

1878 - 1968 — Dr. Lise Meitner

1888 - U.S. physicist and astronomer Sarah Frances Whiting visits Europe to learn the latest developments in physics and astronomy.

1903 - Drs. Marie and Pierre Curie share the Nobel Prize in Physics.

1923 - British physicist and inventor Hertha Marks Ayrton dies.

1932 - The neutron is discovered

1957 - Dr. Chien-Shiung Wu disproves the law of parity in subatomic particles.

Key points:

☞ Inspired by the work of Dr. Marie Curie, Lise Meitner decided to become a "radioactive physicist."

☞ Dr. Meitner and her nephew, Dr. Otto Frisch, coined the phrase "fission" to describe the splitting of a uranium atom.

☞ In 1966 Meitner became the first woman to receive the U.S. Atomic Energy Commission's Enrico Fermi Award.

☞ In the HARNESSING ENERGY Simulation, students will use dominoes to simulate the chain reaction resulting from nuclear fission.

Supplies:

✓ A copy of the "Periodic Table of the Elements" (usually found in chemistry textbooks)

✓ A blackboard and chalk

✓ A copy of "Creating a Chain Reaction" (page 126) for each student.

✓ Blue, red, and green pens (or sharp crayons) for each student

✓ A set of dominoes to be equally divided among teams of 2 - 3 students.

✓ *The Scientific Gazette* for each student

Steps:

1. Point out Berlin, Germany, on a map.

2. Share highlights of Dr. Lise Meitner's life and work.

3. Conduct the HARNESSING ENERGY Simulation.

4. Assist students in clean-up.

5. Add Dr. Meitner's name and a memento to the world map.

6. Distribute *The Scientific Gazette* .

For next time:

• Announce the next scientist.

Bibliography:

Berger, Melvin. **Atoms, Molecules and Quarks**.

Berger, Melvin. **Our Atomic World**.

Crawford, Deborah. **Lise Meitner, Atomic Pioneer.**

McGrayne, Sharon Bertsch. **Nobel Prize Women in Science**.

Mebane, Robert C. and Rybolt, Thomas R. **Adventures with Atoms and Molecules**.

Ogilvie, Marilyn Bailey. **Women in Science.**

Biography of
DR. LISE MEITNER
1878 - 1968

"She should be honored as the most significant woman scientist of this century."
— **Peter Armbruster, physicist**

In 1900, at the age of 22, Lise Meitner decided she wanted a career that would be challenging to her and helpful to others. The papers in Lise's hometown, Vienna, Austria, were filled with news about Marie and Pierre Curie's discovery of radium. Inspired by these articles, Lise Meitner decided to become a "radioactive physicist."

Dr. Meitner

Six years later Meitner became the second woman to receive a doctorate in physics from the University of Vienna. Physics is a branch of science that studies matter, energy, motion, heat, sound, light, and atoms. Deciding to study atoms that emit mysterious rays, or radioactive atoms, Dr. Meitner left Vienna for Berlin where she worked with chemist Dr. Otto Hahn at the Chemical Institute. In 1912 she and Hahn continued their work with radioactive elements at the Kaiser-Wilhelm Institute for Chemistry in Dahlem, a countryside suburb of Berlin.

World War I

World War I and Dr. Meitner's decision to work as an X-ray technician in a field hospital interrupted her scientific work. After the war Dr. Meitner returned to her laboratory in Germany and continued to study radioactive elements. She and Dr. Hahn discovered element No. 91 (protactinium). For this discovery they received awards from the Academies of Science in Berlin and Austria. Dr. Meitner also began lecturing at the university in Berlin. In 1926 she became the first woman in Germany to be a physics professor.

Leaves Germany

When World War II broke out, Dr. Lise Meitner, who was Jewish, escaped Nazi Germany. She found work in Sweden at the Nobel Institute of Theoretical Physics.

Solves mystery

While Dr. Meitner worked in Sweden, Dr. Hahn remained in Germany and continued to conduct experiments with uranium atoms. Meitner and Hahn wrote letters to one another every other day. Hahn confessed that the results of one experiment puzzled him. After studying Hahn's notes, Dr. Meitner concluded that he had accomplished what scientists thought was impossible: Hahn had split the uranium atom! Dr. Meitner and her nephew, Dr. Otto Frisch, coined the phrase "fission" to describe this splitting of a uranium atom.

Isolated

On August 6, 1945, Dr. Meitner learned about the dropping of the atomic bomb on Hiroshima, Japan. Up to this time, she was unaware that scientists and military personnel had been working on ways to harness fission for weapons. Dismayed over this event, Meitner declared that she had never worked with atoms with the intention of creating "death-dealing weapons," but had wanted to unlock the mysteries of the atom to use its energy for peaceful and industrial purposes.

Fermi Award

Dr. Meitner remained in Sweden for 22 years. She did research, traveled, and, until she was 81, climbed mountains. In 1966 Dr. Meitner shared the U.S. Atomic Energy Commission's Enrico Fermi Award with her friend Dr. Hahn and another scientist. This was the first time a woman received the Fermi Award.

Element 109

Two decades after Dr. Meitner's death, physicists in Germany created a new element — Element 109 — the heaviest one. The physicists called this element **meitnerium** in honor of Dr. Lise Meitner, a most significant woman scientist of this century.

Instructor's Guide:

HARNESSING ENERGY Simulation

Background Information:

An atom consists of a small dense nucleus, containing protons and neutrons, encircled by negative charges called electrons. The number of protons in the nucleus of the atom determines which element it is associated with. That number is also called the "atomic number." Nearly all atoms have the same number of neutrons as protons bound together in the nucleus. They are similar in size although the neutrons have more mass.

A chart called the "Periodic Table of the Elements" lists all the elements (adding ones as they are discovered or created). Each element on the Periodic Table is identified in at least four ways: by atomic number (number of protons in that element's atoms); by Symbol (*H* for hydrogen, *He* for helium, etc.); by name, and by atomic weight (mass included in the nucleus).

The splitting of the Uranium-235 atom generates incredible heat (energy). This action is called nuclear fission, a process that causes a chain reaction. If the chain reaction is not controlled, a huge explosion occurs (the idea behind the atom bomb). Nuclear reactors use the elements of cadmium or boron to slow down and control the chain reaction in order to produce heat. More heat is generated from splitting the atoms in one pound of uranium than from burning 3 million pounds of coal.

This activity discusses the atoms of **Uranium-235** (92 protons and 143 neutrons), **Barium-137** (56 protons and 81 neutrons), and **Krypton-84** (36 protons and 48 neutrons). The numbers following the element refer to the specific atom (isotope) used. This number is the sum of the protons and neutrons and is considered its atomic weight.

Instructions:

1. Have copies of the "Periodic Table of the Elements" available. If you can borrow a "Periodic Table" wall chart this will also be helpful. Start your discussion using the chalkboard for illustrations.

Ask . . .
What is the name of the smallest possible unit of a chemical substance? [An Atom.]

2. On the chalkboard, draw the helium atom.

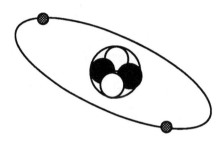

Explain . . .
This is a representation of an atom from the element helium. It has a nucleus that holds 2 protons and 2 neutrons. Orbiting around this nucleus are 2 electrons.

3. On the chalkboard, draw the sodium atom.

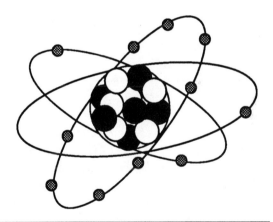

Explain . . .
This is how a sodium atom might look. Its nucleus holds 11 protons and 11 neutrons. Orbiting around the nucleus are 11 electrons, circling on three different planes.

4. Introduce the "Periodic Table of the Elements." Find **helium**. Point out the following things:

- The atomic number is 2 — the same number as its protons and as its electrons.

- Helium's atomic weight is the total of its

---

protons and neutrons plus a tiny bit extra for the neutrons. To make it easier to do calculations, we will round-off this figure.

- Note the symbol for the element (He).

5. Find **sodium**.
   - What is the atomic number? [11]
   - What is the atomic weight? [22]
   - What is its symbol? [Na]

6. Discuss other elements that attract the attention of the students. Point out the elements of gold (Au), silver (Ag), and lead (Pb).

Explain ...
In the Middle Ages, alchemists were often asked to find a way to turn lead into gold or silver. They were never successful. However, in 1939, scientists discovered a way to turn the element uranium into two other elements: barium and krypton. This was done by bombarding a special uranium atom with neutrons.

7. Call the students' attention to the following elements:
   - uranium (U)
   - barium (Ba)
   - krypton (Kr)

Explain ...
*All uranium atoms have 92 protons. Most of the uranium atoms have 146 neutrons. A few uranium atoms have only 143 neutrons. Variations of the same element are called isotopes. It is this isotope (designated as **Uranium-235**) that is used by scientists in creating energy (heat) by nuclear fission.*

8. Distribute copies of "Creating a Chain Reaction."

Explain ...
*This diagram shows a Uranium-235 atom that has been split by a neutron. The result is one barium atom, one krypton atom, and 14 neutrons. Note: The atomic weights of barium (137) + krypton (84)+ 14 = 235 (the atomic weight of the original uranium atom). This splitting of an atom is called **nuclear fission.***

9. On the chalkboard write this equation:
$$14 \times 14 = 196$$

Explain ...
If each of the 14 neutrons released through nuclear fission was to strike a uranium atom the results (besides creating atoms of barium and krypton) would be the release of an additional 196 neutrons.

10. With a blue pen have students mark these neutrons on their diagram (14 clusters of 14 neutrons). See below.

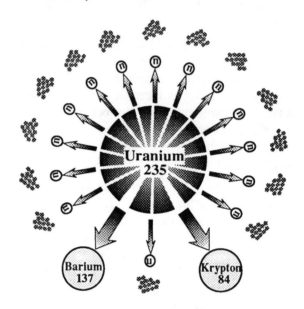

11. On the chalkboard write these equations:

[If you have access to a calculator pass it around so various students can get the answers.]
$$196 \times 14 = 2,744$$
$$2,744 \times 14 = 38,416$$
$$38,416 \times 14 = 537,824$$
$$537,824 \times 14 = 7,529,536$$

Explain ...
If each burst of neutrons hits a uranium atom, the resulting explosions will release 14 times <u>more</u> neutrons.

12. Ask students to use a red pen to indicate the next level of explosions (14 groups of 196). See next page.

13. Finally, ask students to use a green pen to add the "next generation" of explosions. [These will totally cover the rest of the sheet.]

Explain . . .

The process you have just drawn (neutrons splitting atoms that release more neutrons that split more atoms) is called a chain reaction.

A chain reaction of this magnitude would release massive amounts of heat, light, and high-energy radiation. It would devastate everything in its path.

Through the use of nuclear reactors the scientists can slow down and control the chain reaction produced by nuclear fission. Rods of the elements cadmium or boron are placed with the uranium fuel rods. The cadmium (or boron) captures some of the flying nuetrons. When this happens, the nuclear energy becomes an economical source of heat.

14. Bring out dominoes. Form students into teams. Give each team the same number of dominoes. Ask them to use the dominoes to demonstrate two scenarios. The dominoes should be set on their narrow ends and close enough that when one is tipped over it will knock the others down. In each scenario the action is started by tipping only one domino.

Use a watch with a second hand or a stop watch to time the action.

- Set up the dominoes in a pattern that will bring all of them down in the shortest possible time.

- Set up the dominoes in a pattern that will bring them down in the slowest possible time.

Give the teams time to practice (and time) their chain reactions. Suggest that they may wish to add other materials to the "chain" to slow down the action even more.

◆ ◆ ◆

Add notes here:

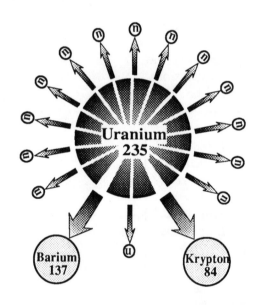

The Scientific Gazette

Meitner suggested that physicists had split the atom

Until 81 years of age, Dr. Lise Meitner climbed mountains. She enjoyed opera, skiing, and walking leisurely through the Berlin Botanical Gardens. But she loved physics. For more than 60 years, Meitner's work in the branch of science that studies atomic particles gave meaning to her life.

Inspired to become a "radioactive physicist" like Dr. Marie Curie, Lise began her university studies when she was 21 and completed eight years of work in only two years. She became the second woman to receive a doctorate in physics from the University of Vienna.

Drawn to Berlin, Germany, to study with world-famous physicist Max Planck, Dr. Meitner assured her parents that her absence from home would not be longer than six months. She remained in Berlin for 31 years. Her work included

Dr. Lise Meitner, 1878 - 1968

the discovery of protactinium for which she and her associate, chemist Dr. Otto Hahn, received awards from the Academies of Science in Berlin and Austria.

After Dr. Meitner escaped Nazi Germany, she and Hahn continued to exchange letters. At one point he described the puzzling results of an experiment. After studying his notes, Meitner concluded that her friend had split the uranium atom! She and her nephew, physicist Dr. Otto Frisch, coined the term "fission" to describe this splitting of a uranium atom.

Dr. Lise Meitner received a number of awards including the Max Planck Medal. In 1966 she became the first woman to receive the U.S. Atomic Energy Commission's Enrico Fermi Award.

How much do YOU know about Atoms?

Draw lines to match the following terms with their correct definitions:

1. atom   **(a)** A particle found in the nucleus of an atom. It carries a positive charge.

2. element   **(b)** The smallest unit of a chemical substance

3. proton   **(c)** A negative charge that normally encircles the nucleus.

4. neutron   **(d)** A simple substance made up of only one kind of atom.

5. electron   **(e)** Found in the nucleus of an atom, this particle carries no electrical charge.

Answers: 1. (b); 2. (d); 3. (a); 4. (e); and 5. (c).

— Inspiration —

The work and intelligence of Dr. Marie Curie inspired Lise Meitner to study physics. Whose life or work inspires you? _____

Why? _____

At the close of World War II, Dr. Lise Meitner was interviewed by Eleanor Roosevelt. During this transoceanic radio broadcast with Roosevelt in the United States and Meitner in Sweden, the physicist must have smiled when Mrs. Roosevelt noted that both Dr. Meitner and Madame Curie were inspirations to women everywhere.

> **At Home:**
> ◆ Read **Lise Meitner, Atomic Pioneer** by Deborah Crawford.
> ◆ Expand your reading to include molecules and quarks.

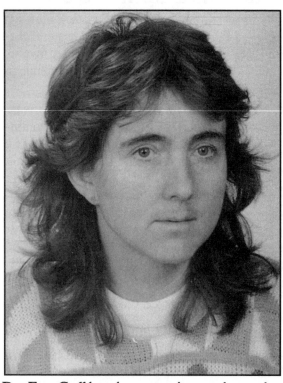

Dr. Eva Cudlínová, economist, works at the Institute of Landscape Ecology in the Czech Republic.

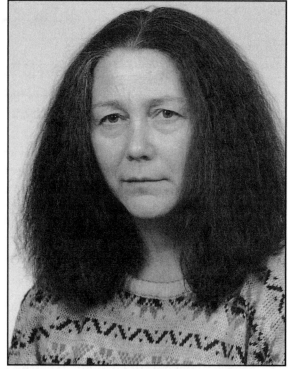

Biologist Irena Hanousková specializes in geobotany (geographical botany).

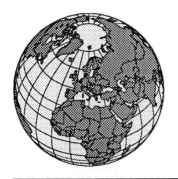

Discovery Unit No. 15

Dr. Eva Cudlínová and Irena Hanousková
Landscape Ecology

A PLAN FOR A BETTER FUTURE Project

Time-line:

1951 - Irena Hanousková is born in Chomutov, Czechoslovakia.

1954 - Dr. Eva Cudlínová is born in Prague, Czechoslovakia.

1975 - Dr. Katherina Zaleska from Poland continues the medical work she began in Africa more than 15 years ago.

1984 - **The Granite Garden: Urban Nature and Human Design** by landscape architect Anne Whiston Spirn is published.

1988 - Dr. Jara Moser, physician and sculptor, serves as a plastic surgeon in the Czech Clinic of Plastic Surgery, King Charles University.

Key points:

☛ The Institute of Landscape Ecology concentrates on a the structure, function, and change in a landscape including the communities of plants, animals, and humans.

☛ Dr. Eva Cudlínová and Irena Hanousková are two of the 25 scientists working at the Institute of Landscape Ecology in the Czech Republic.

☛ Dr. Eva Cudlínová is an economist.

☛ Irena Hanousková is a biologist whose specialty is geobotany.

☛ Both scientists agree that the interdisciplinary approach at the Institute of Landscape Ecology offers enriching opportunities.

☛ In A PLAN FOR A BETTER FUTURE Project students will map the "communities" within a geographical area; will determine the positive contributions of each community; and will design a more nurturing "landscape" for communities coexisting in this geographical area.

Supplies:

✓ Maps that include your classroom neighborhood

✓ A copy of "Map Symbols and Suggestions" or each student. (page 133)

✓ Several sheets of newsprint

✓ A pencil for each student

✓ A collection of green, red, blue, orange, purple, and brown crayons.

✓ A "My Notes" sheet for each student

✓ *The Scientific Gazette* for each student

Steps:

1. Point out Ceské Budejovice in the Czech Republic.

2. Share highlights of Dr. Eva Cudlínová and Irena Hanousková's lives.

3. Conduct A PLAN FOR A BETTER FUTURE Project.

4. Add Cudlínová and Hanousková's names and memento(s) to the world map.

4. Distribute *The Scientific Gazette* .

For next time:

• Introduce the next scientist.

Bibliography:

Cudlínová, Eva. **Letter**, November 18, 1994.

Ecology and Democracy: The Challenge of the 21st Century. Proceedings of the First International Conference, Full Abstracts.

Hanousková, Irena. **Letter**, November 18, 1994.

Levin, Beatrice. **Women and Medicine: Pioneers Meeting the Challenge!**

Macksey, Joan, and Kenneth Macksey. **The Book of Women's Achievements**.

Norwood, Vera. **Made from This Earth**.

Bibliography continues page 132

Biographies of
DR. EVA CUDLÍNOVÁ b. 1954
IRENA HANOUSKOVÁ b. 1951

The Institute of Landscape Ecology in the Czech Republic concentrates on a science that studies the structure, function, and change in a landscape including the communities of plants, animals, and humans. Of the 25 scientists working at the Institute, five are women. Two of these women are Dr. Eva Cudlínová, an economist, and Irena Hanousková, a biologist.

Dr. Eva Cudlínová

Born in Prague, Czechoslovakia, in 1954, Dr. Cudlínová grew up in that city. Her father was a high school teacher and her mother, a clerk. Her favorite subject in primary school was biology and included everything that had "some connection with nature." In high school she changed to the human sciences.

Her husband is also a scientist and they have a 13-year-old son, an 11-year-old daughter, and a small dog.

Cudlínová studied for five years at the Economic Institute in Prague. She graduated in 1978. In 1988 she earned her Ph.D. from the Institute of Economy, Czechoslovak Academy of Sciences.

Irena Hanousková

Irena Hanousková was born in Chomutov, Czechoslovakia, in 1951. She grew up in a small agricultural village. Both parents were teachers. Her father was arrested by the communists for political reasons and spent five years in the uranium mines.

Her favorite subject in school was physical training. A "self-made sportswoman," she excels in long-distance running. Her least favorite subject was descriptive geometry. Her family includes her husband (a private land surveyor), a teenage son, and a teenage daughter both of whom "specialize" in mathematics.

Hanousková earned a master's degree in biology from Charles University in Prague. Preferring the biological disciplines related to observing the "voices, colors, smells" in rural and natural environments, she specialized in geobotany, or geographical botany.

Three years ago

Cudlínová and Hanousková met three years ago in the Institute's Department of Anthropoecology on a project describing the land-use activity of the Czech Republic's private farmers after 40 years of collectivization. The economic and agricultural questions in this issue required Cudlínová's knowledge of economics and Hanousková's specialty in geobotany.

Interdisciplinary approach

Cudlínová believes that interdisciplinary work offers enriching opportunities. She writes, "I have more opportunity than any time before to combine an economic point of view with an ecological dimension." At first it was challenging for Hanousková to modify her knowledge gained from the natural sciences in order to address landscape ecology topics. Although challenging at times, this interdisciplinary approach is a unique and attractive feature of work at the Institute. As women working in a male-dominated field, Cudlínová and Hanousková support and encourage each other.

"We believe that because we are women, we can more easily overcome the barriers between our two disciplines . . . We can set aside our egos and validate each other's, and we have a natural ethic of cooperation that is very helpful."
— **Dr. Eva Cudlínová**

Instructor's Guide:

A PLAN FOR A BETTER FUTURE
Project

Background:

Landscape ecology as a science comes from the ideas and writings of Alexander von Humboldt, 1769-1859, a German scholar and explorer. He defined landscape as the total character of the earth including its cultural, economic and physical dimensions and characteristics.

Around 1855 in the Kingdom of Bohemia, then part of the Austro-Hungarian empire and now the Czech Republic, it was decided to plot the natural landscape into units for the purpose of economic planning and increased forest and agricultural production. These units were identified according to such characteristics as forest or field, geological conditions and climate. The study of the landscape has continued and grown to the present day.

Landscape ecology is the study of the structure, function and change in a landscape including the communities of plants, animals, and humans.

Landscape ecologists come from several fields of study including geography, ecology, botany, landscape architecture, forestry, economics, and regional planning.

In A PLAN FOR A BETTER FUTURE Project students will map the "communities" within a geographical area; will determine the positive contributions made by the plant, animal, and human populations to each other; and will design a more nurturing "landscape" for plants, animals, and humans coexisting in this area.

Instructions — Part 1:

1. Have available maps from the area surrounding the place your class is being held. (Sometimes maps are included in your telephone book. These can easily be duplicated.)

2. Introduce the subject of landscape ecology. Tell students Humboldt's definition of "landscape." Write the definition of "landscape ecology" on the chalkboard. Underline the words structure, function, change, landscape, and communities.

Explain ...

We will refer to the "landscape" as the geographical area we will study. The word "community" refers specifically to a group that includes all the plants, a group that includes all the animals, and a group that includes all the humans.

Structure is documented through mapping the area to be studied. The map includes geological features (water and land formations), locations of plant growth, presence of animals, and concentrations of people.

Function refers to relationships within the plant, animal, and human communities, as well as interactions between these communities.

Change is a result of natural occurrences (such as fire with subsequent regrowth) or human activities (such as clearing forests for agricultural development). Landscape ecologists document this change through aerial photographs, satellite images, and other technical data recording devices. They can also predict changes in the landscape structure or function and the potential consequences of these changes through computer simulation modeling.

First we are going to study the structure of our landscape. [Note: although this activity is written as a group project, it can also be done individually with students studying the landscape ecology of their own neighborhoods.]

---

3. Look at the maps. Where are you on this map. Find nearby parks, shopping centers and commercial areas, residential areas, apartment buildings, farm land, etc.

4. Distribute copies of "Map symbols and Suggestions."

5. Distribute copies of a map showing your surrounding area. [If no map is available, then you should develop your own street map as part of this project.]

6. As a group, walk the nearby streets. Make notes referring to "Map symbols and Suggestions" as necessary.

---

7. Tape sheets of newsprint to the wall or chalkboard.

8. Using a pencil, lightly draw the streets and roads in your landscape. Draw any waterways, lakes, or ponds.

9. Sketch in buildings and patterns of plant communities.

10. With green crayons color in the plant communities.

11. With red crayons color the buildings with a high density population of humans.

12. With blue crayons color the areas of water.

13. With orange crayons color the buildings with medium density population.

14. With purple crayons color the single family dwellings.

15. Show the animal population with brown.

> **Explain ...**
> *A patch is a small community surrounded by a different community structure. For example, a single family dwelling in the middle of a commercial area or a vacant lot (filled with weeds) in a residental area.*

16. Locate "patches" in your landscape.

> **Explain ...**
> *Corridors are linear elements that span portions of a landscape. **Line corridors** (roads, paths) are narrow, usually have a continuous edge, lack plants, and may serve as barriers or movement routes for animals and humans. **Strip corridors** are wider and contain some plant life. They can also support certain animals.*

17. Locate "corridors" in your landscape.

> **Ask ...**
> *Which corridors provide movement? Which provide barriers? What are the advantages of corridors? For whom are they advantageous?*

18. Save your landscape (roll up to store).

19. Assist students in clean-up.

Instructions — Part 2:

1. Distribute "My Notes Sheet."

> **Explain ...**
> *Landscape ecology is the study of the structure, function, and change in a landscape including the communities of plants, animals and humans.*
>
> *Earlier we mapped the landscape around us in order to study its structure. Now we are going to become familiar with the function of the communities within our landscape.*

2. Allow time for students to think of ways that one community contributes to the well-being of another and to write these ideas on their "My Notes" sheet.

3. In a class discussion encourage students to share their ideas with one another.

4. Tape to the wall the drawing of the landscape completed at the beginning of this project.

> **Ask ...**
> *What words would you use to describe this landscape? [Write words on chalkboard.]*
>
> *What words would you like to use? [Write words on chalkboard.]*

5. Tape a new sheet of newsprint to the wall. With suggestions and help from students create a new landscape designed as a better environment for plants, animals, and humans.

6. Compare the two landscapes. Choose one thing that your class can do to make your actual landscape better for at least one of the "communities" living within it. Work on this idea as a class "service project."

Additional Bibliography:

McGraw-Hill Encyclopedia of Science & Technology.

Petch, J.R., and Koleijka, J. "The Tradition of Landscape Ecology in Czechoslavia," **Landscape Ecology and Geographic Information Systems.**

Map Symbols & Suggestions to use with "Landscape"

Plant Communities:

1. Note the places where plants are growing. (Planting areas between street and sidewalk, weeds and wildflowers along the side of the road, flower boxes beneath windows and planters on front steps, cracks in pavement, yards, fields, river banks, rooftop gardens, etc.) Mark these on your map. Are the plant communities concentrated in a cluster or do they form a strip or wide line?

Animal Communities:

2. Animal communities include both wild and domesticated creatures. List all animals. Are there dogs and cats? Do they have specific areas that owners exercise them in or do they run wild? Are there squirrels? What are their travel routes? Do they cross streets using power lines? Are there fences? Do migrating birds stop in your landscape? Do birds build nests? Where? In trees? Mud banks? Beneath the eaves of houses? Barns? What other animals live in your landscape? Don't forget insects. Carefully lift boards to see if an insect community is "hiding" there.

Human Communities:

3. Think in terms of density. A residential neighborhood can contain single dwelling homes (low density), apartment buildings (medium or high density), farms (very low density), etc. How would you describe the density in your downtown area? In your suburban areas? Are there more children or adults?

Use symbols to represent the parts of your communities. Some ideas for symbols are shown at the bottom of this page. You may make up your own symbols. Be sure to keep a "key" to these symbols (a picture of the symbol with the words describing what it stands for).

 Tree

 Field

 Single Dwelling House

 Medium Density Area

 High Density Area

Community: Interacting populations in a common location.

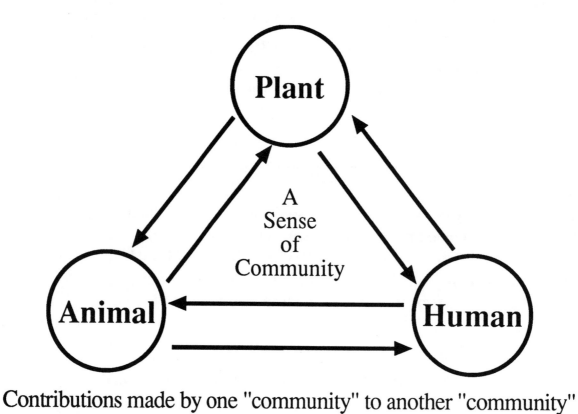

Contributions made by one "community" to another "community"

Plants to Animals _____

_____

Plants to Humans _____

_____

Animals to Humans _____

_____

Animals to Plants _____

_____

Humans to Plants _____

_____

Humans to Animals _____

_____

The Scientific Gazette

Czech scientists continue tradition of landscape ecology

Dr. Eva Cudlínová

At the Institute of Landscape Ecology in the Czech Republic, twenty-five scientists work in a science that studies the structure, function, and change in a landscape including the communities of plants, animals, and humans. Two of the scientists are Dr. Eva Cudlínová, an economist, and Irena Hanousková, a biologist whose specialty is geobotany.

Cudlínová was born in Prague, Czechoslovakia, in 1954. Her father was a high school teacher and her mother, a clerk. In primary school her favorite subject was biology; in high school she changed to the human sciences. Cudlínová studied for five years at the Economic Institute in Prague where she graduated in 1978. In 1988 she earned her Ph.D. from the Institute of Economy, Czechoslovak Academy of Sciences.

Hanousková was born in Chomutov, Czecho-slovakia, in 1951. She grew up in a small agricultural village. Both of her parents were teachers but her father was arrested by the communists for "political reasons" and spent five years in the uranium mines. "A self-made sportswoman," Hanousková excels in long-distance running. From Charles University in Prague, Hanousková earned a master's degree in biology with a specialty in geobotany.

Irena Hanousková

Both scientists use their respective disciplines in landscape ecology, a tradition started in the Kingdom of Bohemia (Czech Republic) around 1855. Cudlínová explains, "It is the possibility to work in a team of scientists from different disciplines instead of solving the whole problem only by myself . . . I enjoy this style of work." Hanousková agrees. Her work in landscape ecology allows her to see the "many faces reality has."

A map of the present
A plan for the future

In mapping the "communities" near our classroom, I discovered:

_____

_____

In comparing our "old" and "new" landscapes, I concluded:

_____

_____

In selecting an activity that could improve our landscape, I decided:

_____

_____

_____

International conference

Cudlínová and Hanousková worked on the organizing committee for the International Conference on Ecology and Democracy: The Challenge of the 21st Century (6-9th of September 1994). This conference brought together scientists, politicians, philosophers, etc. "We discovered more commonalities between our fields," Cudlínová concluded. By inviting a variety of specialists, the intent was, in Hanousková's words to "switch on the bridge between ecology, a scientific discipline, and democracy."

At Home: Map the community around your residence. Design a more nurturing "landscape" and determine an activity your family can do to make your landscape better for one of the "communities" living within it.

Dr. Marie Vasilievna Klenova, marine geologist, participated in geologic expeditions for the USSR every year from 1925 to 1975.

Discovery Unit No. 16

Dr. Marie Vasilievna Klenova
Marine Geology

EXPEDITING A SCIENTIFIC EXPEDITION

Time-line:

1898 - 1975 — Dr. Marie Vasilievna Klenova

1891 - Russian mathematician Dr. Sonya Kovalevskaya dies of pneumonia.

1899 - Dr. Florence Bascom begins teaching petrography at Bryn Mawr College in Pennsylvania.

1928 - Rachel Carson sees the ocean for the first time.

1958 - Negotiations begin on the Antarctic Treaty

1963 - Valentina Vladimirovna Nikolayevna-Tereshkova from the USSR is the first woman astronaut (cosmonaut) in space.

1970 - Sylvia Earle and four other oceanographers live for two weeks in an underwater habitat.

Key points:

☛ Marine geologist Dr. Marie V. Klenova researched the sediments deposited on the floors of seas, lakes, or other bodies of water.

☛ Klenova's discoveries were valuable to her nation's scientific, industrial, and military agencies.

☛ Every year from 1925 until her death in 1975, Dr. Klenova participated in geologic expeditions that included the Arctic and Antarctica.

☛ Klenova wrote **Geology of the Sea**, a "most famous" book which remains a valuable text for students of oceanography.

☛ In EXPEDITING A SCIENTIFIC EXPEDITION, student scientists will plan and carry out an expedition that has a clearly defined purpose, student-directed plans, and a scientific focus.

Supplies:

✓ Sheets of newsprint

✓ Marking pens

✓ Other supplies to be determined during "Planning Stage One"

✓ *The Scientific Gazette* for each student

Steps:

1. Point out Irkutsk, Russia, near Lake Baikal.

2. Share highlights of Dr. Marie V. Klenova's life.

3. Plan and enjoy the EXPEDITING A SCIENTIFIC EXPEDITION.

4. Add Dr. Klenova's name and a memento to the world map.

For next time:

• Announce the next scientist.

Bibliography:

The Shirshov Institute of Oceanology in St. Petersburg, Russia, and the Institute of Oceanology RAS in Moscow, Russia, provided biographical information on Dr. Marie V. Klenova. Translations by Sergei Gulev (Moscow, Russia) and Jana Triskova Thompson (California, USA).

Holloway, Marguerite. "Profile: Sylvia A. Earle," **Scientific American**, April 1992.

Kosheleva, Inna. **Women in Science: Pioneers Meeting the Challenge!**

Levin, Beatrice. **Women and Medicine**.

Terek, Eugenie. **Scientific Expeditions**.

Biography of
Dr. Marie Vasilievna Klenova
1898-1975

Dr. Marie Klenova sailed aboard icebreakers and, equipped with a special underwater suit, descended into freezing Arctic waters. This pioneering marine geologist researched the sediments deposited on the floors of seas, lakes, or other bodies of water. Every year from 1925 until her death in 1975, Klenova participated in geologic expeditions whose discoveries were valuable to her nation's scientific, industrial, and military agencies.

"Petrography of Modern Sediments"

Born in Irkutsk, Russia, on August 31, 1898, Marie was educated in Sverdlovsk in the Ural Mountains. In 1918 she became a student in the Geophysical Department at Moscow State University and worked part-time as a teacher in the evening. By 1924 she had earned a master's degree in geology and, two years later, her doctorate degree for which she wrote a thesis entitled "Petrography of Modern Sediments." Petrography is the science that studies the description or classification of rocks.

Aboard research vessels

By the time she earned her doctorate, Klenova was a research scientist at the Plavuchi Morskoi Institute (Onboard Marine Institute) whose *Persey* was the first Soviet research vessel. In 1930 Klenova organized the first laboratory of marine geology at the Institute and subsequently organized nine more laboratories at important marine locations throughout the country. All laboratories were linked by telegraph; the geologic discoveries at one were quickly telegraphed to others.

From 1933 until 1937, Dr. Klenova explored the "soils" (sediments) of the Barents Sea and Arctic waters. She created a map that was helpful to the Soviet Navy as they built terminals for the country's military ships. In 1939 she received her Doctor of Science Degree.

Her "most famous" book

During World War II, the State Oceanographic Institute (SOI) was established and Professor Zubov, "The Father of Soviet Oceanography," invited Dr. Klenova to chair the laboratory in the Institute's marine geology department. She agreed. Her work was highly praised and in 1948 she wrote **Geology of the Sea,** her "most famous" book which remains a valuable text for students of oceanography.

Underwater explorations

During an expedition aboard the icebreaker *Litke,* Klenova, wearing an underwater suit, descended to the Arctic floor and obtained photographs of a new technique of extracting sea floor materials by geological tube. These one-of-a-kind photographs made evaluation of this tube technique possible.

In 1955 Dr. Klenova began working at the USSR Academy of Sciences. She did scientific work in Antarctica, the Caspian Sea, the Barents Sea, and the Atlantic Ocean. Her comprehensive description of the geology of the Atlantic Ocean was a manuscript of 500 pages. Submitted for publication in 1974, Klenova died on August 6, 1975 — several months before the book's publication.

"Now I am not a woman, but . . ."

Whether Dr. Klenova was the only woman at ice-camp station "North Pole 4," the first woman scientist to work in Antarctica, or a professor supervising an expedition studying sediments in the hope of finding oil, her response to the expressed opinion that the sea was not the right place for a woman was, "Now I am not a woman, but a scientific researcher."

Instructor's Guide:

EXPEDITING A SCIENTIFIC EXPEDITION

Background:

Dr. Klenova collected marine geologic samples during scientific expeditions that traversed the globe. Such expeditions allow scientists to gather new information at its source. The distances traveled may be extensive, the destinations exotic, and the work dangerous. On the other hand, an expedition may be as close, as common, as safe as the nearest library.

Several factors are common to all expeditions: 1. a clearly defined purpose
2. a careful plan of action

In EXPEDITING A SCIENTIFIC EXPEDITION student scientists will plan and carry out a class trip (expedition) that has a clearly defined purpose, student-directed plans, and a scientific focus. The scientists are expected to make some of the arrangements such as scheduling a school bus for transportation, determining the cost of the expedition, and, if necessary, fundraising. A presentation and evaluation follow the expedition. Bon voyage!

Instructions:

Planning Stage One

1. Introduce the subject of expeditions. Relate this experience to Dr. Klenova and scientists such as McWhinnie, Peden, and Ocampo-Friedmann (Antarctica), Obeng and Tima (Africa), Yener and Samish (Asia), Diaz and Hogg (North America), Alconini and Snethlage (South America), and Bennett (Australia).

2. With your student scientists, choose a place to go (explore). [library, zoo, botanical garden, science museum, herb farm, park, etc.]

3. Define the purpose of the trip. [Begin with a verb such as: to collect, observe, explore, investigate, study. An example is — to observe how many zoo animals nap between 1 and 2 p.m.]

4. Choose a name. [The _____Expedition]

5. Identify what scientific field(s) is being explored in this expedition.

6. Divide scientists into four planning teams.

7. Provide each team with its list of considerations, sheets of newsprint, and marking pens.

   Team A — Logistics — How to get there and back.

   —transportation: mode and duration

   —meals: during travel and at the site

   —cost: per scientist with recommendations of ways to cover this cost.

   —insurance, access, permission slips, etc.

   —other

   Team B — On-site Arrangements — What we know about our expedition place.

   —information on expedition site:
     brochures, maps, etc.

   —admission costs

   —dates for expedition

   —what can/cannot be taken onto the site

   —other

   Team C — Research — How do we gather and record our information?

   —materials/supplies needed

   —list of what scientists are looking for (see purpose)

   —what to wear: clothing, shoes, insect repellant, sun screen, etc.

   —other

   Team D — Presentations — How do we present our findings?

   —reports

   —displays

   —press conference

   —audio/visual

   —other

8. Give planning teams time to list their recommendations for a successful expedition.

9. Bring teams together to share plans. Beginning with Team A — Logistics, ask if there are other considerations to be included. Are there parts of the plan that can be eliminated? Display the final plan.

In the same manner, review plans of Teams B, C, and D.

10. Assign each task to an individual or group. Set a date for completion of each task.

Between now and the completion date, occasionally touch base with scientists to learn if they need help in completing their tasks on time.

Planning Stage Two

11. Bring all scientists together to share the information they have obtained and to finalize the Expedition Plan.

The Scientific Expedition

12. At a pre-expedition meeting be sure that all scientists know what is expected of them during the research part of the expedition. Make specific assignments if appropriate.

13. Go on your scientific expedition.

Presentation

14. Immediately following expedition, collect all the research information.

15. Review the Presentation Plan. Modify if necessary. Make specific assignments if appropriate. Set a date for the presentation.

16. Allow time to work on the presentation.

17. Give presentation.

Evaluation

18. Go over the original plan. Compare with what actually happened. Did your expedition fulfill its purpose? Did it stay within its budget? Were the assignments realistic?

19. Write a list of recommendations for the next expedition.

Add information and ideas here:

The Scientific Gazette

In nineteen hundred thirty-three, Klenova sailed the Barents Sea . . .

Dr. Marie Klenova 1895-1975

Dr. Marie V. Klenova was a Russian marine geologist who traveled around the world collecting underwater "soil samples." Klenova:

- descended to the Arctic floor to take photographs,
- prepared an atlas of marine "soils" or sediments,
- studied the magnetic changes in the Atlantic Ocean,
- researched the possibility of oil in the Caspian Sea,
- organized marine geology laboratories,
- wrote **Geology of the Sea**, and
- was the first woman scientist to work in Antarctica.

Her findings were valuable to her country's scientific, industrial, and military interests. In 1949 Dr. Klenova received a government prize for her achievements in marine geology.

Whether Dr. Klenova was the only woman at an ice-camp station or creating a map helpful to the Soviet Navy, her response to the opinion that the sea was not the right place for a woman was always, "Now I am not a woman, but a scientific researcher."

The "science of the earth"

In her work as a marine geologist, Dr. Klenova studied the earth — the floors of seas, lakes, and oceans. Geology means the "science of the earth" and includes many branches of study including *sedimentology*, the science of sedimentary deposits and their origins.

Discover the meanings of the following words. How might these sciences have helped Dr. Klenova in her work in marine geology?

geophysics _____

mineralogy _____

oceanography _____

hydrophysics _____

petrography _____

Aboard the *Lomonosov*

Named for Mikhail Lomonosov, a famous 18th century geologist, the *Lomonosov* is a research ship belonging to Russia's Academy of Sciences' Marine Hydrophysics Institute. During each expedition 30 - 40% of the scientists are women. On one trip the women scientists included: **Nelly Sorokina**, an optical scientist in the Optics Department of the Marine Hydrophysics Institute, who described expeditions as being an opportunity to "collect a great deal of information"; **Anna Gordina**, an ichthyologist in the Ukrainian Academy of Sciences' Institute of the Biology of the South Seas, who studied fish spawn and larvae in the Indian Ocean; physiologist **Kira Alexeyeva**; and, zoo-plankton specialist **Olga Belyayeva**.

There were 60 scientists on this expedition. If 40% of them were women, how many women scientists were aboard the *Lomonosov* on this expedition? _____

At Home:

- "Expedite" an expedition with your family.

Tomorrow Belongs to the Children

Venus Sahihi Pezeshk — b. 1950

Global cooperation on environmental issues was the theme of the **United Nations Conference on Environment and Development** held in Rio de Janeiro, Brazil, in June 1992. Activities focusing on hopes for the future were a part of **Global Forum '92** which ran concurrently with this "Earth Summit."

Artwork and essays by thousands of children from around the world were submitted in a contest on the environment*. Winning entries were published in the book **Tomorrow Belongs to the Children** which, in turn, was given to all Non-Governmental Organizations and world leaders attending the Earth Summit.   * *Organized by an NGO, The Bahá'í International Community.*

In this photograph, Pezeshk is presenting a copy of **Tomorrow Belongs to the Children** to James Grant, UNICEF Executive Director.

Venus S. Pezeshk, then Director of the Bahá'í Environmental office in Brazil, coordinated activities relative to the **Earth Summit** and the **Global Forum**. A landscape architect with her own firm, Pezeshk has served as special advisor to the government of the new State of Tocantins. In view of the state's strategic position in the Amazon region, Pezeshk has assisted in the first initiatives for the establishment of an environmental policy. In 1990 she was honoured with the title of "Comendadora" for important services rendered the government of the State of Tocantins and awarded the Medal of Merit.

She has traveled extensively and photographically documented urban ecology throughout the world including Iran, Israel, Turkey, Egypt, Peru, Paraguay, Portugal and Spain.

Venus Pezeshk's advice to young people:*"Be steadfast in your ideas, sincere and pure in your heart desires, and loving with each other, to ensure a better tomorrow for all of us."*

An hourglass-shaped monument stands as a timeless symbol of the Earth Summit and the Global Forum.

Into the monument's hollow structure children from various countries poured soil from nations around the world. This act symbolized the international cooperation and unity required to establish world peace. Soil samples from other countries have been added yearly on World Environment Day bringing the total to 85 countries.

Enrichment Activity:

Select a theme (such as "Tomorrow Belongs to the Children") and organize a contest for children in your community. Entries can be artwork, essays, poems, drama, video, songs, etc. Ask a department in your local government to sponsor this event by providing an area to exhibit the winning entries. An elected official could present the awards. Notify the media. Coverage of the contest and presentation of awards will help increase community awareness of environmental issues.

Bibliography:

American Bahá'í. August 20, 1992.
Tomorrow Belongs to the Children. Distributed through UNICEF.
Venus S. Pezeshk. **Letter**, May 24, 1995.

North America is the third largest continent covering more than 16% of the earth's land surface. Extending from Alaska south to Panama's eastern border, this continent includes the world's second largest country (Canada) and the world's largest island (Greenland). The highest point in the continent is Alaska's Mount McKinley at 20,320 ft. The lowest point is also the hottest: California's Death Valley at an elevation of 282 ft. below sea level and a record temperature of 134°F set in 1913.

Along the continent's western belt, active volcanoes loom heavenward and earthquakes shake the landscape. In Atlantic waters humpback whales swim the length of the continent twice each year while the golden plover flies 2,400 miles in its migration from eastern Canada to South America. Inland, the world's largest cactus, the saguaro, lives 150 to 200 years and the sequoia tree, more than 3,500. Land animals include: beavers whose front teeth never stop growing, roadrunner birds that attack rattlesnakes, and the inch-long Panamanian ponerine ant who eats fruit and meat. From the treeless tundra dotted with pingos (giant frost-heaves) to the Mayan ruins scattered through Guatemala and Honduras, North America offers a host of natural and cultural wonders.

NORTH AMERICA

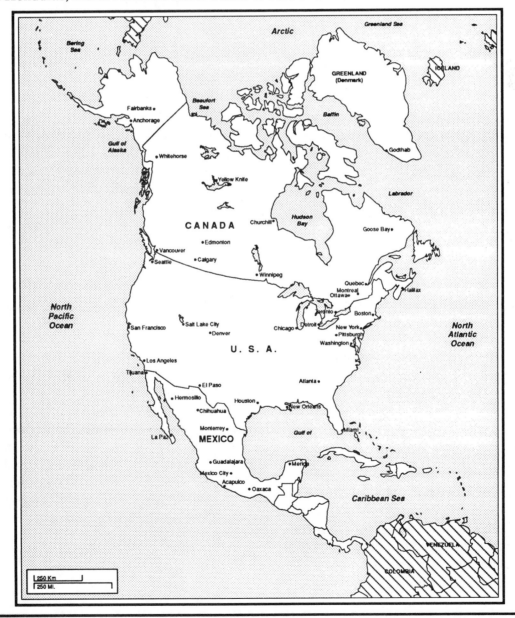

Continental Summary

North America and Science:

Thousands of years ago, the first people coming into North America may have traveled through an ice-free passage between Asia and Alaska. This migration was the first of many spanning hundreds of years and extending from the Arctic Circle to South America.

The history of these people reflects diversity and creativity. **Housing** was a necessity but the "building blocks" varied: the Eskimo built ice igloos with blocks of frozen snow; the Haida in British Columbia used tall trees to construct long houses; and the Zuni, in what is now the state of New Mexico, carved cliffs into dwellings with one residence housing 1,200 people in 800 rooms.

Agricultural methods differed from place to place. The Iroquois fashioned a hoe from a deer's shoulder blade, New England tribes fertilized the soil with fish heads, and the Aztecs created floating vegetable gardens by covering rafts with mud.

Almost 9,000 years ago residents of Mexico began growing maize. By 6500 BC, farmers living in the Valley of Mexico were growing chili peppers, squash, maize, beans, and cotton. Sweet potatoes, onion, avocados, tomatoes, vanilla, and tobacco followed. Both Mayans and Aztecs were fond of cocoa made from grinding beans from cacao trees.

Foods had to be preserved beyond the hunting and growing seasons. Meats and fish were dried, smoked, or, in colder climates, frozen; fruits were sun-dried; and some grains, nuts, and vegetables were ground into flour.

To make the most of the materials at hand, creativity was essential:

- Eskimos used animal fat to fuel lamps whose wicks were made of twisted moss,
- The Iroquois invented a pump drill to start fires,
- The Plains Indians attached dogs to a sled-like vehicle fashioned from two long poles and a connecting net, and
- Aztecs made paper from wild fig trees.

Both men and women intertwined creativity with knowledge and science to transform common substances into ornate baskets, colorful pottery, ceremonial dress, jewelry, musical instruments, and games.

In **literature**, **mathematics**, **astronomy**, and **architecture**:

- the Olmecs of Mexico (1200 to 300 BC) created picture writing called hieroglyphs;
- the Mayans invented "zero" before the Arabs introduced it into Spain;
- the Anasazi and Pueblo of the Southwest recorded in paintings and carvings the formation of the Crab Nebula in 1054 AD., and
- the Mayans constructed large pyramids from which they tracked the moon, planets, and the stars.

Medical tools and treatments seem remarkably modern:

- The Sioux soaked rawhide before wrapping it around a broken bone. The drying and shrinking of the rawhide formed a plaster-like cast holding the broken bone in place.
- Native Americans used an animal bladder and hollow bone or quill to make a syringe-like instrument. They drained deep wounds, and used stoneseed for birth control.
- The participation of women as medicine women and *curanderas* (women healers descended from immigrants from Spain or Spanish colonies) was widespread and highly respected.

The four scientists featured in this unit have contributed to disciplines that reflect peoples' age-old concerns with food, water, numbers, and the stars. These women are **Dr. Lenora Moragne** (nutrition), **Maria Elena Diaz** (aquabiology), **Mildred Bennett** (mathematics), **Dr. Helen Sawyer Hogg** (astronomy).

Continental Facts:

- The name "Canada" possibly came from the Huron-Iroquois word, *Kanata* , which means "village" or "community."
- Mexico City, Mexico, is not only the largest city in North America but also the largest city in the world. Its population numbers more than 17 million people.
- The Mississippi-Missouri is the third longest river system in the world.
- Cuba was the first country in Latin America to offer women access to all educational levels in co-educational institutions.
- In 1843 a half-billion gray squirrels migrated across southern Wisconsin.

Continental Curiosities:

- Archaeologists believe that the Olmecs of ancient Mexico sculpted "mysterious stone heads" weighing more than 20 tons.
- More than 100,000 earthen mounds dot the landscape through the Mississippi Valley. Made by the Adena, these mounds were burial sites, temples, or dwellings. The base of the Cahokia mound in Poverty Point, Louisiana, is 750,000 square feet. Since no tribe in North America had knowledge of the wheel, how did the Adena successfully move an estimated 660,000 cubic yards of earth?

Exploration Questions:

- What would your world be like without wheels?
- What river system is the world's longest?

Enrichment Activities:

- Although maize was a major crop in Mexico by 1500 BC, it was not introduced into New England until around 1400 AD. Two hundred years later, the Iroquois had more than 50 recipes that used corn. Collect recipes that include corn ingredients. Select several to prepare and enjoy.
- Without a potter's wheel, the Aztecs worked coils of clay into pottery shapes. For decoration, the artist added pieces of clay or etched designs with a sharp knife. Imitate this method. Some homemade clay recipes will harden if left exposed to the air overnight. Paint when dry.

Add notes here:

Bibliography:

Beck, Barbara L. **The Aztecs**.

Johansen, Dorothy O. **Empire of the Columbia**.

Perrone, Bobette, H. Henrietta Stockel, and Victoria Krueger. **Medicine Women, *Curanderas*, and Women Doctors**.

Tannenbaum, Beulah and Harold E. **Science of the Early American Indians**.

Mathematician Mildred Bennett was the second woman electrical engineer hired by Westinghouse.

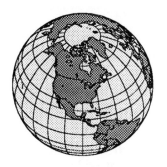

Discovery Unit No. 17

Mildred Bennett
Mathematics

From FISH SCALES to FRACTIONS

Time-line:

- 1921 - Mildred Bennett is born in Portland, Oregon.

- 1928 - Mathematician Dr. Olive C. Hazlett studies in Europe under a Guggenheim Fellowship.

- 1932 - Dr. Emmy Noether becomes the first woman to speak at the International Congress of Mathematics.

- 1954 - Bertha Lamme, first woman engineer hired by Westinghouse Electric and Manufacturing Company, dies.

- 1986 - Rear Admiral Grace Murray Hopper retires from the U.S. Navy. Her career in programming computer languages earned her the title of "First Lady of Software." She was the first woman admiral in the U.S. Navy.

Key points:

- ☛ Mathematician Mildred Bennett is a retired university professor and the second woman electrical engineer hired by Westinghouse.

- ☛ In her math tutoring programs for minority children, Bennett uses math games to get her students enthusiastic about and competent in math.

- ☛ Each year the Oregon Council of Teachers of Mathematics awards the Mildred Bennett Elementary Education Award to an outstanding elementary teacher. In 1992 this council inducted Bennett into their Mathematics Educational Hall of Fame.

- ☛ In From FISH SCALES to FRACTIONS students play two math games designed by Bennett to entertain and instruct.

Supplies:

- ✔ A **Scaling the Fish** gameboard for every 2 - 3 students (page 151)
- ✔ 27 chips per gameboard
- ✔ Three dice —1-6 pattern— (page 150)
- ✔ A **Four Straight** gameboard for every 2 - 4 students (page 152)
- ✔ 18 chips per player — a different color for each player
- ✔ Three dice —1-4,6,8 pattern— (page 150)

Steps:

1. Point out Portland, Oregon, on a map or globe.
2. Share highlights of Mildred Bennett's life.
3. Distribute gameboards and supplies.
4. Enjoy the math games.
5. Assist students in clean-up.
6. Add Mildred Bennett's name and a memento to the world map.
7. Distribute *The Scientific Gazette*.

For next time:

- Announce the next scientist.

Bibliography:

Bennett, Mildred. **Interview**, October 24, 1994.

Bennett, Mildred. **Telephone Interview**, November 21, 1994.

Kass-Simon, G., and Patricia Farnes. **Women of Science: Righting the Record**.

Biography of
MILDRED BENNETT
b. 1921

"I would like to think I was a marvelous 'encourager' to people who were not math majors."
— **Mildred Bennett**

Mildred Bennett is a retired university professor who refuses to stop teaching. At age 73, Bennett's busy schedule includes: teaching for the University of Portland Mathematics/Computer Science Department such courses as mathematics for elementary teachers, statistics for non-math majors, and a fundamental ideas of mathematics course; establishing tutoring programs for minority children; recruiting volunteer tutors; and tutoring. Her truck is a mobile classroom with crates of file folders brimming with math games.

Becomes electrical engineer

A native Portlander, Mildred Bennett lives 12 blocks from the house in which she was born. At Oregon State University she was a mathematics major who was also within three credits of having a major in physics. Following graduation in June 1942, Bennett went to work for Westinghouse and became the second woman electrical engineer ever hired by this company. There were 400 young men and Mildred Bennett hired as Westinghouse engineers that year.

Bennett worked for Westinghouse for three years. She worked in the advanced design section with magnetrons, tubes emitting high frequency waves. These tubes are central to all radar sets and microwave ovens.

A "first" at the Polytechnic Institute

During this time Bennett did graduate work at the Polytechnic Institute in Brooklyn. She accepted the Institute's invitation to teach in their mathematics department and became the first woman hired as a full-time teacher at the Polytechnic Institute.

Returns "home"

In 1948, Mildred and her family returned to Portland where, for the next seven years, she focused her energies on her family. When her daughters were 2, 4, 6, and 8, Bennett resumed her career by teaching evening classes at Portland State University. By 1955 she was teaching full time.

A blackboard and chairs, but no tables

Beginning in 1969 Bennett helped students who were having trouble doing arithmetic but wanted a college degree. She taught at the PSU Educational Center in North Portland where the setting was a warehouse and the supplies included a blackboard and chairs, but no tables. Her courses cost students $6 a credit and for five years Mildred Bennett taught there for free.

Tutoring programs

During 15 of her 20-year full-time teaching career at Portland State (1974 - 1994), Bennett taught daily math classes at inner-east Portland elementary schools before going to PSU to teach. She created peer tutoring programs where "younger friends see older kids who are willing to help them." Her original emphasis was working with African-Americans but now she tutors other groups including Hispanic, Russian, and Asian students. Bennett is committed to getting these students enthusiastic about and competent in math early-on so that they "enter middle school on par with their peers."

Honors

In 1992 the Oregon Council of Teachers of Mathematics established the Mathematics Educational Hall of Fame. Mildred Bennett was one of the three charter inductees. This same council also established the Mildred Bennett Elementary Education Award to be given annually to an outstanding elementary teacher. The first recipient of this award was the deserving Mildred Bennett.

In the spring of 1995, Mildred Bennett was one of ten people from a four-county metropolitan area to receive a J.C. Penney Golden Rule Award. Nominated by the Lutheran Family Services Peer Support Network, the award honors volunteerism to the community.

Instructor's Guide:

From FISH SCALES to FRACTIONS

Background:

"Games are purposeful, but not as dry as mathematical texts." — **Mildred Bennett**

Scaling the Fish and **Four Straight** are only two of the many games designed by Mildred Bennett to nurture the elementary student's enthusiasm and competence in mathematics. The games entertain and instruct since they are designed to give the student mathematician choices of mathematical operations. In most games the throwing of dice dictates movement. In these games the throwing of dice offers choices.

Several days before:

1. Make at least one copy of both gameboards for every 2 or 3 students.
2. Laminate gameboard or slip into plastic sheet protector for durability.
3. Copy (or transfer) dice pattern onto card stock, at least one set for each student.

Today:

1. Distribute dice patterns to all students. Instruct them to cut on the solid lines and fold on the dashed lines. A ruler may be used as a straight edge to help with folding.
2. Assist students with assembly of dice. Tape side and ends.
3. Share instructions.
4. Form groups of 2 to 3 students. Allow time for both games to be enjoyed.

Scaling the Fish

Content: Addition, subtraction, multiplication, division with numbers 1-6.

Number of players: 2-3

Object: To remove the chip from each number, i.e. to "scale the fish."

Materials:

- One gameboard for every 2-3 children
- 27 chips per gameboard
- Three dice, numbered 1-6

How to play:

1. Place a chip in each hexagon.
2. Each player rolls all three dice. The person with the largest sum goes first.
3. When it is your turn, roll all three dice. Use any of the four basic operations to form a covered number. Remove and keep the chip covering the number you made.

Example: You roll 3, 4, and 5. The following are two possibilities out of many.

$$(3 + 4) \times 5 = 35$$
$$(5 - 3) \times 4 = 8$$

Note: If you cannot form a remaining number, then pass the dice to the next player.

4. The winner when there are 2 players, is the first one to get 12 chips. The winner when there are 3 players, is the first one to get 8 chips.

Four Straight

Content: Equivalent fractions using the numbers 1,2,3,4,6 and 8.

Number of players: 2-4 (best with 2)

Materials:

- One gameboard for every 2-4 children
- Three dice, numbered 1,2,3,4,6,8
- 18 chips per player, a different color for each

How to play:

1. Each player rolls all three dice. The player getting the largest sum goes first. The other players take turns in clockwise rotation.
2. When it is your turn, roll all three dice. Choose two to use and one to discard.
3. Form a fraction with the smaller number as the numerator and the larger number as the denominator. Cover that fraction <u>or its equivalent</u> on the gameboard with <u>one</u> of your chips.

Example: You roll 3, 4, and 8. You could form any of these fractions:

$$3/8 \quad 3/4 \quad 4/8$$

The fraction 4/8 is not on the gameboard, but its equivalent 1/2 is.

4. The first player to get four chips in a row horizontally, vertically or diagonally wins.

Ending Discussion:

Discuss how students felt about playing math games. Offer to let them play math games during their free time. Invite students to share other math and number games with the group.

Expansion Activity:

Create a math fair where students display math games they have created.

To make dice: Cut on solid lines. Score on dotted lines. Fold so that the six marked squares are on the outside. Use glue or rubber cement to secure.

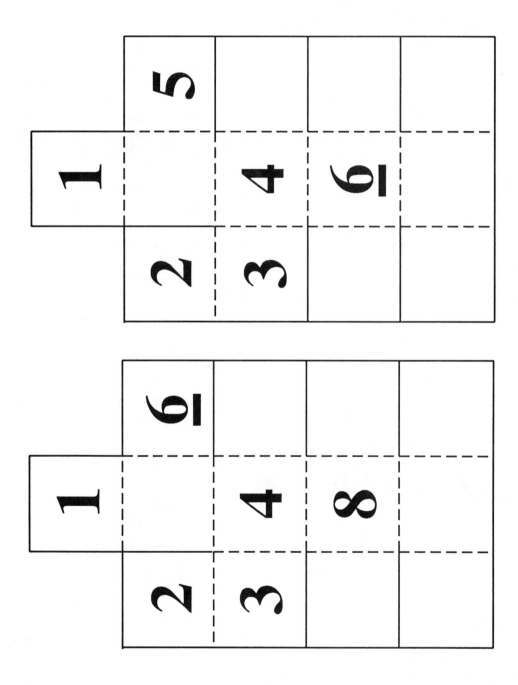

Note: Each game uses a set of three dice. The top pattern is used with **"Scaling the Fish"**; the bottom pattern is used with **"Four Straight"**.

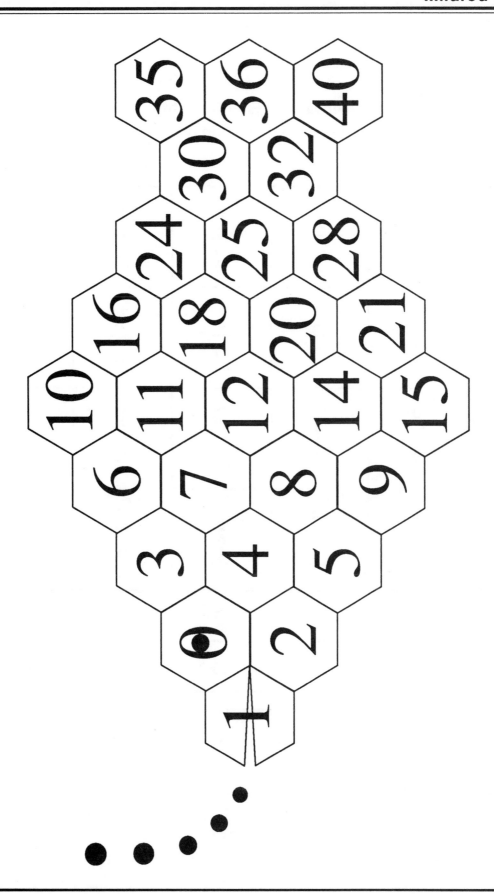

Gameboard for Scaling the Fish

Gameboard for Four Straight
(Equivalent Fractions)

1	$\frac{1}{2}$	$\frac{1}{3}$	$\frac{1}{4}$	$\frac{1}{6}$	$\frac{1}{8}$
$\frac{1}{2}$	1	$\frac{2}{3}$	$\frac{1}{2}$	$\frac{1}{3}$	$\frac{1}{4}$
$\frac{1}{3}$	$\frac{2}{3}$	1	$\frac{3}{4}$	$\frac{1}{2}$	$\frac{3}{8}$
$\frac{1}{4}$	$\frac{1}{2}$	$\frac{3}{4}$	1	$\frac{2}{3}$	$\frac{1}{2}$
$\frac{1}{6}$	$\frac{1}{3}$	$\frac{1}{2}$	$\frac{2}{3}$	1	$\frac{3}{4}$
$\frac{1}{8}$	$\frac{1}{4}$	$\frac{3}{8}$	$\frac{1}{2}$	$\frac{3}{4}$	1

The Scientific Gazette

Mathematics

Mildred Bennett

Fish Scales and Fractions

Mildred Bennett is a retired university professor and recent inductee into the Mathematics Educational Hall of Fame established by the Oregon Council of Teachers of Mathematics. At age 73, her busy schedule includes teaching math and education courses at a local college and creating tutoring programs for minority students. Her truck is a mobile classroom fueled by Bennett's love of mathematics.

In that "classroom on wheels" are folders of games like "Scaling the Fish" and "Building Four Straight" in which you throw the dice and then add, subtract, multiply, and/or divide. These games entertain and instruct.

Born in Portland, Oregon, in 1921, Bennett lives 12 blocks from the home in which she was born. She majored in mathematics at Oregon State University and, for three years following her graduation in June 1942, worked for Westinghouse as an electrical engineer. She was the second woman electrical engineer hired by Westinghouse.

Mildred Bennett is the mother of four daughters, two of whom were math majors in college. One is a city engineer in Milwaukie, Oregon and the other, an actuary with an insurance company. A grandson recently earned a mechanical engineering degree from the University of Southern California. In her spare time, Bennett plays the trumpet with the Brass Ensemble.

Like Mildred Bennett, I have created a math game. Its name is

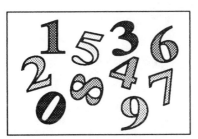

1st woman engineer at Westinghouse

Bertha Lamme (1869 - 1954) was the first woman electrical engineer at Westinghouse Electric and Manufacturing Company and the second woman to receive an engineering degree in the United States. Her work with Westinghouse began following her graduation from Ohio State University in 1893. During her twelve-year employment at the company's East Pittsburgh plant, Lamme designed motors and generators. She was particularly skilled in mathematics. Her daughter Florence became a physicist for the U.S. Bureau of Mines in Pittsburgh.

Math fun for the family

Family Math and *Math for Girls and Other Problem Solvers* are two publicationS parents might select for home entertainment and instruction. *Family Math* uses simple, everyday objects such as beans, blocks, toothpicks, and pennies. Activities are designed for intergenerational use. Write EQUALS, Lawrence Hall of Science, University of California, Berkeley, CA 94720, or call (510) 642-1910 to request a brochure on these and other publications.

At home:

- ◆ Read through the newspaper and select stories dealing with numbers.
- ◆ Critically read newspaper articles with numerical data; try to verify data.
- ◆ Work with fractions in a recipe i.e. double or triple the recipe.
- ◆ Work with fractions in cutting up things in a workshop.

Dr. Lenora Moragne, Chief Executive Officer of Nutrition Legislation Services, is one of the nation's leading nutrition professionals.

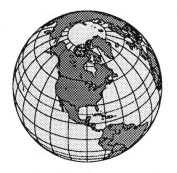

Discovery Unit No. 18

Dr. Lenora Moragne
Nutrition

FAT-in-FOOD DETECTOR Test

Time-line:

- 1931 - Dr. Lenora Moragne is born in Evanston, Illinois.

- 1939 - Agnes Chase Smith retires as senior botanist from the U.S. Department of Agriculture (USDA).

- 1944 - "Miss Farmer's School of Cookery" closes. Its founder, Fannie Farmer, was the "inventor" of measured ingredients in recipes.

- 1956 - Dr. Dorothy Crowfoot Hodgkin announces the structure of vitamin B_{12}.

- 1977 - Microbiologist Dorothy Fennell (USDA) receives the Federal Women's Award for her scientific drawings and photomicrographs of penicillin molds.

- 1988 - Pacific West Area Scientist of the year is Dr. Betty Klepper, Research and Location Leader (USDA), Columbia Plateau Conservation Research Center.

Key points:

☛ Dr. Lenora Moragne is one of the nation's leading nutrition professionals.

☛ Dr. Moragne has worked as a nutrition publicist for General Foods Corporation, a professor of foods nutrition at several universities, Head of Nutrition Education and Training for the U.S. Department of Agriculture, an author, and was the first female professional staff member of the U.S. Senate Agriculture, Nutrition, and Forestry Committee.

☛ She is founder, owner, and Chief Executive Officer of Nutrition Legislation Services.

☛ In The FAT-in-FOOD DETECTOR Test, students will collect and study "nutrition facts" labels from their favorite foods.

Supplies:

✓ An assortment of food labels from crackers, chips, cookies, cereals, etc. Have students help collect these labels.

✓ Nutrition Facts label (from instructor's guide, page 157) drawn ahead of time on newsprint.

✓ Supplies for student posters and displays

✓ *The Scientific Gazette* for each student

Steps:

1. Point out Evanston, Illinois, and Washington, D.C., on a map.

2. Share highlights of Dr. Lenora Moragne's life.

3. Conduct The FAT-in-FOOD DETECTOR Test.

4. Create posters or displays featuring "nutrition facts" labels.

5. Assist students in cleanup.

6. Add Dr. Moragne's name and a memento to the world map.

7. Distribute *The Scientific Gazette* .

For next time:

- Announce the next scientist.

Bibliography:

McGrayne, Sharon Bertsch. **Nobel Prize Women in Science**.

Moragne, Lenora. **Résumé**.

Moragne, Lenora. **Telephone Interview**, October 6, 1994.

Vare, Ethlie Ann, and Greg Ptacek. **Mothers of Invention**.

Wiser, Vivian. **Women Scientists in USDA** (U.S. Dept. of Agriculture).

Biography of
LENORA MORAGNE, PH.D., R.D.
b. 1931

"African-Americans are under-represented in the sciences and math. Because nutritionists must have a strong science base, African-Americans are absent from this field."

— Dr. Lenora Moragne

Lenora Moragne learned to drive when she was 12 years old so she could drive herself to work. "My parents had a very strong work ethic. You had a job all of the time." In the eighth grade, Lenora's job as "tray girl" at Evanston Hospital in Illinois introduced her to dietetics, the study of quantity food preparation and nutrition. Thirty years later Dr. Lenora Moragne was one of the nation's leading nutrition professionals.

In 1950 she graduated from Evanston Township High School in Evanston, Illinois. She spent her freshman year at Ohio Wesleyan University in Delaware, Ohio, but transferred to Iowa State University in Ames, Iowa.

A "professional person"

Following graduation from Iowa State University, Moragne became a Dietetic Intern at the Veterans Administration Hospital in Hines, Illinois. One year later she returned to Evanston, Illinois, to work as the Chief Dietitian at the Evanston Community Hospital, an eighty-bed facility serving the African-American community. Her salary was $4,100 per year. "This was more than my father made and he was so proud." Lenora had grown up in this part of town so her work at the hospital made her a "professional person from the neighborhood." This was "a big deal."

Door-to-door interviews

Moragne supervised the six-person dietetic staff for two years before attending Cornell University where she earned a M.Sc. degree in 1959 (Institutional Administration). For her doctorate she researched how people's lives impacted their food habits. From her door-to-door interviews in Harlem, she concluded that people who worked outside of their neighborhoods and thus were exposed to different people and new experiences practiced improved food and health habits.

Central America and Africa

Moragne continued her study of food habits at the Institute of Nutrition for Central America and Panama in Guatemala City. She interviewed rural Indian households and studied their nutrition deficiencies by examining skin, hair, blood samples, and height and weight measurements. Traveling to Africa, Moragne studied quantity food service operations in Ghana, Nigeria, Guinea, Liberia, and Sierra Leone.

Back in the United States, Lenora Moragne received her Ph.D. in 1969 (Rural Sociology, Education, and Nutrition) and worked as a nutrition publicist with General Foods. There she developed a public information and nutrition campaign that targeted African-Americans. Moragne initiated the use of Black models in the company's advertising.

In 1972 Dr. Moragne left General Foods to become the Head of Nutrition Education and Training in the Food and Nutrition Service of the U.S. Department of Agriculture. This agency administers the Federal nutrition programs (school meals, food stamps, elder meals, WIC, etc.).

Popularity of nutrition newsletter

Dr. Moragne left the Department of Agriculture to become the first female professional staff member of the U.S. Senate Agriculture, Nutrition, and Forestry Committee. Senator Robert Dole from Kansas was the chairman and Dr. Moragne, his staff person. While there, she worked on proposed legislation, drafted speeches, staffed hearings, and started a nutrition newsletter for the Senator. The newsletter became so popular that it was picked up by the national press. In 1979 Moragne left the U.S. Senate to become a nutrition advisor with the U.S. Department of Health and Human Services in Washington, D.C. where she worked on the dietary guidelines and the nutrition objectives for the nation.

Eight years later, Dr. Moragne started the **Nutrition Legislation News**, a publication sharing information and public policy documents pertaining to nutrition. Two other publications followed: **The Nutrition Funding Report** and the **Black Congressional Monitor** featuring information and documents of interest to the African-American community.

Instructor's Guide:

The FAT-in-FOOD DETECTOR Test

Background Information:

Our bodies require energy to function. This energy comes from food — particularly from **carbohydrates**, **proteins**, and **fats**.

Carbohydrates:

- fuel muscular activity and the functioning of the central nervous sytem,
- metabolize fats, and
- are concentrated in foods called starches and sugars.

If the diet is severely restricted in carbohydrates, the normal breakdown of fats cannot take place.

Proteins:

- are essential for growth, repair, and maintenance of body tissue,
- help the body fight disease, and
- are found in animal products such as eggs, meat, fish, poultry, and milk.

Consumers who want to reduce their intake of proteins in the form of animal fat will obtain healthy energy by combining certain plant proteins in the same meal i.e. legumes and grains - or - grains, nuts, and seeds.

Fats:

- are the most concentrated source of energy, and
- can raise <u>and</u> lower cholesterol levels.

The consumption of **saturated fat** can raise cholesterol levels and place a person at risk for heart attack, heart disease, stroke, and other cardiovascular diseases. Animal sources of saturated fat include butter, lard, and fatty meats. Vegetable sources of saturated fat are found in many processed foods and include coconut, palm, and "partially hydrogenated" oils. **Monounsaturated fat** and **polyunsaturated fat**, both from vegetable sources, can help lower cholesterol.

Calories:

The potential energy value of foods and how much energy the body uses to do work is measured in units of heat called **calories**. A calorie is the amount of heat required to raise the temperature of 1 kilogram of water 1 degree Centigrade. One gram of fat yields 9 calories. Carbohydrates and proteins yield 4 calories per gram.

Prior to this activity:

Ask students to bring the "nutrition facts" labels from their favorite foods, or take-home menus from their favorite fast-food restaurants. Many of these menus have the calorie and fat content of the food items. If the fat content is not listed in calories, multiply the number of grams of fat by 9 to get this figure.

Instructions:

1. Discuss energy, calories, energy sources, etc.

> **Ask . . .**
> *How many of you have heard about reducing the amount of fat we eat?*

> **Explain . . .**
> *Nutritionists say it is healthier to reduce the amount of fat in our diet, but some foods, such as cereals, can fool us with their high level of fat. For example, one national brand of cereal containing natural oats, honey, and raisins has 27% of its calorie content coming from fat; but, another leading brand of round oat cereal with apple and cinnamon flavoring has 0% fat.*

> **Ask . . .**
> *How can we find out the fat content in foods?*
> [Study the labels.]

2. Show an enlarged newsprint copy of the following "Nutrition Facts" panel from a food label.

Nutrition Facts		
Serving Size 1 cup		
Servings Per Container 4		

Amount Per Serving		
Calories 225		Calories from Fat 135

		% Daily Value
Total Fat 15g		23%
Saturated Fat 7g		35%
Cholesterol 36mg		12%

Ingredients: Butter, cheese, hydrogenated oil, chicken, carrots, cornstarch, cream, salt, spices.

3. Discuss what the information on the label really means.

Explain . . .

- *Serving size: Always determine if this is appropriate for you. For example, if the serving size is 2 cookies, but you always eat 4, then you need to double the figures given on the label.*

- *Calories per serving and calories from fat. These are the important figures.*
  Divide the calories from fat by the calories per serving. 135 ÷ 225 = 60% fat.

  This percentage does not coincide with any of the figures shown beneath the % Daily Value column. This is because the percentages listed on the label are based on a 2,000 calorie diet in which 30% of the total energy from that day's food can come from fat (in this case, almost half of which is saturated fat!).

- *Ingredients are listed in the order of percentage of total weight. In this product butter is present in the highest percentage, by weight. Cheese and hydrogenated oil are listed next. Conclusion: this food is likely to be a high-fat product.*

---

4. Calculate the actual fat content on each label collected by the students.

   Determine a "fat scale" and sort labels into cleverly named categories. The scale should be from 0 to 100% fat. Categories might be 30-40% fat — "Oh, Oh let's take a second look," 0-30% "Pass a second helping," etc.

5. Students may now arrange their labels, pictures, and captions into attractive and eye-catching posters or displays.

   Make Dr. Moragne's photograph and quote "Education is Essential" central to the display.

◆ ◆ ◆

Enrichment Activities:

- Write and reproduce a nutrition newsletter highlighting information discovered in this unit. Distribute copies to students, teachers, and parents.

- Create a nutrition resource center in your classroom. Request literature from the American Heart Association, community hospital, extension service, etc.

- Since March is both National Nutrition Month and National Women's History Month, create a display featuring Dr. Moragne and the importance of reading and understanding food labels.

- Build a collection of misleading labels. Contact the companies and ask for information supporting their claims. Display these labels with the companies' explanations.

Add notes here:

The Scientific Gazette

From "Tray Girl" to Nutrition Professional

When she was 12 years old, Lenora Moragne (pronounced More-RAIN-knee) learned to drive so she could get to work as a "tray girl" at Evanston Hospital in Illinois. This was Lenora's introduction to dietetics, the study of quantity food preparation and diet therapy. Thirty years later, Dr. Lenora Moragne was one of the nation's leading nutrition professionals.

To conduct research for her doctorate (Cornell University, 1969), Moragne studied the food habits of African-Americans in Harlem. She traveled to West Africa to observe quantity food service operations. In Winneba, Ghana, she helped establish a four-year home-economics college.

Dr. Moragne has been:

◆ A nutrition publicist with General Foods;

◆ Professor of Food and Nutrition at Hunter College in New York City and North Carolina College in Durham, North Carolina;

◆ Head of Nutrition Education and Training in the Food and Nutrition Service of the U.S. Department of Agriculture;

◆ Co-author with her physician brother, Rudolph, of **Our Baby's Early Years**, a guide to infant care with illustrations featuring African-Americans; and co-author of a junior high school textbook for McGraw-Hill Book Co., titled **Focus On Food**;

◆ The first female professional staff member to serve on the U.S. Senate Agriculture, Nutrition and Foresty Committee; and

◆ Founding Editor and Publisher of the **Nutrition Legislation News**.

Dr. Lenora Moragne's commitment to nutrition and education has spanned half a century.

A favorite memory of Dr. Moragne's

While a student at Iowa State University, Lenora Moragne received $5 and $10 dollar bills from home since her father, a construction laborer, paid her $40-per-quarter tuition. Although neither of her parents (her mother worked as a domestic) went beyond the third grade, both valued education. Lenora was the first of four children to attend college. Of her three brothers, one is in sales, another is a physician, and the third is an engineer. In their parents' honor, Lenora and her three brothers established a scholarship fund at Evanston Township High School in Evanston, Illinois.

What is one of your favorite memories?

Dr. Moragne's advice to parents

"I feel that parents are standing around and watching children grow up, instead of directing their growth and development. Someone needs to help children with discipline, values, a healthy work ethic, or working with hands and head, volunteerism, and expressing themselves."

A more intelligent choice

As we examined labels from food products we sometimes discovered misleading statements. Advertising is done to convince people to buy one brand instead of another. The Nutritional Facts panel on the food labels gives us information to make a more intelligent choice when choosing which foods or brands to buy.

Professor Maria Elena Diaz teaches courses in limnology at the University of Guadalajara.

Discovery Unit No. 19

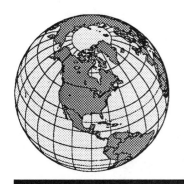

Maria Elena Diaz
Water Biology

WATER, WATER EVERYWHERE Experiments

Time-line:

- 1958 - Maria Elena Diaz is born in Ensenada, Mexico.
- 1968 - Explorer-scientist Jeanne Gurnee and associates discover a Mayan ceremonial cave in Guatemala.
- 1975 - West Indian Ruth Nita Barrow becomes the first black president of the World Wide YWCA. Her sister, Ena, was the Associate Director of Public Health in St. Croix; her sister, Sybil, worked as a pharmacist; and her brother, Errol, served as the first Prime Minister of Barbados.
- 1982 - For her contributions to marine biology, Dr. Isobel Bennett receives the Mueller Medal from the Australia and New Zealand Association for the Advancement of Science.

Key points:

- ☞ Maria Elena Diaz, professor at the School of Biology at the University of Guadalajara, studies water.
- ☞ Diaz teaches courses in limnology, the study of the biological, chemical, geographical, and physical features of fresh waters, and aquaculture, the cultivation of bodies of water for food production.
- ☞ Diaz enjoys field trips to such places as Lake Chapala, one of the Mexico's most important bodies of water and the primary source of Guadalajara's water supply.
- ☞ In The WATER, WATER EVERY-WHERE Experiments, students observe microorganisms and minerals in water, create a filtering system to remove impurities, and explore the source and quality of their community's drinking water.

Supplies:

- ✓ Equipment for WATER, WATER EVERYWHERE Experiments:

"HAY INFUSION"
- 1 glass jar, at least quart-size
- weeds and grass
- clean tap water
- magnifying glass

TESTING FOR MINERALS
- 3 clear glass bowls or glasses
- distilled water
- tap water
- salt water (can dissolve salt in distilled water)

FILTERING SYSTEM
- 1 two-liter plastic soft-drink bottle
- 4 cups sand
- 4 cups 1/4" (pea) gravel
- mesh-like material
- glass jar or pitcher
- dirty water

✓ "My Notes" sheet(s) for each student
✓ *The Scientific Gazette* for each student

Steps:

1. Point out Ensenada, Mexico, and Guadalajara, Mexico, on a map.
2. Share highlights of Professor Marie Elena Diaz's life.
3. Begin The WATER, WATER EVERYWHERE Experiments.
4. Assist students in cleanup.
5. Invite a water quality specialist from your community to visit.
6. Add Professor Maria Elena Diaz's name and a memento to the world map.
7. Distribute *The Scientific Gazette* .

For next time:

- Introduce the next scientist.

Bibliography — see page 164.

Biography of
MARIA ELENA DIAZ
b. 1958

So far, the scientific world has been a happy-ending story for me. Just about everything I have tried to do since I went into kindergarten has turned out to be possible, and even successfully done." — **Maria Elena Diaz**

Born in Ensenada, Baja California, Mexico, Maria Elena Diaz was raised in a Catholic home, and attended a private Catholic school where she learned English, sewing, embroidery, and singing "along with the regular subjects you learn in elementary, junior high, and high school. In high school, Maria won awards in Spanish Literature and was encouraged by her professors to study this subject in college. But she had other plans.

"Happiest days"

Raised near the ocean, Maria had always "loved the sea." This love, her liking of Biology, Physics and Chemistry, and the fact that Mexico's best school of oceanography was located in her hometown made Maria realize "that all of these factors intertwined just fine for me to decide on studying something I found a lot more fascinating and challenging than a career in literature. She enrolled in the school of oceanography where she spent some of her "happiest days, learning a lot of interesting things."

In 1983 Maria Elena Diaz graduated from the School of Marine Sciences with a Bachelor of Science degree and began teaching at the School of Biology at the University of Guadalajara in Guadalajara, Mexico. Five years later she left Mexico to earn a master's degree in Fisheries Science at Oregon State University in the United States. By July 1992 she had returned to her position of tenured professor at the University of Guadalajara.

Limnology & aquaculture

Diaz studies water. Her classes include limnology, the study of the biological, chemical, geographical, and physical features of fresh waters, particularly lakes and ponds, and aquaculture, the cultivation of bodies of water for the purpose of producing food. As part of her "Principles in Aquaculture" course, students visit local hatcheries where they conduct water quality tests and assist in the harvest of the fish being cultured, particularly carp and catfish.

Some of Diaz's time is spent advising students and assisting them with their thesis work. She also gives lectures to high school and elementary teachers on topics like the ecology of the oceans and how global change impacts oceans. She edits papers, writes articles, and attends regional and international science meetings and workshops.

"Never stays the same"

Diaz enjoys the field trips "where I get to be close to nature," and the meetings with colleagues where she can "network with people who have interests similar to mine but who live in a very different geographic region of the world." Professor Maria Diaz has discovered that in both teaching and research, the work "never stays the same." A teacher enjoys "new topics, new information, new subjects, as the science advances." In research, "you are always uncovering the unknown, you never find the same situation twice..."

Future generations

Although Diaz has lately encountered the "glass ceiling" that limits her opportunities in her career, she can "hardly think of a more interesting activity in life than getting to know and be the 'guide' for the generations of the future!"

Instructor's Guide:

WATER, WATER EVERYWHERE
Experiments

Background Information:

Water is a precious resource required by all living things. We have the same amount of water on the earth now as we did millions of years ago. It simply recycles itself. Water evaporates from rivers, lakes, and oceans. It is blown by the winds across land where it forms clouds. The water then returns to the earth as rain, hail, or snow. This process is called the water cycle.

In order to keep healthy, our drinking water must be free of bacteria and other harmful impurities. EPA (Environmental Protection Agency) sets the standards to keep our drinking water safe. Many states impose even stricter laws. Our drinking water comes from various sources: wells, lakes, rivers, and desalinized from oceans and seas. Most of our drinking water is provided by a municipality (funded by fees and taxes) that accepts the mandate to keep water safe according to state or federal standards.

Instructions:

Today

1. Discuss the water cycle and importance of pure drinking water.

2. Discuss drinking water — What do the students already know or believe about:
   - where their drinking water comes from,
   - what could be the sources of harmful microorganisms in this water,
   - what other contaminates could be in this water, and
   - how is this water purified and kept clean?

3. Distribute "My Notes" -Hay Infusion sheet.

> **Explain . . .**
> *We are going to set up an experiment that will allow us to observe some microorganisms. It will take about 5 days to see the results.*

4. **Conduct the "Hay Infusion" experiment.**
   - Gather stalks of grass with some weeds

mixed in. Cut off dirty or muddy base.
   - Stuff into glass jar, fill with water, and place in a window.

5. Students fill in Part A of "My Notes"

> **Explain . . .**
> *Certain minerals can also be present in drinking water. These cannot be seen by eye. Arsenic and nitrates can be harmful to humans while other minerals can be helpful. We are going to do an experiment to help detect minerals in water. It will take several days to observe the results.*

6. **Conduct the Testing for Minerals experiment:**
   - Fill one clear glass bowl with 2" distilled water — label it.
   - Fill a second clear glass bowl with 2" tap water — label it.
   - Fill a third clear glass bowl with 2" salt water (you may dissolve table salt in distilled water) — label it.
   - Place bowls on a sunny window sill while water evaporates.

> **Explain . . .**
> *Our public drinking water goes through many stages to assure its safety. Some stages include holding in a reservoir, circulating through mixing and settling basins, flowing through sand and gravel filters and piping into a storage tank. Chemicals are often added at this last stage. We are going to create a sand and gravel filter.*

7. **Create a filtering system.**
   - Thoroughly wash 2 cups of sand and 2 cups of gravel.
   - Cut bottom out of a two-liter plastic soft-drink bottle.
   - Turn bottle upside down (like a funnel) and position a piece of nylon net or other fine mesh-like material inside the bottle to cover the spout opening. (This will keep the sand and gravel in the bottle.)

- Layer sand and gravel to a depth of 2".
- Pour dirty water i.e. from a mud puddle, through the funnel capturing it in a clear jar or pitcher. How does it look?
- Add more layers of sand and gravel to a depth of 4".
- Pour dirty water through the filter and examine its clarity.
- Experiment with the thicknesses of the sand and gravel layers and the depth of the total filter until you get the most efficient combination.

8. Distribute "My Notes" - Water Filtering System sheet and allow time for students to do the cross section drawing of the "most efficient" water filter.

9. Collect "My Notes" - Hay Infusion sheet.

10. Assist students in clean-up.

One Week Later

1. Re-distribute "My Notes" - Hay Infusion sheet.

2. Examine jar with grass and weeds in it. How does the water look? Do you see movement in the water? Examine the water more closely with a magnifying glass. Little organisms on the grass have been growing.

3. Allow time for students to complete Part B of "My Notes."

4. Examine the glass bowls used in testing for minerals. Even if the water is not entirely evaporated you should be able to detect deposits on the sides of the bowl. Can students detect differences in the deposits? Which bowl has no deposits? This is a good time for forming questions and speculations.

Preparation for a visitor:

> **Explain . . .**
> *By law, our drinking water must be kept pure from contaminants. We are going to prepare for a visit from a representative of the municipality responsible for our safe drinking water. Let's think of questions in advance and write them on the board (or on newsprint?)*

1. List questions from students. Questions might include: What is the source of our drinking water? How is it filtered for impurities? What minerals are in our water? How is our water treated?

2. Telephone the water company and arrange for a visit from their representative.

3. When the visitor arrives, share information the class has learned through its experiments.

4. Ask for suggestions of ways the students can help keep our water safe and pure.

Enrichment Activity:

Students from Vancouver, Washington, have developed a program with the Public Works Department to help stop the contamination of water. Storm drains throughout the city collect rain water and other types of ground water. This water is carried through pipes to the Columbia River. To help raise the awareness of the citizens of Vancouver (so that poisons, oil, and other dangerous liquids are not dumped into the storm drain system), the students stencil the figure of a fish on the curb by each storm drain opening. They also stencil the words "Don't pollute, I live here."

Explore ways your students can help share their awareness of the importance of keeping our water pure and clean.

Bibliography:

Davies, Delwyn. **Fresh Water: The Precious Resource**.

Diaz, Maria Elena. **Letters,** July 1994, 9/16/94, 9/28/94, and 11/21/94.

Haniff, Nesha Z. **Blaze a Fire: Significant Contributions of Caribbean Women**.

LaBastille, Anne. **Women and Wilderness**.

Wallander, Diane. "A Science Career and a Family Too — There are options . . .," **AWIS Magazine**, November/December 1993.

My Notes by _____ Date _____

"Hay Infusion" Experiment

Part A

Question: How do microorganisms get into the water? _____

_____

_____

Hypothesis: If plants are growing near and in our drinking water, then they might be a source of microorganisms.

Experiment: (Describe) _____

_____

_____

Part B

Results:

This is what I saw happening inside the jar:

This is what I saw through a magnifying glass:

Conclusion: _____

_____

A Water Filtering System

This is a cross section of our most efficient sand and gravel water filtering system.

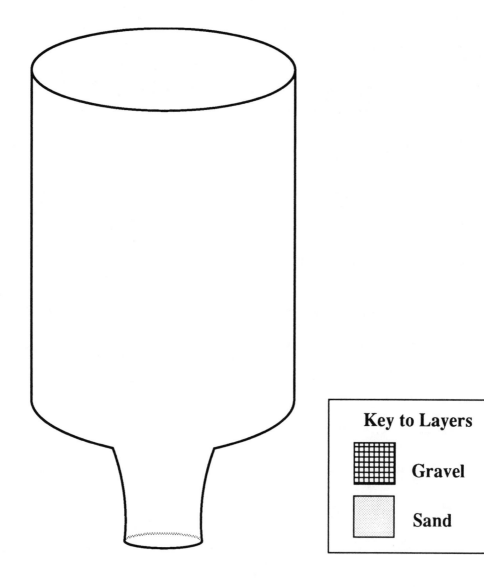

Key to Layers

Gravel

Sand

Efficiency Scale — How our filtered water looked:

☐ Looked really clean   ☐ Looked cleaner   ☐ Noticed no difference

The Scientific Gazette

Reaching New Frontiers

Born in Ensenada, Mexico, Maria Elena Diaz was raised near the ocean and always "loved the sea." She was one of 8 children. In high school Diaz won awards in Spanish Literature but decided to study oceanography instead. She is now a tenured professor of Biology at the University of Guadalajara in Guadalajara, Mexico.

In addition to teaching, conducting research, and writing, Diaz takes her students on field trips. At Lake Chapala, one of Mexico's most important bodies of water, they study the biological, chemical, geographical, and physical features of fresh waters (**limnology**). At hatcheries they learn how fish are raised and harvested. The cultivation of bodies of water for food production is called **aquaculture**.

Diaz lectures to high school and elementary teachers on the ecology of oceans and how global change impacts oceans. She also convened a "Workshop on the Study of the Impacts of Global Change on Biodiversity" which was attended by scientists from 12 different countries in North, Central, and South America.

"My work is always different," Diaz says. "It is always evolving, it never stays the same. You are always reaching new frontiers: if it's the teaching, the programs are always changing to include new topics, new information, new subjects, as the science advances. If it is the research, you are always uncovering the unknown — you never find the same situation twice while researching something."

Professor Marie Elena Diaz Advises Students to . . .

- Express yourself! Don't let anybody tell you what a girl should do. You can do just about anything you want to do — whether it's being an astronaut, an engineer, a marine biologist, or a lawyer. Many of us grow up thinking there are "certain things" a woman can't do and then when we realize that it's not true, it's too late to go back and re-start all over again.
- Be persistent and work hard!
- Be serious about your work, so people can take you seriously.
- Take advantage of the opportunities women have these days.
- Try to decide as soon as you can what it is that you would like to do. Too much wandering and too much changing careers may end up wasting your energies for what you end up doing for a lifetime.

At Home:

- Read the delightful book **The Magic School Bus at the Waterworks** by Joanna Cole.
- "Bio" means "life" and "**diversity**" means "variety." Biodiversity can be all the different kinds of life — plants and animals — in a given area. Explore your backyard or local park. List all the kinds of life you discover.

Fun Facts:

- 6000 BC - The large agricultural settlement of Jericho was developed around a sweetwater spring.
- 2500 BC - In Mesopotamia wells were dug to supply clean drinking water.
- 1500 BC - Minoan palaces had tile drainage systems and pipes to bring in fresh water.
- In the colonial U.S., residents hollowed-out logs for use as water pipes.
- At McMurdo Station in Antarctica nuclear power extracts fresh water from sea water.
- Our community's drinking water comes from

Dr. Helen Sawyer Hogg, distinguished astronomer and brilliant educator, wrote **The Stars Belong to Everyone**.

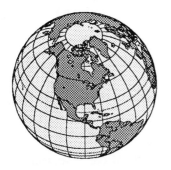

Discovery Unit No. 20

Dr. Helen Sawyer Hogg
Astronomy

TWINKLE, TWINKLE MANY STARS Activity

Time-line:
- 1905 - Dr. Helen Sawyer Hogg is born in Lowell, Massachusetts.
- 1956 - Dr. Dorrit E. Hoffleit, astronomer, becomes the director of the Maria Mitchell Observatory on Nantucket.
- 1972 - Asteroid 2917 was named "Helen Sawyer Hogg."
- 1979 - Astronomer Dr. Vera Rubin identifies galaxy NGC 1961, a giant galaxy containing billions of stars.
- 1992 - Astronaut Dr. Roberta Bondar, medical doctor and neurologist, becomes the first Canadian woman to be a member of a space flight.

Pronunciation guide:
- Pleiades (PLEE-ya-deez)
- Betelgeuse (BEE-tahl-juice)
- Rigel (RYE-jel)
- Aldebaran (al-DEB-a ron)

Key points:
☞ Dr. Helen Sawyer Hogg was a distinguished astronomer, brilliant educator, inspiring role model, and a warm, genuine person.

☞ Dr. Hogg researched variable stars in globular clusters.

☞ Astronomers believe globular clusters hold clues to the age and evolution of the universe.

☞ Through Hogg's teaching and writing, she encouraged everyone to enjoy the stars.

☞ In The TWINKLE, TWINKLE MANY STARS Activity, students will observe star clusters, adjacent constellations, and a variable star, and document their observations.

Supplies:
✓ Star and constellation charts from astronomy books found in the library
✓ 1 round balloon
✓ Celestial Observation Log (page 173)
✓ Observation Log for the Variable Star "Mira" (page 174)
✓ *The Scientific Gazette* for each student

Steps:
1. Point out Toronto, Canada, on a map.
2. Share highlights of Dr. Helen Sawyer Hogg's life.
3. Begin The TWINKLE, TWINKLE MANY STARS Activity assignments.
4. Add Dr. Hogg's name and a paper star to the world map today. When students complete both assignments, add a memento to replace the star.
5. Distribute *The Scientific Gazette* on the day the unit begins.

For next Ttme:
- Announce the next scientist.

Bibliography:
Chartrand III, Mark R. **Skyguide: A Field Guide for Amateur Astronomers.**

Docekal, Eileen M. **Sky Detective: Investigating the Mysteries of Space.**

Hogg, Helen Sawyer. **The Stars Belong to Everyone: How to Enjoy Astronomy.**

Lafferty, Peter. **Science Facts — Space.**

Pipher, Judith L. "Helen Sawyer Hogg (1905-1993)," **Publications of the Astronomical Society of the Pacific,** December, 1993.

Rey, H. A. **The Stars: A New Way to See Them.**

VanCleave, Janice. **Astronomy for Every Kid.**

Biography of
DR. HELEN SAWYER HOGG
1905 - 1993

Very little time is required to see and enjoy the beauties of the sky; once you come to know them, they never lose their appeal.

> — Dr. Helen Sawyer Hogg in the Foreword to her book, **The Stars Belong to Everyone: How to Enjoy Astronomy**

Dr. Helen Sawyer Hogg was a distinguished astronomer. She received prestigious awards including the Fellow of the Royal Society of Canada (1946), the Companion of the Order of Canada (1976), and the City of Toronto's Order of Merit (1985). The National Museum of Science and Technology in Ottawa dedicated The Helen Sawyer Hogg Observatory in 1989 and the University of Toronto dedicated "The Helen Sawyer Hogg Telescope of the University of Toronto Southern Observatory" in Chile in 1992. She was a brilliant educator, an inspiring role model, and a warm, genuine person who believed "anyone can follow the beautiful and interesting events in the sky..."

Solar eclipse sparks interest

Born in Lowell, Massachusetts, in August 1905, Helen earned an undergraduate degree from Mt. Holyoke College and, a master of arts (1928) and Ph.D. (1931) from Radcliffe College. She credited her family, a solar eclipse in January 1925, and a mentor at Mt. Holyoke College as the factors behind her initial interest in astronomy.

In 1931 Dr. Helen Hogg and her husband, Dr. Frank Hogg — also an astronomer, were appointed to the staff at the Dominion Astrophysical Observatory in Victoria, British Columbia. Through the Observatory's 72-inch telescope, Dr. Helen Hogg researched variable stars in globular clusters. These clusters are immense groupings of hundreds of thousands or millions of stars that astronomers believe were the first to form in the Milky Way Gal-axy. Astronomers believe that these clusters hold clues to the age and evolution of the universe.

2119 variables found

Dr. Helen Hogg continued her research of globular clusters when she and her husband joined the staff at the University of Toronto's David Dunlap Observatory in 1935. By 1973 she had found 2119 variables in 108 globular clusters. Her **Catalogue[s] of Variable Stars in Globular Clusters** is useful to both professional and amateur astronomers.

In 1951 Dr. Helen Hogg began teaching astronomy at the University of Toronto. She taught for 25 years. On leaves of absence she served as the Acting Chair of the Astronomy Department at Mt. Holyoke, her *alma mater,* and Program Director for Astronomy at the National Science Foundation. Also in 1951 Dr. Hogg began writing a weekly astronomy column for the *Toronto Star* — a task she joyfully continued for more than 30 years.

"The Stars Belong to Everyone"

In both her teaching and her writing, Dr. Hogg aspired to persuade the average student and the ordinary citizen that they could understand the basics of astronomy. The enjoyment of "attending moonrise and moonset," of observing an eclipse, following "the arch of the Milky Way" or gazing at "the old moon in the new moon's arms" were not celestial sights intended for the privileged few because, as her book title says, **The Stars Belong to Everyone.**

◆ ◆ ◆

Instructors Guide:

TWINKLE, TWINKLE MANY STARS

Instructor's Note:

Due to the changing positions of the stars, you should determine in advance which months the constellations of Orion, Taurus and Cetus will be visible in your latitude. There are two assignments in this unit. Each assignment consists of: 1. the lesson,
2. independent observation time, and
3. follow-up and sharing time.

Assignment 1 — Star Clusters

Background:

Clusters are groups of stars formed at the same time and traveling together through space. Open clusters contain from a few dozen to many hundreds of stars. Some are younger in age than our earth. Globular clusters are groups of about a million stars. Globular clusters are the oldest objects in the Galaxy.

A beautiful open cluster named the Pleiades can be easily seen in the Northern Hemisphere. The Pleiades appear as a tiny silver cloud in the constellation of Taurus, the Bull. A person with sharp eyesight can discern 7 individual starlets in this group, although only 6 are easily visible. Binoculars will reveal dozens of stars and a telescope can see hundreds.

The Pleiades was formed during the age of the dinosaurs, about 100 million years ago.

Greek mythology named the stars after the seven daughters of Atlas and Pleione. Maia, the first born and most beautiful of the sisters, is referred to as the brightest. The other stars are named Asterope, Taygeta, Celaeno, Electra, Alcyone, and Merope. According to legend, Electra's light dimmed when she witnessed the destruction of Ilium.

Instructions:

1. Tell students about open star clusters. Tell them about the Pleiades.
2. Distribute astronomy books and examine the star charts. Encourage students to work together. Look for charts (sky maps) showing the constellations of Orion and Taurus.

Ask . . .
Who can locate the Pleiades? What constellation is it in? [Make sure everyone has located the Pleiades on the star maps.]

Explain . . .
It can be difficult to locate stars in the sky because lines are not drawn to show constellations and there are many more stars than are shown on the star maps. It is important to establish a starting point. Since the constellation of Taurus is difficult to see, we will learn to find the Pleiades by sighting a path through the stars. You will practice drawing this path in the classroom so it will be easier to find it at night.

---

3. Review the following steps for locating the Pleiades. (See diagram below.) Draw the diagram on the chalkboard and ask students to draw it on scrap paper. They should also trace this path with their finger on the star charts.

   • Locate the constellation of Orion. (First look for the three stars in the belt.) Locate the stars Betelgeuse and Rigel.

   • Draw a line from the star in Orion's right "shoulder" through a large red star. This star is Aldebaran (the fiery red eye of Taurus).

   • Continue with line until it intersects with a tiny silver cloud. This cloud of stars is the Pleiades.

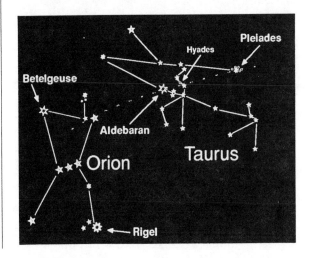

> **Explain . . .**
> *Another open cluster is located in Taurus. It is called the Hyades.* [Help students find this cluster on the star charts.] *There are probably 350 stars in this cluster that is a mere 120 light years away. After locating the Pleiades, students should easily find the Hyades.*

4. Distribute Celestial Observation Log.

> **Explain . . .**
> *Some of the phenomena on this log will be discovered after our next assignment.*

5. Distribute **The Scientific Gazette**.

Observation:

6. Instruct students to go out at night and start trying to locate the celestial objects shown on their observation logs. They might need to try observing at different times at night because of the movements of the stars. They should ask family members to help them.

7. Whenever they have located an object on their log they should record the observation information.

8. After a week, discuss their progress. Students should observe on a clear night when the moon is not in the sky.

Evaluation:

9. Ask students to share observation logs and their experiences.

Assignment 2 — Variable Stars

Background:

Variable stars, or variables, change the intensity of the light they produce. Some variables are **extrinsic.** These produce contant light but are completely or partially blocked by another star for periods of time ranging from minutes to several days. With **intrinsic** variables this light output actually varies because there are internal and surface changes in the stars themselves.

The variable star Mira (latin for "wonderful") is in the constellation Cetus. It is an intrinsic variable that changes from a 3rd magnitude star to a 10th magnitude star (invisible without a telescope) and back to a 3rd magnitude star in a total of 331 days.

Instructions:

1. Tell students about variable stars. Explain about the variable star "Mira"

Conduct pulsating demonstration:

> **Explain . . .**
> *Most stars are at equilibrium. This means gravity pulling inward equals the light and heat pressure pushing outward. However, the star Mira pulsates, acting like this . . .*

- Partially inflate balloon. [Keep opening in your mouth throughout demonstration.]
- Force more air into balloon.
- Let some air escape.
- Repeat, establishing a pulsating pattern.

> **Explain . . .**
> *The balloon stretches and shrinks as the air changes within it . . . just as the star Mira changes size due to internal pressure .*

2. Pass around astronomy books and begin examining star charts. Look for charts that show the constellation Cetus (sometimes referred to as sea monster or whale.) Look at the constellations and bright "named" stars around it and determine a strategy for locating Cetus in the sky. Be sure that everyone sees the location of "Mira" in Cetus.

3. Distribute star map of Cetus with observation log to each student.

4. After a week, discuss progress. Be sure all students have located Cetus.

Observation (several months):

5. Over a period of several months students should observe the position of Mira and record the magnitude. If she is not visible, write this into log. It may take as many as five months for Mira to become visible or to "disappear."

Evaluation:

6. Ask students to share observation logs and their experiences.

Celestial Observation Log by _____

Phenomenon	Observing Location	Date	Time	Remarks
Star Clusters				
Pleiades				
Hyades				
Constellations				
Orion				
Taurus				
Cetus				
Stars				
Betelgeuse				
Rigel				
Aldebaran				
Variable Stars				
Mira				

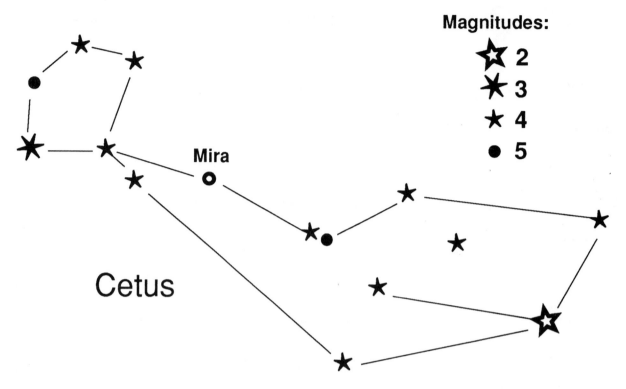

Magnitudes:
☆ 2
✶ 3
★ 4
● 5

Mira

Cetus

Measure Mira's brightness against other stars with known magnitudes. Use the stars in Cetus's "tail" as a guide. Observe Mira every 2-3 weeks.

Observation Log (Variable Star "Mira")

Date	Magnitude	Date	Magnitude	Date	Magnitude

The Scientific Gazette

Canadian astronomer studied variable stars

Dr. Helen Hogg

Distinguished astronomer Dr. Helen Sawyer Hogg believed that her family, a solar eclipse in January 1925, and a mentor at Mt. Holyoke College were the factors influencing her to study astronomy.

After earning a Ph.D. degree from Radcliffe College in 1931, Dr. Hogg was appointed to the staff at the Dominion Astrophysical Observatory (DAO) in Victoria, British Columbia. Through the DAO's telescope, she researched variable stars in globular clusters, groupings of hundreds of thousands or millions of stars. Astronomers think these clusters hold clues to the age and evolution of the universe.

Several years later Dr. Hogg joined the staff at the University of Toronto's David Dunlap Observatory. In 1951 she began teaching astronomy at the University of Toronto and writing a weekly astronomy column for the **Toronto Star** newspaper. She taught for 25 years and wrote the column for 30. The title of her book, **The Stars Belong to Everyone**, reflects Dr. Hogg's belief that anyone can understand the basics of astronomy and enjoy gazing at the wonders in the night sky.

Star cluster inspires legends and names

The Pleiades are an easily seen open cluster of stars in the Northern Hemisphere. Named by the Greeks in honor of the seven daughters of Atlas and Pleione, other cultures have created varied stories and names for this stellar cluster:

★ In China they were called the "Seven Sisters of Industry,"

★ Native Americans saw seven young men dancing,

★ In Arabia they were seen as a group of camel riders, and

★ Others called them the "Seven Little Nanny Goats" and a "Man with Six Chickens."

After observing the Pleiades, what name would you choose for this cluster of stars?

◆ Dr. Helen Sawyer Hogg has Asteroid 2917 named in her honor. A crater on the moon is named for her husband, astronomer Dr. Frank S. Hogg.

◆ A light year is the distance that light travels in one year, or about 6 million million miles. It takes 8.5 minutes for light to travel from the sun to the earth.

TWINKLE, TWINKLE MANY STARS

Today marks the beginning of two astronomy activities that will take several months to complete. My family and I will be making observations about star clusters and constellations as well as observing a variable star named "Mira" which means "wonderful" in Latin. Together, our family listed the name's of stars we knew.

They are:

"My Country Needs Professionals"

Yasmin Sequeda — b. 1976

"I am willing to work at any company in my country after I finish my studies, provided it helps the well-being of my country."

— **Yasmin Sequeda**

Yasmin Sequeda (left) with a member of her "host" family in the United States.

Yasmin Sequeda from Venezuela is helping her country's future by studying Management Engineering at Stevens Institute of Technology in New Jersey. "My country needs professionals, especially those that are interested in the well-being of our country." After completing her undergraduate studies in the United States, Yasmin will return home where her work will strengthen the economic and political future of Venezuela.

Born in San Fernando de Apure, Venezuela, Yasmin grew up in a two-parent family with two older sisters. In high school her favorite subjects were math, physics, and English. For being the second best student in her high school, Yasmin received three certificates. She also received honors in the Mathematics Olympics and the Chemistry Olympics, and earned a National Merit Scholarship Commendation for her grades. Active in environmental and service clubs, she wrote for the school newspaper and was the captain of the volleyball team.

For her outstanding scholastic record and demonstrated leadership skills, Yasmin was nominated her junior year in high school to be a Galileo

Scholar. Initiated by Venezuela's Fundación Gran Mariscal de Ayacucho in 1989, the Galileo Program's purpose is to identify outstanding high school students and grant scholarships for studies in Venezuela and selected countries abroad.

The selection is highly competitive. Students are nominated their junior year. For one year they complete studies with an enhanced curriculum and meet regularly to deepen their understanding of national issues. At the end of their senior year, candidates participate in a month-long program to demonstrate their leadership skills. The top 100 candidates are selected for scholarship abroad, the next 250 for scholarships in Venezuela. Yasmin was one of the 100.

Galileo scholars complete one year of language and cultural studies before being admitted to competitive colleges and universities. In the fall of 1993 Yasmin left Venezuela to begin this year of study at the Institute for American Language and Culture at Lewis & Clark College in Portland, Oregon. By the following spring she had applied to and was accepted at Stevens Institute of Technology.

"I chose to study Management Engineering because it "combines engineering with business." Originally Yasmin wanted to study Electrical Engineering but realized she also liked administration and business. "Today, most engineers will take on managerial positions. Technology-based companies typically recruit and promote engineers not only for their technical expertise but also for their potential as effective managers."

Yasmin's education and leadership skills will surely contribute to her country's well-being as she intends her professional career to make a difference "where it is needed."

Enrichment Activities:

◆ Foreign exchange travel/study programs are two-way opportunities: Be a Host Family for an international student or explore travel-abroad programs available through school or community service groups.

◆ Correspond with a student in another country.

South America is the fourth largest of the continents with an area of about 6,780,000 square miles. Bounded by the Pacific Ocean on the west, Atlantic Ocean on the east, and the Caribbean Sea on the north, the continent is connected to North America by the Isthmus of Panama.

One of South America's most distinguishing features is its 5000-mile long Andes mountain range. Extending from Venezuela south to Chile along the continent's western coast, the Andes are part of the "Ring of Fire" chain of volcanoes that edge the Pacific Basin. The range's highest peak is Mt. Aconcagua at 22,831 feet.

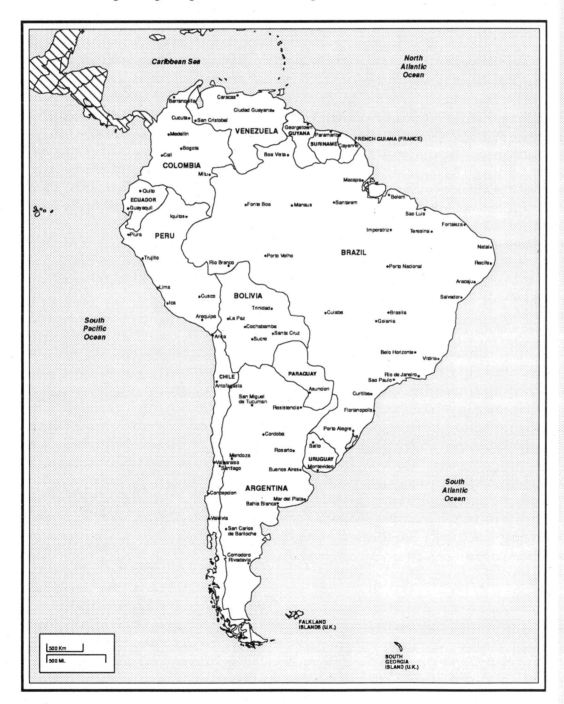

SOUTH AMERICA

South America and Science:

"Then, linked arm and arm with virtuous, honest, and just men in the garden of spiritual civilization women will climb the steps of light to have their ephemeral physical beauty crowned with the immortal diadem of true beauty, of science and creativity."
— **Francisca S. da M. Diniz**
"Equality of Rights" - April 1890

In Chile

Women's access to public university education came first in Chile. On April 11, 1881, **Eloísa Díaz Inzunza** received her bachelor's degree and earned a medical degree five years later. In 1887, the president of Chile awarded her a diploma of medical surgery and praised her accomplishment at becoming the first Chilean woman to earn a professional title. Most of Dr. Inzunza's career was spent in public health including work as a medical inspector of Santiago's primary schools.

Ernestina Pérez Barahona followed in Inzunza's footsteps. After earning her medical degree in Chile, she studied gynecology in Europe. Dr. Barahona is the first physician from South America to be elected to the Academy of Medicine in Berlin.

By the 1920s, 49 Chilean woman had earned medical degrees, 115 had degrees in dentistry, and 130 were pharmacy graduates.

In Brazil

The Brazilian government did not grant women admission to public universities until 1879. In 1887 **Rita Lobato Velho Lopes** became the first woman to earn a medical degree from a school in Brazil. Drs. **Maria Augusta Generosa Estrella** and Dr. **Josefa Agueda Felisbella Mercedes de Oliveira** were two Brazilian women who received medical degrees prior to Lopes but studied in the United States.

In Argentina

"I have known in Buenos Aires some forty female doctors who practice medicine, surgery, dentistry, anthropology and obstet-rics. I visited a class at the Academy of Medicine which was directed by a woman."
— Travel Diary of **Gina Lombroso Ferrero**, 1907

In 1889 Dr. **Cecilia Grierson** became the first woman to earn a medical degree from the University of Buenos Aires. She practiced medicine as well as spearheaded the organization of the National Council of Women in Argentina (1900) and the Argentine Association of University Women (1902). In May 1910 she presided at the first International Feminist Congress in Buenos Aires. More than 200 women from Argentina, Uruguay, Peru, Paraguay, and Chile attended.

From a handful to hundreds, professional women in South America were becoming increasingly optimistic about the future of women. They agreed with Dr. **Julieta Lanteri de Renshaw**, recipient of a degree in pharmacology from the National College of La Plata in 1898 and a medical degree from the University of Buenos Aires in 1906, who declared:

"Hope begins to shine on the dark horizon. Woman is awakening to the consciousness of her own worth."

Bibliography:

Beck, Barbara L. **The Incas.**

Carlson, Marifran. **¡Feminismo!: The Woman's Movement in Argentina from its Beginnings to Eva Perón.**

Hahner, June E., Editor. **Latin American History: Their Lives and Views.**

Lavrin, Asuncion, Editor. **Latin American Women: Historical Perspectives.**

Miller, Francesca. **Latin American Women and the Search for Social Justice.**

Mindell, Earl. **Earl Mindell's Food as Medicine.**

Continental Facts:

- According to recent findings by a Peruvian research team, the Amazon River, not the Nile, is the longest river in the world. Believing the Ucayali River is the Amazon's source (instead of the Maranon), the Amazon becomes 4,131 miles long compared with the Nile's 4,003 miles.
- The Amazon River drains one-sixth of the globe's runoff into the ocean.
- One day's discharge of the Amazon River — 4.5 trillion gallons — could supply the water needs of all U.S. households for 5 months.
- Lake Titicaca drains southward into Lake Poopó.

Continental Curiosities:

- Humboldt Penguins live on the coasts of Chile, Peru, Argentina, and the Galapagos Islands.
- The annual precipitation in Arica, Chile, is .003 inches.
- The annual precipitation in Quibdo, Colombia, is 345 inches.

Exploration Questions:

- The Amazon Basin is rich in natural resources but development threatens the ecology of the area. What are the area's resources? What forces are at work to change this area?
- What is the largest bird found in South America? Can it fly?

Enrichment Activities:

- In the 1500s AD, the Incas of South America raised a variety of crops including corn, beans, potatoes, squash, peppers, and quinoa. Quinoa (KEEN-wah) was so highly regarded by the Incas that they called it "the mother grain" — a misnomer since quinoa is a dried fruit whose seeds are used in broth and baked goods. Find quinoa in a grocery store and follow package directions to create a taste sensation enjoyed for hundreds of years.

Add notes here:

Dr. Ana Aber is an instructor and researcher at the University of Uruguay.

Discovery Unit No. 21

Dr. Ana Aber
Environmental Science
"LOS CICLOS" Activity

Time-line:

1948 - Dr. Ana Aber is born in Montevideo, Uruguay.

1951 - Dr. Margarita Delgado de Solis Quiroga begins her two-year presidency of the Pan American Medical Women's Alliance.

1962 - In her book *Silent Spring*, marine biologist Rachel Carson describes how pesticides are harming the environment.

1979 - Lidia Gueiler Tejada is serving as the president of Bolivia.

1983 - Dr. Symphorose A. Nesbitt from Tanzania earns her Doctorate in Entomology/Parasitology.

1993 - Claudia Freitas teaches science to sixth-graders at the Escola Americana do Rio de Janeiro, Brazil.

Key points:

☛ Dr. Ana Aber is an instructor and researcher at the University of Uruguay.

☛ She specializes in termites, members of the Isoptera order, who cause extensive damage in Uruguay. Dr. Aber hopes to discover the best way to control termite plagues.

☛ Through her advisory work with the National Ministry of Environment, Dr. Aber informs citizens about the dangers of toxic chemicals and the benefits of recycling. She wants each person to become "un consumidor responsable."

☛ In "LOS CICLOS" Activity, students will complete worksheets created by Dr. Aber in her work with the National Ministry of Environment.

Supplies:

✓ Worksheets (pages 184-186) for each student or group of 3 to 4 students

✓ A Spanish-English dictionary or a student with Spanish-language skills

✓ *The Scientific Gazette* for each student

Steps:

1. Point out Montevideo, Uruguay, on a map.

2. Share highlights of Dr. Ana Aber's work.

3. Enjoy "LOS CICLOS" Activity.

4. Add Dr. Aber and a memento to the world map.

5. Distribute *The Scientific Gazette*.

For next time:

• Announce the next scientist.

Bibliography:

Aber, Ana. **Letters and Worksheets**, October 1994 and March 1995.

Carson, Rachel. **Silent Spring.**

Dirección Nacional de Medio Ambiente. Educational Brochures.

Farb, Peter, and The Editors of LIFE. **The Insects.**

Gross, Susan Hill, and Bingham, Marjorie Wall. **Women in Latin America: The 20th Century.**

Lovejoy, Esther Pohl. **Women Doctors of the World.**

Scott, Jackie. **"Death, Daybreak and Education Highlight Tour of Rio de Janeiro,"** The Oregonian, April 15, 1993.

Biography of
DR. ANA ABER
b. 1948

"I like researching, I like the world of the laboratory, and I like the world of cellular biology. " — **Dr. Ana Aber**

When student Ana Aber gave a report on termites to her high school biology class, she had no idea that these social insects would be "the subject of study during my life." Thirty years later Dr. Ana Aber has written more than 30 articles about termites in her native Uruguay, conducted seminars on how to control termite plagues, and organized the first Conference of Termite Specialists/Scientists in MERCOSUR (Argentina, Brazil, Paraguay, and Uruguay).

An "inclination" for science

Born in Montevideo, Uruguay, on March 1, 1948, Aber attended public primary school where she discovered an "inclination" for science. She dissected fish and taught this skill to her friends. At home she raised fish and carefully studied them.

After high school Aber studied at the University of Uruguay where she first earned her BSc degree in Medical Science, became a Clinical Laboratory Technician of the Faculty of Medicine, and earned a master's degree in Biology.

Left Uruguay

Since no university in Uruguay offered a doctorate, Aber moved to Argentina and attended the University of Buenos Aires. "Doing my post-graduate far from my family was very hard but I was compensated by the satisfaction of completing my vocation." Her thesis concentrated on the behavior of a particular species of termite common in Uruguay.

Termites - social insects

Returning to the University of Uruguay - where Aber has spent a total of 25 years as either a student or a professional — she conducted research and taught in the Cellular Biology Department and, later, in the Ethology Department. Termites, members of the Isoptera order, remain her specialty.

Termites eat "wood, books, trees, and live where there are electric lines." They "destroy houses" and cause extensive damage in Uruguay. By studying the behavior of termites, Dr. Aber hopes to discover the best way to control them. She doubts that pesticides offer the best solution since they are harmful to human health and the environment.

"Un consumidor responsable"

At the university, Dr. Aber is now teaching environmental studies, specifically biodiversity and environmental education. She is also an advisor for the National Ministry of Environment. Through publications that discuss the dangers of toxic chemicals, encourage the purchase of products with an ozone-friendly symbol, and inform citizens about the benefits of recycling, Aber hopes that each person will become "un consumidor responsable" (a responsible consumer) and a conscientious recycler. A healthy environment is "necessary for the survival of human beings."

Her greatest challenge

She is married and the mother of three children. Of her busy schedule Aber says: "The greatest challenge that I face every day is to be a married woman with three children with the responsibilities that this means."

Instructor's Guide:

"LOS CICLOS" Activity

Background Information:

Uruguay is a Spanish-speaking country. Although different peoples on the earth speak different languages, we all occupy the same planet and share the responsibillity for keeping it habitable for future generatons.

"Los Ciclos" is a two-step activity: 1) translation of pages 184-186, and 2) completion of pages 184 and 185. Translation may require:

- **Guesswork** since some Spanish words resemble English words.

- **Spanish-speaking students** becoming "Activity experts." These "experts" circulate to answer vocabulary questions.

- **Duplication** of "The Glossary of Spanish Words" printed on this page. Enlarge and distribute to groups or individuals.

Los Ciclos activity sheets emphasize the energy the sun gives to our world and how this energy is utilized in the continents' waters, air, earth, and life (plants and animals).

In "LOS CICLOS" Activity, your students will have several experiences. They will be sharing a lesson with students from a different continent and hemisphere of the world — a lesson that has relevance regardless of the country in which the student lives. Many students will be working in an unfamiliar language. This activity may help them empathize with students for whom English is a second language. By treating this activity as a "puzzle," the students are encouraged to make "educated guesses" and search out sources to confirm their answers.

Instructions:

1. Distribute worksheets (pages 184-186).

2. Describe the content of these sheets (see Background Information).

3. Let students work together.

4. Discuss what they have learned.

5. Ask the following questions:

   - Was it fair for you to be expected to do this lesson in Spanish?

   - How did you feel when you didn't understand some of the words?

   - How do you think people for whom English is a second language feel when they are still learning English words and meanings?

> **Explain . . .**
> *Spanish-speaking countries have a rich heritage in literature, music, drama. We would know more of the richness of this culture if we could speak and read the language.*
>
> *Language is a powerful tool for understanding and communicating with people all over this planet.*

Glossary of Spanish Words:

antepasadas -	ancient	agua salada -	salt water
árboles -	trees	arriba -	above
bosque -	forest	cada -	each
cercano -	close, near	ciclos -	cycles
comida -	food	como -	as, like
cómo -	how	compartir -	to share
de compartir -	sharing	comunidades -	communities
corriente -	current	cosa -	thing
Creencias -	beliefs	da -	gives
donde -	where	ellos -	them
entendidos -	understood	entre -	among
escoje -	choose, select	este -	that
juntos -	together	lugar -	place, site
mensajes -	messages	miembro -	continent
modo -	manner, way	mundo -	world
mundial -	of the world	playa -	beach, shore
poder -	power	pradera -	meadow, prairie
proveen -	provide	sueños -	dreams
viven -	live	travajan -	work
trabajando -	working	única -	unique

la cúal cubre - that which covers
un cuerpo de agua - a body of water
tiene que ver con - It has to do with
tratando de obtener - complete

Translation of Ecolocacion -

Echo-location: In order to locate others, bats and dolphins emit a high frequency sound, that reaches the prey and returns to the enemy (the predator) who is capable of detecting the size and distance of the desired object.

Name.

COMUNIDADES DEPENDEN EN
LOS CICLOS

Como el CORRIENTE DE ENERGIA del sol le da el poder a cada CICLO del universo los ciclos proveen comida, aire, agua y vida a cada miembro del la COMUNIDAD mundial.

Escoje uno de los siete miembros de la comunidad en el mundo arriba. Describe cómo este miembro depende a cada uno de los ciclos.

El aire:_____

El agua:_____

La tierra:_____

La vida:_____

Name:

VOCABULARIO

1. Comunidad:_____

2. Habitat:_____

3. Cooperación:_____

4. Cultura:_____

5. Global:_____

6. El Bosque:_____

7. La Playa:_____

8. Arqueología:_____

9. Nicho:_____

10. Comunicación:_____

11. Cooperación:_____

12. Local:_____

13. Idioma:_____

14. El Mar:_____

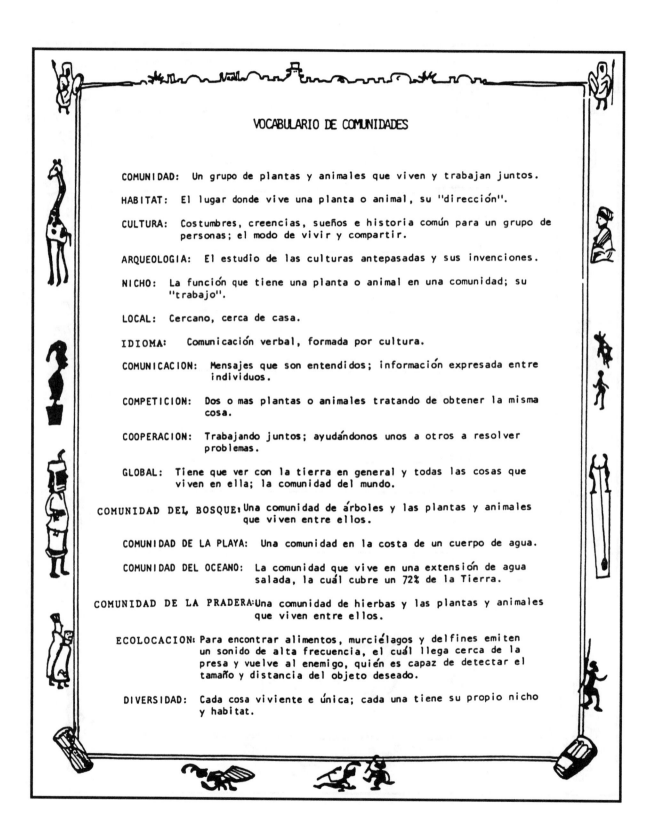

VOCABULARIO DE COMUNIDADES

COMUNIDAD: Un grupo de plantas y animales que viven y trabajan juntos.

HABITAT: El lugar donde vive una planta o animal, su "dirección".

CULTURA: Costumbres, creencias, sueños e historia común para un grupo de personas; el modo de vivir y compartir.

ARQUEOLOGIA: El estudio de las culturas antepasadas y sus invenciones.

NICHO: La función que tiene una planta o animal en una comunidad; su "trabajo".

LOCAL: Cercano, cerca de casa.

IDIOMA: Comunicación verbal, formada por cultura.

COMUNICACION: Mensajes que son entendidos; información expresada entre individuos.

COMPETICION: Dos o mas plantas o animales tratando de obtener la misma cosa.

COOPERACION: Trabajando juntos; ayudándonos unos a otros a resolver problemas.

GLOBAL: Tiene que ver con la tierra en general y todas las cosas que viven en ella; la comunidad del mundo.

COMUNIDAD DEL BOSQUE: Una comunidad de árboles y las plantas y animales que viven entre ellos.

COMUNIDAD DE LA PLAYA: Una comunidad en la costa de un cuerpo de agua.

COMUNIDAD DEL OCEANO: La comunidad que vive en una extensión de agua salada, la cuál cubre un 72% de la Tierra.

COMUNIDAD DE LA PRADERA: Una comunidad de hierbas y las plantas y animales que viven entre ellos.

ECOLOCACION: Para encontrar alimentos, murciélagos y delfines emiten un sonido de alta frecuencia, el cuál llega cerca de la presa y vuelve al enemigo, quién es capaz de detectar el tamaño y distancia del objeto deseado.

DIVERSIDAD: Cada cosa viviente e única; cada una tiene su propio nicho y habitat.

The Scientific Gazette

Dr. Ana Aber — Termite expert in Uruguay

In high school Ana Aber gave a report on termites to her high school biology class. Little did she dream that some day these social insects would be "the subject of study during my life."

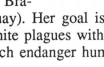

As an instructor and researcher at the University of Uruguay, Dr. Ana Aber researches termites, members of the Isoptera order. She has written more than 30 articles about termites in Uruguay and organized the first Conference of Termite Specialists/Scientists in MERCOSUR (Argentina, Brazil, Paraguay, and Uruguay). Her goal is to learn how to control termite plagues without the use of pesticides which endanger human health and harm the environment.

Believing that a healthy environment is "necessary for the survival of human beings," Dr. Aber is an advisor for the National Ministry of Environment. Through publications and student worksheets that discuss the dangers of toxic chemicals and list the benefits and how-to of recycling, Aber hopes each person will become "un consumidor responsable" (a responsible consumer).

Dr. Aber is active in several scientific organizations including the International Isoptera Society, Entomology Society of Brazil, and the Zoology Society of Uruguay.

Termites around the world

Almost 2,000 different species of termites exist worldwide. Their complex social life requires a rigid caste system with each insect performing a specialized task. Workers labor to build and maintain the nest; soldiers defend the nest; and the royal pair, a primary queen and primary king, produce eggs.

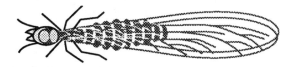

Termites:
- Cannot live in sunlight,
- May number more than 3,000,000 in one colony,
- Are not born with the ability to digest wood products,
- Regulate the temperature and humidity in the nest, and
- Build a variety of nests including mounds 20' high.

Women physicians met in Montevideo

In 1951, 150 women physicians from North and South America attended the Third Congress of the Pan American Medical Women's Alliance in Uruguay's capital. One of these physicians was Dr. Marie Luisa Saldun de Rodriguez from Uruguay. A pediatrician and professor, she worked in the hospitals of Montevideo, wrote four books on children's diseases, and lectured in Mexico, Peru, Colombia, Ecuador, and Brazil.

At Home:
- Set up a recycling center. Learn how products are recycled. If possible, tour a facility that converts recyclables into new products.

- Join an organization committed to improving the environment.

- Explore the world of other social insects i.e. bees and ants.

Professor Sonia Alconini and her team of Aymara workers at the site of Chiji Jawira (ceramic workshop) in the prehispanic city of Tiwanaku. They found 13 complete vessels which are now in the museum of Tiwanaku.

Discovery Unit No.22

Sonia Alconini
Archaeology

The HUNT for LITHIC TOOLS

Time-line:

- 1965 - Sonia Alconini is born in La Paz, Bolivia.
- 1970 - 1978 - Cynthia Irwin-Williams directs the archaeological excavation of a pre-historic Pueblo site at Salmon Ruins, New Mexico.
- 1985 - Sonia Alconini decides to study Archaeology at the University of La Paz.
- 1989 - Archaeologist Aslihan Yener discovers a bronze-age tin mine and ancient mining village in southern Turkey.
- 1991 - Working on a joint project with the University of Chicago, Sonia Alconini excavates a craft shop dating back to the Tiwanaku (300 - 1200 AD).
- 1992 - In a joint project with archaeologists from the University of Minnesota, Alconini helps excavate Chiripa (500 BC - 100 AD), a site that pre-dates the Tiwanaku.

Key points:

☛ Archaeologist Sonia Alconini believes it is important to share Bolivia's prehistory with the indigenous Aymara and Quechua people.

☛ Sonia Alconini is the first Bolivian woman to earn a degree in archaeology.

☛ In 1993 Professor Alconini became the first woman in Bolivia to chair a department of archaeology.

☛ Currently she is enrolled in a Ph.D. program at the University of Pittsburgh and is looking forward to returning home to share her newly-acquired knowledge with "the young archaeologists of the future."

☛ The HUNT for LITHIC TOOLS was designed by Sonia Alconini to help students

"become more familiar with techniques of excavation and archaeological analysis."

Supplies:

✓ A "My Notes" sheet for each student

✓ Bags to carry stones

✓ Outdoor location for The HUNT for LITHIC TOOLS

✓ Roll of masking tape

✓ Marking pen

✓ *The Scientific Gazette* for each student

Steps:

1. Point out La Paz, Bolivia, on a map or globe.

2. Share highlights of Sonia Alconini's life and work.

3. Conduct The HUNT for LITHIC TOOLS. (See instructor's guide, page 191.)

4. Assist students in clean-up.

5. Add Sonia Alconini's name and a memento to the map.

6. Distribute *The Scientific Gazette.*

For next time:

- Introduce the next scientist.

Bibliography:

Alconini, Sonia. **Letter**, June 17, 1995.
Encyclopaedia Britannica.

Biography of
SONIA ALCONINI
b. 1965

"Since I belong to the first generation of professional archaeologists in our country, I feel that we have a great responsibility to study our country's prehistory."

— Sonia Alconini

Bolivian archaeologist Sonia Alconini has excavated a Tiwanaku craft shop that was more than 800 years old, analyzed ceramic vessels dedicated to pre-Incan deities, and surveyed land between the Titicaca basin and the Amazon River basin. From these experiences she discovered ancient manufacturing and production patterns, the impact of economic and political changes on religious ideas, and prehispanic society's relationship to their natural environment.

"Their glorious past"

For Alconini, "studying her country's prehistory" is a great responsibility. "For me, it is particularly important to be able to transfer the knowledge we gain of our prehistory through archaeology to the indigenous Aymara and Quechua people of Bolivia so that they can really feel proud of their glorious past . . . Knowledge of their cultural heritage empowers ethnic groups and allows for their more equitable integration into Bolivian society."

Personal roots

This sense of responsibility has personal roots. Alconini's mother is Aymara and her father has Quechua ancestors. Both the Aymara and Quechua enjoyed a rich history prior to the Spanish Conquest of the Americas in 1492. "My mother has always been proud of the culture and history of her indigenous heritage." Sonia credits her mother as being "the person who influenced my life the most when I was growing up."

The majority of Bolivia's population "are indigenous people who continue to live in the rural areas and maintain the culture of their ancestors." Although Alconini was born and raised in the city of La Paz, Bolivia, her parents "still have ties with relatives who live in the country-side." These contacts, plus classes at the Catholic school, "Desmaissieres R. R. Adoratrices," sparked Sonia's interest in Bolivia's prehistory and led to her decision to study Archaeology at the University Mayor de San Andres in La Paz in 1985.

A couple of "firsts"

Upon her graduation, Alconini became the first Bolivian woman to earn a degree in archaeology. In the early 1990s, Alconini worked as a researcher at the Instituto Nacional de Arqueologia de Bolivia and as a professor in the Archaeology Department at the University of La Paz. In a series of "archaeological projects at the international level," she conducted excavations with archaeologists from the University of Chicago and the University of Minnesota.

When Professor Alconini was elected chairperson of the Archaeology-Anthropology Department at the University of La Paz in 1993, she became the first woman in Bolivia to chair a department of archaeology. Alconini believes this responsibility was "one of the greatest challenges of my career."

"The process of achieving these goals has not been easy, especially since I am a woman. In general, in Bolivia, most of the administrative chairperson positions are held by men. Archaeology in Bolivia is still a profession dominated by men . . .. Today, changes are occurring in which both men and women are overcoming their gender and ethnic differences in order to create a more democratic and participatory society."

The future

Currently Alconini is enrolled in the Ph.D. program in the Department of Anthropology at the University of Pittsburgh. Upon returning to Bolivia Professor Alconini will continue to teach archaeology at the university in order to share her newly-acquired knowledge with "the young archaeologists of the future."

Instructor's Guide:

The HUNT for LITHIC TOOLS

Background Information:

Archaeologist Sonia Alconini defines technology as "the optimal use of available resources." The technology of prehistoric humans during the Lower Paleolithic Period (Old Stone Age) made the best use of available resources i.e. stones and bones. To **COLLECT** and **CLASSIFY** prehistoric artifacts requires scientific know-how and analysis. First, the artifacts are collected "in archaeological contexts." Then, archaeologists must classify them.

Classification requires analysis since archaeologists must identify the functions of these artifacts in order to classify them. Basically, there are two ways to identify functions: 1) the context in which the artifacts are found, and 2) "the shape and use-wear" of the artifact.

For example, if there is other evidence of cooking activities, then an archaeologist finding a thin, sharp stone, with an elongated shape might **HYPOTHESIZE** that the lithic artifact was a knife used for preparing food. Under a microscope, an archaeologist can observe the "use-wear left on the knife's surface," and, consequently, obtain more evidence of the artifact's function and a better understanding of that culture's technology.

In The HUNT for LITHIC TOOLS, students will become familiar with techniques of surface collection and archaeological analysis, and will better understand the relationship between shape, function, and technology.

Instructions:

1. On the chalkboard list, with the help of the students and school resources, the basic needs of Paleolithic humans (food, shelter, etc.).

2. Explain that the class will go on a walk (on a field trip) and will pick up lithic artifacts that they see on the ground. This is called "surface collection." They will select lithics that are similar to tools.

   Students must remember that Paleolithic humans learned to use some rocks as stone tools, taking advantage of the type of the material and the initial shape of the stone.

3. Distribute "My Notes."

Instruct students to pretend that they are Paleolithic humans so they must assign a function to each stone according to its material, hardness, and shape. The basic categories to be considered are scrapers, polishers, knives, and grinding stones. Discuss why each of these categories are important. Have students write these reasons on their "My Notes."

Collect

 Collecting artifacts is often illegal. Do not infringe on a potential archaeological site.

1. Go on a walk or field trip. In groups or individually, students collect possible lithic artifacts or tools. They must remember that a good selection of these artifacts depends on the Paleolithic diet and subsistence. Remember that if the students do not collect good stones they will starve!

2. Place rocks in a bag to carry back to class.

Classify

1. Using "My Notes," students classify their artifacts according to the following categories:
   - scrapers
   - polishers
   - knives
   - grinding stones

2. Number stones using marking pens and masking tape.

Hypothesize

1. On "My Notes" explain why each stone could fulfill the function of its category.

2. Complete "My Notes."

3. Discuss the following questions:
   - How do you think you would function in a prehistoric culture of this kind.?
   - How has your knowledge of modern-day technology prepared you to survive in a culture where the only tools are stones and bones?

4. Assist students with clean-up.

My Notes by _____ Date _____

SCRAPERS: Used for _____

_____

I.D. number	Why I think this stone will fulfill the function of a scraper

POLISHERS: Used for _____

_____

I.D. number	Why I think this stone will fulfill the function of a polisher

KNIVES: Used for _____

_____

I.D. number	Why I think this stone will fulfill the function of a knife

GRINDERS: Used for _____

_____

I.D. number	Why I think this stone will fulfill the function of a grinder

The Scientific Gazette

Sonia Alconini and Bolivia's "Glorious Past"

Bolivian archaeologist Sonia Alconini has excavated a Tiwanaku craft shop that was more than 800 years old and analyzed ceramic vessels offered to pre-Incan deities. At Chiripa, she helped excavate one of the oldest archaeological sites in Bolivia (500 BC - 100 AD).

For Alconini the study of Bolivia's pre-history is a great responsibility:

"For me, it is particularly important to be able to transfer the knowledge we gain of our prehistory through archaeology to the indigenous Aymara and Quechua people of Bolivia so that they can really feel proud of their glorious past..."

Her mother is Aymara and her father has Quechua ancestors. These personal ties and high school classes in Bolivia's history inspired Alconini to study Archaeology at the University Mayor de San Adres in La Paz. Upon graduation, Sonia Alconini became the first Bolivian woman to earn a degree in archaeology.

In the early 1990s, Alconini became a professor in the Archaeology Department at the University of La Paz. Elected chairperson in 1993, she became the first woman in Bolivia to chair a department of archaeology.

Currently, Alconini is enrolled in the Ph.D. program at the University of Pittsburgh. She is looking forward to returning home to share her newly-acquired knowledge with "the young archaeologists of the future."

The Hunt for Lithic Tools

In the Lower Paleolithic Period (Old Stone Age) humans had yet to learn how to start and control fires. Their only tools were made of stones and bones. Ceramics, baskets, cloth, and metal were unknown. Humans hunted game, collected plant food, and lived in stone shelters or open encampments.

The HUNT for LITHIC TOOLS was designed by archaeologist Sonia Alconini to help students "become more familiar with techniques of surface collection and archaeological analysis." Students pretend they are Paleolithic humans and search for stones to perform specific functions essential to survival.

> *"Today, changes are occurring in which both men and women are overcoming their gender and ethnic differences in order to create a more democratic and participatory society."* **— Sonia Alconini**

This is an illustration of a lithic I discovered:

It falls into the category of a _____ and will fulfill the function well because

_____

_____

_____ .

At Home:

Locate **Hatchet**, an adventure survival book by Gary Paulsen. "Armed" only with a hatchet, a boy attempts to survive in the woods.

Ornithologist Dr. Emilie Snethlage ignored health risks and personal dangers to collect avifauna on Amazonia. On one collecting expedition, she was forced to amputate one of her fingers.

Discovery Unit No. 23

Dr. Emilie Snethlage
Ornithology

FLIGHT DESIGN LAB

Time-line:

1868 - 1929 — Dr. Emilie Snethlage

1874 - 14-year-old Maria Augusta Generose Estrella leaves Rio de Janeiro, Brazil, to study medicine in the United States.

1881 - Estrella obtains her medical degree.

1906 - In New Mexico U.S. ornithologist Florence Bailey discovers a three-toed woodpecker.

1910 - The International Feminist Congress convenes in Buenos Aires, Argentina.

1916 - National Council of Women is organized in Montevideo, Uruguay.

Pronunciation guide:

- ornithologist (or-nuh-THAWL-uh-just) — a bird specialist

Key points:

☛ In 1905 ornithologist Dr. Emilie Snethlage moved from Germany to Brazil where she became one of the country's "most remarkable scientists."

☛ Her collecting expeditions into Amazonia posed health risks and personal dangers. On one occasion she amputated one of her fingers.

☛ Her collection of avifauna became the cornerstones of the bird collections at museums in Belém and Rio de Janeiro, Brazil.

☛ The FLIGHT DESIGN LAB will give students the opportunity to learn how "lift is the secret to flight."

Supplies:

✓ Library books on paper airplanes
✓ Paper (recycled paper from the office etc.)
✓ Rulers
✓ Scissors
✓ Tape
✓ Paper clips
✓ Tape measures
✓ Watches with second hands or digital watches with chronometers
✓ "My Notes" sheets A and B for each student
✓ *The Scientific Gazette* for each student

Steps:

1. Point out Belém, Brazil, and Rio de Janeiro, Brazil, on a map.
2. Share highlights of Dr. Emilie Snethlage's life.
3. Conduct FLIGHT DESIGN LAB.
4. Assist students in clean-up.
5. Add Dr. Snethlage's name and a memento to the map.
6. Distribute *The Scientific Gazette*.

For next time:

- Enter the World of Possibilities

Bibliography:

Bonta, Marcia Myers. **Women in the Field: America's Pioneering Women Naturalists.**

Carlson, Marifran. **Feminismo!: The Woman's Movement in Argentina from its Beginnings to Eva Perón.**

Churchill, E. Richard. **Fabulous Paper Airplanes.**

Francis, Neil. **Super Flyers.**

Goodman, Harvey D. & others. **Biology Today.**

Sick, Helmut. **Birds in Brazil: A Natural History.**

Biography of
Dr. EMILIE SNETHLAGE
1868 - 1929

"Emilie Snethlage was the only woman scientist in all of South America to occupy a high administrative position in a well-known scientific institution."
— **Oswaldo Rodrigues da Cunha**
Historian, Pará Museum, Brazil

In 1905 at the age of 37, Dr. Emilie Snethlage left the Berlin Museum in Berlin, Germany, for the Natural History Museum (Museu Paraense Emilio Goeldi) in Belém, Brazil, where she became one of the country's "most remarkable scientists." Her scientific specialty was ornithology, the study of birds, but her scientific interests included animals, insects, plants, geography, and native peoples living in the Amazon River basin (Amazonia).

Health risks and personal dangers

Two years after arriving in Brazil, Snethlage became the director of the museum's zoological section and garden. To expand the museum's collections, Snethlage became active in field work. Traveling on foot, by canoe, and on horseback, she hired only canoe paddlers and horse handlers. No other scientist or assistant went along. These expeditions posed health risks and personal dangers to which Snethlage bravely responded. On one occasion she even amputated one of her fingers after it was "seriously mangled by piranhas."

An expedition between the Xingui and Tapajós Rivers in 1909 not only gave Snethlage the opportunity to collect plant (floral) and animal (faunal) specimens but to correct maps of the area and record vocabularies from several of the native languages.

An impressive catalogue of birds

Avifauna are kinds of birds in a region, period of time, or a particular environment. Dr. Snethlage concentrated on the avifauna in Amazonia. In 1915 she published her **Catalogue of the Birds of Amazonia**, an impressive work featuring 1117 species of birds. The Catalogue served two purposes — to be a manual for bird students visiting Amazonia and a reference work for ornithologists elsewhere in the world.

Published in Germany, copies of the Catalogue intended for American correspondents of the museum were held in Hamburg, Germany, since World War I had just begun. A 1915 issue of **The Auk**, a quarterly journal of ornithology, quotes Dr. Snethlage as requesting the journal "to announce that these [copies] will be forwarded as soon as possible."

Becomes a traveling naturalist

In 1922 Dr. Snethlage became a traveling naturalist for the National Museum of Rio de Janeiro and, during the next seven years, traveled extensively through Brazil. Her collection of avifauna became the cornerstones of the bird collections at museums in Belém and Rio de Janeiro, Brazil.

In 1929, while on an excursion to the Rio Madeira, Dr. Emilie Snethlage suffered a heart attack and died on November 25, 1929. Dr. Roquette Pinto, director of the National Museum of Rio de Janeiro, expressed the thoughts and feelings of many when he said: "The scientific world suffered a heavy loss and most of all, we in the museum, where she had in every colleague a respectful friend."

◆ ◆ ◆

Instructor's Guide:

FLIGHT DESIGN LAB

Background Information:

Parallels between the aerodynamics of bird flight and aircraft include the forces of **thrust** and **lift**.

In takeoff a bird pushes down with its wings and its feet to create the power neccesary to leave the ground and, once airborne, to continue moving forward. The same is true of a jet plane. Instead of wings and feet creating the takeoff power, hot gases forced out of the rear of a plane "kick back" and move the plane skyward. Once airborne, its engines suck in the resisting air, combine air and fuel, and release hot gases which continue to "kick back" and move the plane forward. (The kick back is like releasing a balloon filled with air. The balloon contracts releasing air which kicks back against the balloon and moves the balloon forward.) This movement is **thrust**.

Air pressure under the wings helps keep birds and planes airborne. This is **lift**. The shape of the wings allows air to move faster over the top of the wings thereby creating an area of lower air pressure. The normal air pressure under the wing pushes the wing into the region of lower air pressure above the wing, thus providing an upward movement of the wing, or **lift**.

Two other forces that influence the way birds and aircraft fly are **drag** and **gravity**. The amount of drag is influenced by the area of surface exposed to the air, while gravity is a factor to overcome in leaving the ground and while "flying" in the air.

In the FLIGHT DESIGN LAB students will learn that some shapes are more "air-friendly" than others. The student's toss-strength determines the craft's thrust; the wing area and shape determine lift. These forces combined must be greater than the total forces of drag and gravity for the aircraft to fly effectively.

Instructions:

1. Set out supplies for the FLIGHT DESIGN LAB.
2. Give flat sheets of paper from the supplies table to two students. Ask them to throw the paper. (Return paper to table for reuse.)

Ask . . .
How far did these sheets of paper fly?

Explain . . .
The FLIGHT DESIGN LAB is an opportunity to design a paper aircraft that will fly farther and better than a flat piece of paper. Dr. Snethlage studied birds because she loved birds; other scientists have studied birds because they wanted to create flying machines. Birds and planes are similar.

Ask . . .
In what ways do you think birds and planes are alike? How can these ideas help you design your paper aircraft? [This is a good place to discuss **thrust** and **lift**.]

---

3. Instruct students to work as individuals or divide into design teams.
4. Distribute "My Notes."
5. **Stage 1:** Sharing the resource books, allow students time to choose a design to fold or make a plane of their own design. Remind them to name their plane. Tell them NOT to test or modify their design at this point.
6. **Stage 2:** Have design teams test their models. Using Part A of "My Notes," ask them to record distances and flight times. They should also make notes on any erratic behaviors—i.e. always veering to the left.

Ask . . .
What are some of the flight behaviors you have been observing that are interfering with the efficiency of your plane? [Have teams demonstrate these behaviors as they discuss their observations.]

Ask . . .
What forces do you think are contributing to these problems? [Discuss **drag** and **gravity**.]

Explain . . .

Two problems your aircraft may be experiencing are stalling and diving.

When it hesitates or almost stops in midair it has gone into a stall. This can be corrected by slipping one or more paperclips onto the nose of the plane. This is adjusting your plane's "trim."

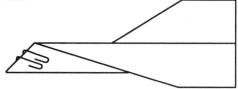

When a plane goes into a dive it has too much weight near the front. Moving paper clips close to the tail can correct this movement.

Another way to "stabilize" your plane is to make four cuts in its tail. Bend the paper flaps between the cuts.

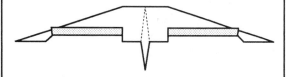

Bending the flaps up slightly will help pull the nose up during flight.

7. **Stage 3:** Design teams should try various design modifications to help their planes fly farther and better. These modifications should be recorded on "My Notes" sheet Part B.

8. **Stage 4:** Each team should demonstrate its aircraft model and explain the modifications made to the basic design. Team members should point out strong points of the aircraft and accept suggestions from other students on any identifiable weaknesses.

9. **Stage 5:** Display the aircraft. Include the name of the plane, members of the design team, and the Flight Performance Record (which includes distance and duration).

10. Assist students in clean-up.

Expanded Activity:

Stage an air show. Plan competitions to determine which design flies the farthest and which design stays in the air the longest. Students may wish to design stunt planes for entertainment and/or for competitive events.

Add notes here:

My Notes by _____ Date _____

FLIGHT DESIGN LAB

Part A

Name of experimental aircraft _____

Members of Design Team: _____

_____

_____

_____

Baseline Data — Flight Performance

Distance	Duration (Time)
1. _____	1. _____
2. _____	2. _____
3. _____	3. _____
4. _____	4. _____
5. _____	5. _____
6. _____	6. _____
7. _____	7. _____
8. _____	8. _____
9. _____	9. _____
10. _____	10. _____

Observations (erratic behavior):

_____

_____

_____

_____

_____

FLIGHT DESIGN LAB

<u>Part B</u>

Name of experimental aircraft _____

Modifications made to aircraft: _____

_____

_____

_____

Data — Flight Performance — After Modifications

Distance	Duration (Time)
1. _____	1. _____
2. _____	2. _____
3. _____	3. _____
4. _____	4. _____
5. _____	5. _____
6. _____	6. _____
7. _____	7. _____
8. _____	8. _____
9. _____	9. _____
10. _____	10. _____

Performance Averages:

Distance	Duration (Time)
_____	_____

Signatures of Design Team Members: _____

_____

_____

The Scientific Gazette

Brazilian birds from the Amazonia intrigue ornithologist

For almost a quarter of a century, Dr. Emilie Snethlage explored the Amazon River basin (Amazonia) to collect animal (faunal) and plant (floral) specimens for museums in Brazil. Her specialty was avifauna with a particular fondness for woodpeckers, antbirds, and vireos, small insect-eating singing birds. The lower Amazon she explored is respectfully called "Snethlage's area."

To acquire information about little-known species, Snethlage battled insects, disease, and personal injury. On one occasion she was forced to amputate her own finger. Her travels were so extensive that she corrected maps of the area and recorded vocabularies of native peoples.

Snethlage's scientific work included the discovery of almost 60 new bird species and subspecies. In her **Catalogue of the Birds of Amazonia**, she featured 1117 species of birds giving the common and scientific names for each species, statements about their geographic location, descriptions of the male and female, and a list of specimens at the museum.

Not only was she regarded as one of Brazil's "most remarkable scientists," but was internationally recognized for her contributions to ornithology. The British Ornithological Society made her an honorary member as did the Berlin Geographical Society and the Academy of Sciences of Brazil.

Secret design revealed at last!

The aerodynamics of bird flight and aircraft share many parallels including **thrust, lift, drag,** and **gravity.** In our FLIGHT DESIGN LAB we discussed how birds and planes are similar and used this information to design paper aircraft. The members of our Design Team created an aircraft that looked like this:

After modifications our aircraft flew an average distance of _____ and stayed aloft for an average time of _____.

Common names & scientific names

Every living thing fits into a scientific category ranging from the most generalized to the most specific. For example, a tiger belongs in the animal **kingdom**, the **phylum** *Chordata*, the **class** *Mammalia*, the **order** *Carnivora,* the **family** *Felidae* (cats), the **genus** *Panthera*, and, finally, the **species** *tigris*.

Since a scientific name includes the genus name followed by the species (or specific) name, the tiger is *Panthera tigris*. If you know that an African lion's scientific name is *Panthera leo*, what categories do the tiger and lion have in common?

> **At Home:**
> ◆ Research the scientific name of your pet(s).
> ◆ Make a list of the avifauna in your neighborhood. A bird identification book will provide common and scientific names.

Certificate of Completion

This certifies that

_____

has completed

The Scientist Within You

Discovery Units

_____   _____
Date   Signature

Discovery Unit No. 24

Entering the World of Possibilities in Science and Mathematics

Exploring Careers through the Scientists Within Them

Time-line:

- 1990s - Students enter the world of possibilities in science and math.

Key points:

☞ Careers using science and math are generally interesting and well paid.

☞ When students drop out of math and science, they seriously limit their career options.

☞ Girls tend to drop out of the more difficult higher level math and science classes.

☞ In the EXPLORING CAREERS Activity girls *and* boys will meet role models and possible mentors in scientific occupations.

Supplies:

✓ Copy of the Discovery Unit template sheets for each student

✓ Telephone books and other occupational directories

✓ Use of a copy machine, typewriter or computer [optional]

✓ Artwork representing the occupation (science) being explored (look through magazines for ideas)

Steps:

1. Ask students to choose an interesting occupation, where math or science is an important criteria.

2. Help students find the name and address of a person working in that occupation.

3. Instruct students to write a letter mentioning that they are doing a class project featuring a person working in a scientific field and they will be developing an experiment or activity based on the science used by that person. Students should ask for an appointment for an interview.

4. Assist students in developing a list of questions to ask during the interview, such as

   - What do you like most about your job?

   - What classes in math and science did you need to take?

   - What special benefits come from working in your field?

   - Is there an experiment or activity you can tell me how to do that will give me a sense of your job?

   Look at career materials from your library or resource center to help in formulating other questions.

5. Students should ask their scientists if they can borrow a picture for this project. Photocopy the picture (reducing or enlarging it if necessary) and use this copy on the unit's photo page.

6. Students can make copies of their Discovery Units to give to the featured scientists along with a thank you note.

Using "Discovery Unit" format pages:

Templates include the following:

- **Title page** — Identify occupation on first line, write name of scientist on second line, student's name appears on the third line, and the date project completed goes on the last line.

- **Photo page** — Attach a photocopy of scientist's picture here. If the scientist doesn't have one to lend, student may ask to take a photograph.

- **Overview of Discovery Unit** — Draw (or clip from another source) simple artwork that relates to the occupation or science represented in this unit. Place the artwork within the circle. Number the Discovery Unit. Write the scientist's name and discipline on the next two lines and use the third for a catchy name to identify the experiment or activity. Fill in the rest of the information

- **Biography page** — The story of the scientist is typed or clearly written on this page.

- **Instructor's Guide** — The experiment is placed here. "Background Information" refers to general information on the scientific discipline that will be helpful to understand the experiment or activity. The steps of the experiment are included under "Instructions."

- **"My Notes"** — Design the "My Notes" sheet to answer relevant questions for the experiment.

- *The Scientific Gazette* — Write a newsletter. This is a good place for information that does not fit into the rest of the unit.

Certificate of Completion:

- Sign and present to students in recognition of their efforts.

What to do with completed units:

- Ask students to teach them to the class.
- Use them as projects at a science fair.
- Teach to a classroom of younger students.

Add ideas here:

Entering a World of Possibilities

Exploring Careers in Science and Mathematics

_____

through the eyes of

_____

Researched and written by

_____

_____

Date

_____

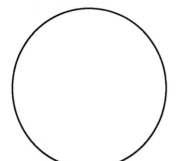

Discovery Unit No. ___

_____

_____

_____

Time-line:

•

•

•

•

Key points:

☞

☞

☞

☞

Supplies:

✓
✓
✓
✓
✓
✓
✓

✓
✓
✓
✓ "My Notes" for each student
✓ *The Scientific Gazette* for each student

Steps:

1.

2.

3.

4.

5.

Bibliography:

Biography of

_____

b. _____

— Quote

Instructor's Guide:

_____

Experiment

Background Information:

Instructions:

My Notes by_____Date_____

The Scientist Within You

The Scientific Gazette

Certificate of Completion

This certifies that

_____

has developed

a Discovery Unit on the scientist

_____

Date _____

Signature _____

Index

Photo Credits

Letitia Eva Obeng — Courtesy of Martha Stewart, Cambridge, MA, p. 10

Symphorose A. Tarimo Nesbitt — Courtesy of Dr. Symphorose A. Tarimo Nesbitt, p. 18

Grace Ngemukong Tima — Courtesy of Grace Ngemukong Tima, p. 26

Sara C. Beck — Courtesy of Dr. Sara C. Beck, p. 34

Mary Alice McWhinnie — National Archives Trust Fund, College Park, MD, p. 38

Irene Carswell Peden — Courtesy of Dr. Irene Carswell Peden, p. 46

Roseli Ocampo-Friedmann — Courtesy of Dr. Roseli Ocampo-Friedmann, p. 54

Rachel Carson — Prints and Photographs Division, Library of Congress, p. 62

Aslihan Yener — Courtesy of The University of Chicago Office of News and Information, Chicago, IL, p.66

Zdenka Samish — Courtesy of Zdenka Samish, p.74

Pham Thi Tran Chau — Courtesy of Dr. Pham Thi Tran Chau, p. 82

Mullick Family — Courtesy of Meera Mullick Batra, Portland, OR, p. 90

Christine Graves — Courtesy of Christine Graves, p.98

Joan Freeman — Courtesy of Dr. Joan Freeman, p. 102

Isobel Bennett — Courtesy of Dr. Isobel Bennett, p. 108

Esther Pohl Lovejoy — Oregon Historical Society, Negative # OrHi 27736, p. 116

Lise Meitner — Prints and Photographs Division, Library of Congress, p. 120

Eva Cudlínová — Courtesy of Dr. Eva Cudlínová, p. 128

Irena Hanousková — Courtesy of Irena Hanousková, p. 128

Marie Vasilievna Klenova — Computer Enhancement by Mark Smith, Eugene, OR, p. 136

Venus Sahihi Pezeshk and Monument honoring the Earth Summit and the Global Forum — Courtesy of National Spiritual Assembly of the Bahá'ís of Brazil, p. 142

Mildred Bennett — Courtesy of Mildred Bennett, p. 146

Lenora Moragne — Courtesy of Dr. Lenora Moragne, p. 154

Maria Elena Diaz — Courtesy of Maria Elena Diaz, p. 160

Helen Sawyer Hogg — The Toronto Star/J. Schenk, Toronto, Ontario, CANADA, p. 168

Yasmin Sequeda — Courtesy of Holly Myers Warren, Portland, Oregon, p. 176

Ana Aber — Courtesy of Dr. Ana Aber, p. 180

Sonia Alconini and crew — Courtesy of Sonia Alconini, p. 188

Emilie Snethlage — File Photo, p. 194

Authors' photographs:
Rebecca Lowe Warren — Thomas Berkemeier
Mary H. Thompson — Jack Liu

Cover Design — Mark Smith

Order Form

<table>
<tr><td>Mail Orders To:

ACI Publishing
Post Office Box 40398
Eugene, OR 97404-0064</td><td>Credit Card Orders To:

ACI Publishing
800/935-7323
Or by mail</td></tr>
</table>

Quantity	Book		Amount
_____	**The Scientist Within You:** Experiments and Biographies of Distinguished Women in Science. **Volume 1** Ages 8 - 13, (192 pages)	$21.95	_____
_____	**The Scientist Within You:** Women Scientists from Seven Continents — Biographies and Activities. **Volume 2** Ages 10 - 15, (224 pages)	$24.95	_____
	Shipping: $4.00 first book $1.50 each additional book		_____
		TOTAL	_____

❏ Paid by check   ❏ Paid by VISA   ❏ Paid by MasterCard

Card Number _____   Exp. Date _____

Name on Card _____   Signature _____

Please ship to:

Name _____

School or Organization _____

Address _____

City/State/Zip _____

Wk. Ph. _____   Hm. Ph. _____   Fax _____

Additional Instructions or Comments _____

_____

_____